the Cheeky Monkey

For my brother, Simon,
a very funny man

the Cheeky Monkey

WRITING NARRATIVE COMEDY

TIM FERGUSON

Currency Press
Sydney

First published in 2010 by
Currency Press Pty Ltd
PO Box 2287
Strawberry Hills NSW 2012 Australia
www.currency.com.au
enquiries@currency.com.au

National Library of Australia Cataloguing-in-Publication Data:

Author:	Ferguson, Tim.
Title:	The cheeky monkey : writing narrative comedy / Tim Ferguson.
ISBN:	9780868198613 (pbk)
Subjects:	Television comedies--Study and teaching--Australia.
	Television comedies--Authorship--Style manuals.
	Comedy--Technique.
Dewey Number:	
	808.066791

Cover and book design by Emma Vine, Currency Press

Cover image by ImageEnvision.com/JVPD

Printed by Hyde Park Press, Richmond, SA

Contents

Acknowledgements

This book could not have been written without the help, savvy and skills of Nick Parsons (editor), Victoria Chance, Claire Grady, Emma Vine, Mark Ryan, Stephanie Mills, Edwina Stuart, Zilla Turner, Kate Richter, Jimmy Thomson, Kelly Lefever, Edwina Exton, Paul McDermott, Richard Fidler, John Clarke, Cynthia Ferguson, Melissa Peres, Peter Abbott, Marc Gracie, Michael Scott, Ted Robinson, May Yeung, Paul Livingston, Clare Renner, Cameron P. Mellor, Liza Birmingham and Michael Pope.

Disclaimer

Much humour is inherently offensive. Therefore, this book, which aims to provide insights and techniques for the writing of comedy, includes offensive content. Potentially offensive topics discussed include, but are not limited to, race and ethnic humour; religion and religious humour; sexual, sexist and gender humour as well as vulgar language. Though offence is innate to some humour, it is not intended here.

Every effort has been made to attribute original author to quoted material, but jokes are often passed around and changed in the process, and their authorship is lost.

A note on the exercises

Sample answers to the exercises may be found in the appendix.

Introduction:
The Purpose and
Function of Humour

Nobody expects the Spanish Inquisition. Our chief weapon is surprise ... surprise and fear ... fear and surprise.

—'The Spanish Inquisition', *Monty Python's Flying Circus*

One man's joke is another man's sentence, so finding common ground between *all* jokes seems impossible. There are, however, certain timeless principles that underlie all jokes and narrative comedy. These principles are not rules or formulae, but the framework within which comedy occurs. They were discovered by writers as far back as Aristotle, although not invented by them. Comedy goes to the core of every human being and always has. It is the world's highest and lowest art form.

In a way, you already know everything in this book. The blueprint for creating comedy is in your DNA. If the principles seem familiar, perhaps bleedingly obvious, it's because you know them instinctively. Humans have evolved into civilised and sophisticated beings. Comedy, however, originates from and speaks to our primate brain, the 'cheeky monkey' within us. If you already write comedy (and it's funny) you're most likely applying the principles whether you know it or not. If you've never written a joke in your life, applying the principles may help you get underway.

The principles of comedy writing offered in this book result from discussions with writers, producers and comedians about their craft, and from my own experience in stand-up, musical comedy and narrative comedy.

This book does not, could not, provide comprehensive definitions of every form of gag and narrative joke. Nor is it an empirical study of comedy itself. The aim is to offer comedy writers some broad principles and practical methods for devising and assessing their work.

Though many of the topics covered in this book can be applied to writing stand-up material or comic plays, stories and movies, the central purpose is to aid screenwriters in developing sitcom. This manual covers the process from the germ of an idea to a fully-fledged series ready for pitching. But be warned: those who know the principles of comedy can come to look on it in much the same way a gynaecologist looks at human reproduction: with too much knowledge to find it sexy.

There's every chance you won't agree with everything in this book, or even with the proposition that a valid theory of comedy is possible. But, as you'll see from the examples in this book, countless comedians and comic writers have successfully applied these principles.

Writing comedy is not for the faint-hearted. It is one of the most challenging creative experiences there is. But it's also one of the most rewarding. Seriously.

The Principles of Comedy

For as long as it's been recorded (the earliest satires date back to ancient Greece), comedy has been comprised of a range of elements and principles that have not changed. Comedy may have a thousand skins but its bones remain the same.

Just as any story must feature a protagonist who faces obstacles to their goal, comedy relies upon a specific range of principles. These principles are based upon primal understandings shared by every human being on the planet.

Though the higher cognitive processes of the brain vary from person to person, the same raw human instincts drive us all. We all have a funny bone.

Sure, each culture may have its own comedy traditions. The Germans, despite appearances, love to laugh. They particularly enjoy *Schadenfreude*, laughter at the misfortunes of others. The Japanese have *Manzai*, a comic tradition first developed in the Heian Period (794–1185). *Manzai* features a two-man team made up of the '*Boke*' (an enthusiastic idiot with a short memory who misunderstands things) and the '*Tsukkomi*' (a dour straight-guy who constantly interrupts the *Boke* to correct him and hit him on the head with a stick). The Italians have *Commedia Dell'Arte*, a tradition dating back to the 16th century that gave birth to Punch and Judy.

Each nation's comedy traditions, however, operate on the same principles. Laughter at a man slipping on a banana peel, the slapstick of the Three Stooges and the psychological cruelty of David Brent in *The Office* are all manifestations of *Schadenfreude*. Comic duos such as Abbott and Costello, Lano and Woodley (Colin Lane and Frank Woodley) and Mark Wary and Jerry (Jason Gann and Dailan Evans) all share a similar dynamic to the ancient *Boke* and the *Tsukkomi*. Mr and Mrs Castanza in *Seinfeld* and Frank and Marie in *Everybody Loves Raymond* share qualities with the ever-battling, baby-taunting Punch and Judy.

Given these contemporary examples of ancient traditions from far-flung countries, it's clear that successful comedy is not so much about what you do, it's about how you do it. This book presents the *what*. The *how* is up to you.

Below are ten principles of comedy. They don't all have to be present in a character, scene or joke for it to be funny, and many apply equally to drama. But they represent the 'territory' of comedy. If you're laughing at something, at least one of these fundamentals will be at work.

- Comedy deals with the abrupt negation, reversal, equation, furthering or exaggeration of given elements.
- It compares, combines, associates, deconstructs or changes the context of given elements.
- It uses stories, characters, rhythms and repetition to build and then defy assumptions and expectations.
- It presents nonsense scenarios or propositions, uses random elements to create absurdities, and applies faulty logic to known absolutes or truisms.
- It inverts values, portraying the trivial as important, the irrational as rational, the incomplete as complete—and vice versa—to illuminate larger truths, or expose the fallacies in accepted truths.
- It examines human nature and relationships by distilling and compressing character and narrative.
- It offers bare truths, not fanciful escapism.
- It examines individual human behaviour, often to highlight common behaviour or broader social concerns.
- It distils complexities and makes the simple complex.
- It uses metaphor to highlight aspects of situations or themes.

Above all, comedy uses any of the above to provoke laughter through affinity, anxiety and surprise.

There isn't a successful comedian or comedy-writer on earth that doesn't rely on one or more of the principles above. The principles do not change between centuries, nations, or artists. Nor do they vary between degrees of sophistication, public taste, age, social awareness or political leanings.

Once learned, the principles can never be forgotten. The fact is, we know them already without being told. For example, if a comic hero finds a pot of gold, how long do you think he will keep it? The answer is, of course, 'not for long'. He'll either lose it, trade it or give it away. There's no way he'll have it at the end of his story, unless it's the last thing he wants.

Somehow, we all know this. It's an inevitable scenario that chimes a primal bell in all of us. A comedy-writer's job is to ring that bell like it's going out of fashion, safe in the knowledge that it never will.

The Nature of Laughter

Everyone laughs, even Methodists. Though the trigger may vary, it's a behaviour shared by virtually all human beings. The ability to laugh is deeply ingrained in our psychological make-up. For all we know, it has been with us since caves had ensuites.

Scientists, biologists and psychologists have put forward countless theories on the origins, causes and effects of human laughter. But getting a laugh is a science only comedians and comedy writers must master.

Laughter has several mysterious qualities. Like blushing, adrenalin rushes and erections, laughter is involuntary. We've all had the giggles at inappropriate times. In fact, the greater the threat of reprisal, the more we giggle. Furthermore, we can't *decide* to be amused. We might expect to laugh at a stand-up comedian, but that doesn't mean we will. Neither can we delay a laugh until we're ready—as anyone who's snorted beer out their nostrils will attest.

By the same token, we can't convince ourselves something is funny any more than we can make ourselves believe someone is sexy—unless we're drunk, and even then it doesn't always work.

Few jokes can make us laugh twice. Yet if we *do* find one, it's likely to keep us laughing for the rest of our lives, whenever we think of it.

Laughter stimulates the release of endorphins—peptide hormones with properties similar to morphine—that can lower stress levels, increase stamina and act as painkillers. A small amount of adrenaline may also be released during laughter. These are chemicals one might associate with fighting or fleeing rather than sitting and watching comedy or dining with funny friends. The descriptors for laughter and comedy also tend towards the violent. Audience members speak of comic material that is 'close to the bone', 'painful to watch' or 'so very *wrong*'. A comedian who has a bad show might say 'I died', but if the show went well they'll say 'I killed 'em', 'It was slaughter' or 'There was blood on the floor'. A comedy audience member who's had a good time might say 'I cried', 'I couldn't breathe' or 'I pissed myself'. Unless you're into sadomasochism, none of the above sound like entertainment.

So what's going on? If we have no control over when we laugh, what we laugh at and how our bodies respond to excessive laughing, then why do we seek it out?

The perspective on laughter that I have found most useful as a writer is one I like to formalise as the 'Underlying Primal Response' theory. It may be simplistic (or even completely wrong) but it works for me.

The theory describes how the key elements of humour, namely surprise and human vulnerability, generate laughter. In essence, laughter is a response to danger averted, avoided or denied.

According to the UPR theory, laughter is a primitive response to simulated danger—danger to our social status, our equilibrium or our physical survival. When we hear an embarrassing joke or a surprising punchline, only the nub of the information is understood by our primitive fight-or-flight brain. A joke that makes an unexpected connection between two otherwise unrelated things registers in the primate brain simply as 'Surprise!' in the same way that it might register a tiger's camouflage in a bamboo jungle. Though our higher brain knows the difference between real and simulated danger, the primal brain is not geared to take chances. It initiates basic fear-and-flight responses such as making noises of alarm, releasing adrenalin and endorphins and bladder evacuation. Our conscious mind diverts this response to the laughter mechanism. As American comedian Bob Newhart says, 'Laughter gives us distance. It allows us to step back from an event, deal with it, and then move on'. We rarely laugh at the same thing twice because, having learned, we're less susceptible to surprise a second time. If we laugh repeatedly at the same thing, it's because it remains a consistent (if only notional) threat to our equilibrium.

The reason the fight-or-flight response is diverted to the laughter mechanism rather than simply suppressed is that laughter is also a social tool, helping people bond and find affinity with one another. The presence of others makes us socially vulnerable, and this may explain why we tend to laugh more when others are around. It's no accident that many sitcoms fake the group-laughter experience by using 'canned' or live-audience laughter on their soundtracks. Producers know that adding a laugh track both highlights the show's humour to the viewing public and boosts the laughs the show generates. Sixty years of broadcasting has yet to prove them wrong.

Live comedy audiences also enjoy laughing together. A sense of togetherness evolves as our private fears and weaknesses are dragged into public view. We are united by our shared vulnerability. When a comedian singles out an individual audience member for ridicule, the rest of the audience laughs, partly from relief that it's not them (although they know they remain in danger) and partly from an affinity with the victim's pain.

The victim is usually blushing and helpless with laughter. They laugh hardest when they interpret the laughter around them as essentially benign: audience identification proves that they have survived the social danger and are still part of the group. Sometimes, however, people interpret this laughter as unfriendly. That is, they feel the audience is laughing *at* them because there is something genuinely different about them. This may be why comedians tend not to pick on, say, disabled people, as this can too easily be construed as the humour of exclusion rather than inclusion.

Comedians like to pick on people who've chosen the limelight, such as celebrities or politicians, because this makes them fair game. And if an audience member provokes an exchange with a comedian by heckling, they have singled themselves out and must cop whatever comes to them.

Laughter can also signal to others that an apparently threatening situation is actually okay, as when we witness someone falling over. If they sit up and laugh, this immediately signals that they are unhurt. Likewise, to an observer, someone being tickled could look like an attack. It's only the laughter that tells us it's actually enjoyable.

Even the act of smiling bears similarities to the fight-or-flight response. Sure, good teeth are a sign of healthy breeding stock but the other signal conveyed by bared teeth is, 'Stay back or I'll bite'. In both smiling and expressing fear, lips are stretched wide, teeth are bared and eyebrows are raised. A frightened face is all teeth and eyeballs, a smile without joy. To most of us an easy smile suggests a positive personality. This may be because we feel a smiling person is one whose insecurities are on display, and that therefore they're an honest, open person we can trust.

The evolutionary imperative has also equipped men and women with subtly different senses of humour. In 2009, research by psychologists Kristofor McCarty at Northumbria University in England, showed that women find a man's sense of humour a key attribute in his attractiveness—findings confirmed by every women's magazine on the planet. ('Why is humour so sexy? Exploration into quality humour production as a possible indicator of intelligence').

While there are many situations in which a light-hearted outlook is desirable in itself (such as smiling in the face of hardship), the research suggests that a sense of humour demonstrates an ability to think quickly and laterally, to surprise and anticipate, showing confidence and cleverness—attributes directly relevant to the ancient skills of hunting, fighting and shelter-building. A man who makes a woman laugh is proving to her that he is capable of meeting danger. Sadly, as we all know, time erodes a man's ability to surprise his partner. 'His jokes used to be funny, but now I'm tired of them. Besides, he's already built the hut.'

Men also include a sense of humour on their list of a woman's desirable attributes, but it rates lower than long legs, big boobs and intelligence (also, incidentally, survival attributes). When was the last time you heard a guy say, 'I just want to meet a woman with a sense of humour'? According to McCarty, the average man would rather a woman laugh at *his* jokes than he laugh at hers.

Learning to Laugh

The most reliable stimulus for laughter is tickling. And yet even here the laughter response can be enhanced by mock-threatening behaviour.

For instance, imagine you are about to tickle a toddler. Do you simply reach out your hands and tickle? Is any part of the baby—e.g. their shoulders or scalp—as ticklish as any other? Do you remain silent as you tickle? Do you tickle the same spot throughout the exercise?

Of course not. To be effective, tickling should be an unfolding drama. A popular tickling routine follows the form of the rhyme below:

Round and round the garden,

Like a teddy-bear.

One step, two step,

Tickly under there!

The routine accompanying the rhyme goes as follows:

1. The tickler begins by ever-so-lightly drawing circles in the victim's palm, using a voice that is light but full of portent: 'Round and round the garden, like a teddy bear ...'

2. The tickler finger-steps up the victim's arm with the delicacy and care of a stalking cat, using a tone that increases tension in the victim: 'One step ... two step ...'

3. Finally, the tickler pounces swiftly, using misdirection to evade the victim's defences. The tickler's voice changes to a rapid and threatening attack: 'Tickly under there!'

The tickler strikes at the armpits, neck, waist, groin, inner thighs, the back of the knees or the soles of the feet. Nowhere else on the body will reliably induce laughter. Why these points?

Our DNA got its act together when savage predators were a fact of life. An attack on the vulnerable points mentioned above would sever vital arteries, gouge essential organs or, in the case of the soles of the feet, render the victim incapable of flight. The caveman might survive without his elbows. His skull and shinbones might withstand a tiger's jaws and he might even have a chance with a chomp out of his buttock. But a savage bite to the neck? Forget it.

When vulnerable body parts are threatened we react instinctively by moving and making noise. In the stone age this behaviour would alert fellow tribe members to the presence of danger, increasing the victim's and the tribe's chances of survival. By training a child to respond to play-danger, parents are unconsciously teaching their kids to recognise their vulnerable points and respond effectively when genuinely threatened.

To make an audience laugh, however, we don't have to inspire fear or savage their vital organs. If that were the case, *Dawn of the Dead* would be a comedy instead of a horror film. But the trappings of horror (surprise, disorder, an assault on vulnerable points) are an integral part of any comic strategy. Ralph Waldo Emerson called comedy the 'balking of the intellect'. When the intellect is confounded, the primal mind responds. Comedy upsets order, reveals hidden meaning, finds unexpected connections, reverses situations, exploits blindspots, exposes vulnerabilities, highlights logical flaws and subverts expectations.

Fear! Surprise! Yes, these are our weapons.

Chapter One:
Gag Principles

'If only smart people like your shit, it ain't that smart.'

—Chris Rock

The first two chapters deal with straight-up gags. Though they are often used in comic dialogue, straight-up gags are essentially stand-alone jokes that don't rely on character humour. They're the domain of stand-up comedy and wisecracks. Narrative gags, that is, gags that drive a comic story, are covered later in the book.

Every joke contains its own 'DNA': its own combination of known qualities, albeit often in an original context. Both straight-up and narrative gags share characteristics that are drawn from the overriding principles of comedy such as surprise, negation, metaphor, irony and character-comedy. Using successful examples from comedians and narrative comedies, this chapter explores the basic components, the individual genes that represent the principles of comedy.

The purpose of outlining the principles is to help you on the days when nothing funny is coming to mind. Instead of eyeing the sharp objects in the house, you can apply these principles to the theme, characters and situation of your comic story.

Simplicity and Surprise

Comedy demands simplicity. If it takes ten seconds to work out the meaning of a punchline, you won't get a laugh; the audience has already moved on. Clarity is key.

But don't be fooled—simplicity ain't easy. Many a comedy writer has come unstuck by layering their comedy with clever ambiguities. Any monkey can make a fruitcake, but it can take years of practice to get a soufflé right every time—even though it must be the simplest dessert on the planet.

Every comic scene must have a clear purpose, though its machinations may be complex. Farce, in particular, can involve a lot of doors opening and closing as characters bustle about to achieve their goals. This farcical chaos, however, must be driven by a simple idea. The core qualities and objectives of each character must be crystal clear.

Why? Because the best ideas are simple. We see them and slap our foreheads—'Why didn't I think of bulldog clips?' Einstein's formula, $E=mc^2$, turned the world of physics on its head. A DNA strand is an elegant double helix, a far simpler form than scientists Watson and Crick had imagined. Genius in any field can be found in those who distil a complicated set of variables into a simple principle. Or, to put it another way, simple ideas can generate complex meanings.

In terms of gag-writing, brevity and simplicity keep a joke a step ahead of the audience while keeping them in touch with what the joke is about. As for writing sitcom, cutting unnecessary story—or character—complications and maintaining a brisk pace are vital to making an episode work. This is not to say that a joke, story or characters can't be dense with detail. *Arrested Development* (created by Mitchell Hurwitz) is a sitcom with complex characters and multiple inter-connected storylines. But each of these elements are presented with clarity. The show moves at a breakneck pace, averaging sixty scenes per twenty-one-minute show compared to, for instance, *The Golden Girls* (created by Susan Harris) which averages eight scenes per show. (Twenty-one minutes, by the way, is referred to as a 'commercial half-hour'. It excludes credits and ad breaks.) To cope with this pace, the audience needs the clearest possible story. Bewilderment has its place (for instance, when the audience momentarily shares a character's confusion at events that have escaped their control), but too much bewilderment leads the audience to conclude the writers are also confused. There is no room for embellishment or diatribe. The elegant clarity of *Arrested Development* is testament to the writers' discipline; they surrender to the fundamental law of narrative: the story is king.

Clarity begins with the questions, 'What is the heart of this story? What is the heart of this character?' This does not discount subtlety as a comic tool, but the subtlety is in the delivery, not the substance. A character can expose their qualities and intentions through choices that are delicate or even implied, but they must nevertheless be clear or the audience will miss the point. A slight nod can mean the end of the world or the beginning of a great love—or both—but we must understand, in that moment, what it means.

In comedy, simplicity serves. All else is vanity.

All punchlines, even the most straightforward, have an element of surprise. If they didn't, we'd duck the punch. Like boxers, comedians and comedy writers use misdirection to get past our defences. The primal mind doesn't like surprises: they could be life-threatening. Laughter is an involuntary expression of the relief that follows.

Humans are capable of the most outlandish flights of fancy, yet when hearing a story, we tend to make logical connections based on what is familiar. Humour exploits this tendency. Just when the audience thinks they know where a joke is headed, it hits them with an entirely different outcome. The result is laughter. (This is why knowing the principles of joke construction can suck the fun out of hearing them: you're aware of all the possibilities in the set-up. Maybe that's why comedians are so depressed.)

> An Englishman, a Scotsman and an Irishman walk into a bar—and nothing fucking happens.
>
> —Jerry Sadowitz

Characters are more interesting when, while remaining true to their fundamental qualities, they still surprise us. When a comic character is in a fix, their distortions and cover-ups should exceed or defy our expectations. After all, if we might have come up with the same solution, how can we be surprised? We laugh when a clever character ties themselves in knots or an idiot solves a complex problem with a simple solution.

Misdirection in comedy plays on an audience's tendency to assume a certain meaning from given words, phrases, titles, the flow of a scene or a popular song or quote.

> I hate it when you fall asleep on the wheel—and it's a pottery-making wheel.
>
> —Elliot Goblet

In the right context, even the obvious can be a surprise:

> If you're being chased by a police dog, try not to go through a tunnel, then on to a little seesaw, then jump through a hoop of fire. They're trained for that.
>
> —Milton Jones

No-one is safe. Assumptions about identity, sensibility and intention can all fall prey to a comedy-writer's trickery. There's a well-known guessing-game scenario that goes:

> A man takes his sick son to the hospital. But at the hospital, the doctor looks at the boy and says, 'This is my son!' How can this be?

It's particularly troubling to see educated women scratch their heads at this quandary because the doctor is, of course, a woman. For some reason the first image most people conjure is a man in a white coat wearing a stethoscope. Similarly, we tend to assume footballers, boxers and terrorists are all male, though there's no reason for us to do so.

But it's not just sex-role assumptions that are open to manipulation …

> *A wife is in the bedroom. Her husband walks in with a duck under his arm.*
> HUSBAND: Darling, this is the pig I've been screwing.
> WIFE: That's not a pig, it's a duck.
> HUSBAND: I was talking to the duck.

Most of the time assumptions work in our favour. Traffic, for example, moves with relative safety due to countless assumptions made by drivers. The colours red, amber and green have an agreed (though arbitrary) meaning to everyone with a licence. Comedy relies heavily upon an audience drawing upon this cognitive lexicon.

Surprise can be generated by misdirection concerning a character's beliefs or intentions:

> I'm on a hunger strike. Three weeks—no hunger.
> —Michael Klimczak

> They lie about marijuana, tell you pot-smoking makes you unmotivated. Lie! When you're high, you can do everything you normally do just as well—you just realise it's not worth the fucking effort.
> —Bill Hicks

Or misdirection concerning a character's role or situation:

> People come up to me and say, 'Steve, what is film editing?' And I say, 'How should I know? You're the director.'
> —Steve Martin

> A girl phoned me the other day and said, 'Come on over, there's nobody home'. I went over. Nobody was home.
> —Rodney Dangerfield

The primary reason for keeping jokes as brief as possible is to maintain surprise. While an audience listens to a joke, unconsciously their minds dart ahead to anticipate the punchline. With enough time, unless it's a gob-smacking surprise, they may work out where the joke is going. Brevity keeps the teller one step ahead.

Brevity also means that the audience is given the minimum information. The less they know, the more assumptions they make and the easier they are to misdirect. Essentially, it's sleight of hand using words instead of florid hand gestures and a drugged rabbit.

Shaggy-dog gags may take a long time to execute but they too are built on the sparest information—it's simply repeated ad nauseum. The following gag can be drawn out to epic proportions as the man crawls over laneways, parks, major highways, neighbours' gardens or Mount Kilimanjaro. Yet these details, as colourful as they may be, are redundant to the gag itself. They provide the misdirecting 'shagginess' while the 'dog' is still simple and spare. Despite the apparent surfeit of detail a vital piece of information is omitted from the set-up.

A man at his local pub is so drunk, he crawls home, pulling himself hand-over-hand, inch by exhausting inch. (Elaborate at will.) When he finally gets home, his wife says, 'Paddy, you're drunk! And you left your wheelchair at the pub again'.

—Unattrib.

Note that the punchline does not state directly that the man is a paraplegic, but uses a new story element, the wheelchair, to imply the crucial information. A punchline such as, 'When he gets home he's exhausted because he's a paraplegic' falls flat because the information is given outside the context of the story. A justifiable story element keeps the audience within the fictional scenario—and implies the truth rather than states it. A punchline that implies a comic contradiction is usually superior to one that is baldly stated.

For example, there are many ways to highlight a wife's talent for remembering every mistake her husband has made. An example of a *good* gag on this topic:

Any married man should forget his mistakes—there's no use in two people remembering the same thing.

—Vicky'sjokes.com

Seventeen words can say so much!

The words in this gag are kept to a bare minimum. The gag doesn't even mention wives—their role in the joke is implicit in the use of the term 'married man'.

The gag is simple. No examples of married men's mistakes are listed.

The contrast between women and men that the joke suggests is clear—men forget and women remember.

The punchline asks the audience to work albeit for a split second. The punchline *assumes* that a wife is certain to remember her husband's mistakes. The audience has to draw this conclusion to get a laugh. The lead-in offers advice to married men. The punchline draws on the common knowledge that partners divide chores, e.g. 'You remember to pick up the kids and I'll remember to mow the lawn'. The punchline accords with general conceptions about married life, so the reasoning behind the observation isn't confusing.

An example of a *bad* gag on this topic:

'There's no point in a married man remembering the time he set fire to the house. Wives remember everything—she'll remind him if he forgets.'

Twenty-five words can say *too* much. The mention of the man setting fire to the house pushes the joke in a specific direction when the topic is general.

The punchline doesn't refer to the fire so the listener can lose the main drift of the gag.

'Wives remember everything' is a direct declaration of the message of the joke. The audience doesn't have to think—they are passive.

'She'll remind him if he forgets' fails for the same reason. A female comedian might make it work by delivering it with a wry or threatening inflection, but without that, the punchline does the audience's thinking for them.

So how can we tell if a gag is good or bad?

Comedy is not an exact science, but the principles above can be boiled down into the following criteria you can match against all gags.

BREVITY

A gag should be boiled down to its bare minimum. Even a shaggy-dog joke needs a tight punchline. While audiences listen to a gag, their minds are racing to guess where the joke is going. The longer the gag takes, the longer they have to devise their own punchlines. Keeping a gag lean helps the teller stay a step ahead of the listener. Packing in as much implied information as possible gives a gag punch.

SIMPLICITY

Avoid distractions. The elements of a given gag should relate directly to the punchline.

CONTRAST

The contrasts in negations, juxtapositions, distortions or misinterpretations should be stark.

LET THE AUDIENCE DO THE WORK

Instead of openly declaring the gag's message, you can allow the audience to draw their own conclusion from the bare information the gag gives them.

EXERCISE

1. Create a commonplace scenario:

    For example, A man crawling home.

2. Identify every likely assumption associated with it: the setting, the characters, the dialogue …

For example: The man lives in a city or town, he has been drinking in a pub or club, alcohol has robbed him of the ability to walk but he is otherwise able-bodied, the home he crawls towards is his home …

3. Look for other circumstances that would support the scenario. These can range from the commonsense to the ridiculous.

For example: The man is literally legless, he's dying of thirst, he's smelling his way home, he's left crumbs of salt-and-vinegar crisps on the asphalt to guide his way, he's crawling to a home—not his home …

4. Select a simple story element that will infer missing information that transforms the assumed scenario.

For example: The man's wife remarks that he's lost his wheelchair, implying that he is crippled, or she remarks that he's the publican and they live above the pub.

Irony and Sarcasm

There is controversy over the true meaning of the term 'irony'—possibly even more than over the meaning of the word 'No' in certain circles.

Some say irony is sarcasm, or a type of sarcasm, or that sarcasm is a type of irony. Or neither. Or both. Irony and sarcasm, however, are distinct. There are two essential qualities for irony: intentionality and unintended consequence. The Iraq War is ironic because its stated intention was to stabilise the Middle East. Sarcasm is related because the unintended consequence is there, but the intention is always attributed after the fact by the sarcastic observer, as in seeing someone trip over their shoelace and saying, 'That was smart.' The person falling over may or may not have believed they were smart. But if Steve Jobs tripped on his shoelaces while demonstrating the high-tech iPhone, that would be ironic. God is reminding us that He has control. If sarcasm is a shotgun, irony is a dirty First Aid kit. Irony comes in various forms.

COMIC IRONY

Although *all* categories of irony have comic potential, 'comic irony' occurs in only two forms:

a) Because of their own actions, a character's intention or desire is denied. For example, Karl flirts with a woman, hoping his wife will become enraged and leave him. His wife however thinks he's flirting with the woman so they can all have a threesome and desires him all the more.

b) Because of their own true nature, a character's intention or desire is denied. For example, Karl's natural inability to make emotional connections is misread by his wife who thinks he's merely playing hard-to-get—an irresistible challenge!

A security guard with chronic insecurities, a would-be Casanova with Tourette's Syndrome and a doctor who can't stand the sight of blood are all ironic characters because they are doomed to frustration. A rocket scientist, despite his brilliance, might be so absent-minded he can't walk home without company: that would be ironic. In a similar vein, one Gary Larson cartoon depicts a student trying to enter the Midvale School for the Gifted. He is pushing as hard as he can against a door marked 'Pull'.

EXERCISE

Devise your own comic ironies using the following set-ups:

1. Brunhilde is a sweet and shy woman who wants to find a husband.

2. Vladimir is a chronic gambler who wants one last win.

3. Rex is a superhero who wants to win a local weight-lifting competition.

SITUATIONAL IRONY

The outcome of an action differs from, or is contrary to, the expected or intended outcome.

A claustrophobic man from the city decides to avoid close spaces by climbing to the top of a mountain. But the weather turns bad and he's forced to spend the night in a cramped cave on the mountainside, where his claustrophobia is worse than before.

EXERCISE

Devise ironic events and outcomes for these scenarios:

1. Claudio is tired of being ignored. He wants to meet someone who will listen to his problems and arranges some dates over the internet.

2. Jemima is a realist. She wants her best friend, Sybilla, to abandon her belief in God. She takes Sybilla to a church and calls upon God to appear.

3. The Archangel Gabriel is given a new assignment: impregnate a virgin in Sydney's western suburbs.

DRAMATIC IRONY

Due to a character's lack of knowledge, their every action or word is laced with a different or opposite meaning for the other characters in the story and also for the audience.

In Act One of *Three Amigos!* (by Steve Martin, Lorne Michaels and Randy Newman), the villagers who hire the amigos to save them from the dreaded bandit El Guapo have no idea the Amigos are actors, not gunfighters. The Amigos themselves are unaware that their identity has been mistaken and happily prepare to do a 'show' for the villagers with El Guapo (whom they assume is an actor). The audience knows all and watches the two groups labour under their respective misapprehensions.

EXERCISE

Devise dramatic ironies that undermine the following scenarios:

1. Davo excitedly shows Suzie his plans for a bank robbery.

2. Detective Smith leads the Chief of Police through a murder scene.

3. John weds Marsha.

VERBAL IRONY

The intended meaning differs from or is contrary to the actual meaning. Verbal irony can be intentional:

> (On Donald Rumsfeld) He's described as the architect of the war on Iraq. And he should be very proud because he's built something that is going to last for years and years.
>
> —Jay Leno

Or unintentional:

> World War I was waged 'to end all wars'. World War II followed soon after.

Put the horse before the cart. Layering a script with ironies is a process best begun in the planning or treatment stage. Imposing ironies once characters and stories are built can involve undoing much of the work you've done.

SARCASM

According to the *Oxford Concise*, 'sarcasm' is used 'to improve the mood and self-esteem of others; an innocent diversion'.

Yeah, right …

Sarcasm is to state the opposite of one's meaning in a way deliberately intended to ridicule, injure or criticise. It's derived from the Greek 'sarkazo' meaning 'to tear flesh' and 'gnash the teeth'.

Sarcasm is as witty as the person who applies it. When Oscar Wilde said that sarcasm 'is the lowest form of wit' he was, of course, being sarcastic, given that he used it with such deftness.

> I often take exercise. Why only yesterday I had breakfast in bed.
> —Oscar Wilde

Sarcasm cuts to the chase. It can sum up a situation, character or idea with deadly accuracy. By the same token, its directness means that sarcastic characters can become monotonous. To stay a step ahead of the audience, sarcastic characters need to vary their technique. For instance, they can—

- Invert the truth:
  GARY: Does my arse look fat in these shorts?
  GRACE: Fat? In those miniscule things? Not at all.

- Invert their meaning:
  GARY: I thought I'd wear the shorts to the dinner party.
  GRACE: Oh, wonderful. Fabulous. Terrific …

- Exaggerate while implying the opposite:
  GARY: Come on, these shorts are quite stylish.
  GRACE: Yeah, you look like Brad Pitt.

- Unfairly compare:
  GARY: But don't I look sexy in these shorts?
  GRACE: Oh, yes … sexy like a hippo in a g-string.

- Suggest an unpleasant consequence:
  GARY: I'm wearing these shorts to the dinner party whether you like it or not.
  GRACE: Great. Just give me a minute to kill myself.

Of course, sarcasm is a trait that implies cynicism or wisdom, and thus is not suitable for every character. Sarcasm in the mouth of a sweet or innocent character distracts from the story because it violates their nature, unless the change is dramatically justified.

Observation Humour

Most things become silly if you look at them closely enough. Many comedians make careers out of highlighting the silliness of everyday events, actions or objects. Their skewed observations can surprise us with anomalies, contradictions and paradoxes that are plain once we think about them. This kind of comedy is devised through deconstructing the subject matter by observing it from a fresh perspective, or changing its context.

Audience familiarity with the subject matter is crucial in observation comedy: it works by making the familiar strange, seizing on common behaviour that would otherwise go unnoticed. Holding the commonplace but unconsidered action up to scrutiny plays upon our mild, but genuine, embarrassment.

The devilishly clever Irish-Australian comedian Jimeoin performs a routine about stifling yawns. He imitates the various faces people pull, and the strange voices in which they speak, as they struggle to conceal their yawns from others. The audience laughs at Jimeoin's canny identification of this insignificant but revealing behaviour and the obsessive detail with which he portrays it gives the humour another layer. Reverence is given to the trivial.

DECONSTRUCTION

The absurdity concealed in the mundane can be revealed by deconstructing something and examining its individual components. Robin Williams has a routine in which he explains the basics of golf. In typical Williams' style, he portrays both a mad Scotsman and a polite, well-spoken questioner.

> Here's my idea of a fucking sport—I knock a ball into a gopher hole. 'Oh, you mean like pool?' Fuck off pool! Not with a straight stick. With a little fucked-up stick …
>
> —Robin Williams

The golf routine goes on to detail all the elements essential to golf: the laborious process by which a little ball must be propelled into a tiny hole deliberately placed among sandpits, long grass and ponds. It requires a stick, a flag in the hole ('to give you hope') and he caps the routine with a declaration that the process doesn't take place once—it must be repeated eighteen times. Along the way his polite interlocutor suggests comparisons: is golf like pool? Croquet? Bowling? Each are robustly rejected by the Scotsman: 'Fuck, no!'

It's a funny routine and golf is revealed as an inane pastime comprised of unlikely elements that only an idiot or a bastard would devise. But not once does Williams stray from the truth. He may exaggerate the frustration of trying to get a ball into a faraway hole with only a 'little fucked-up stick', and he may use his own funny turns of phrase, but he tells us the facts. His explanation is rendered comic by the way he isolates the elements of golf, none of which, by themselves, seem in any way enjoyable or worthwhile. Taken as a whole they might make a fun game, but detailed separately they sound like a form of torture.

Any process with which the audience is familiar can be deconstructed in the same way. Even the other games mentioned in Williams' golf routine (pool, croquet and bowling) would not stand up to scrutiny of their individual elements. Similarly, rituals such as weddings, marriage proposals and funerals are comprised of odd or incongruous elements (e.g. veils, going down on one knee, open coffins) that can be held up to the light one by one to comic effect.

PERSPECTIVE

The commonplace can also appear quirky or unique when examined from an original perspective.

In the following routine Steven Wright takes a bird's perspective on annual migration. Wright begins by reporting that he saw a bird wearing a badge saying 'I ain't flying nowhere'.

> He said, 'I'm sick of this stuff. Every year it's the same thing—winter here, summer there. I dunno who thought this up but it certainly wasn't a bird'.
>
> —Steven Wright

Wright's bird is given the human characteristics of a bored truck driver stuck on the same route, back and forth, day after day. He's *over* it.

Seeing things through the eyes of a character or archetype can make common activities new and surprising. Robin Williams' Scotsman above is fiercely proud that golf is the most cruel and pointless of sports. His enthusiastic description juxtaposes some unlikely ideas: leisure and cruelty, pride and inanity.

CHANGING CONTEXT

The question, '[Subject]: what's *that* about?' is a cliché of stand-up comedy. Changing the context of familiar things can highlight their silliness and reveal a larger truth in the same way as a metaphor. For instance, throwing rice at newlyweds is a traditional part of the wedding ritual. But what about other foods that often go with rice? How would the newlyweds react if we pelted them with beef casserole or soy sauce? What if the rice was cooked? What if we threw rice at our married friends every time we saw them? All these absurdities highlight the larger truth that throwing rice at newlyweds has lost its traditional meaning. It's become something we do without thinking.

Thoughtless group behaviour is prime material for a context change. For instance:

> The Mexican wave: what the hell is that about? Thousands of football fans throw their arms up and shout in sequence. I wonder, when a Mexican waves at his friend in the street, does everyone else in the street wave in sequence? And, once the wave starts, where does it stop? No wonder the Mexico economy's in trouble—every thirty seconds, everyone has to stop working and wave.
>
> —Tallulah Lowe

Even a whistling kettle can be turned to comic effect with a change of context. Kettles are inanimate household objects, but whistling is a human pastime. Comic juxtapositions emerge when, for instance, we imagine other common household items also doing entertaining things:

> I have a kettle that whistles when the water boils. Now I want a toaster that sings.

Specifics can make a gag more vivid and immediate. A generality such as 'sings' is okay—we get the idea. But the gag has more kick if it contains a detail that tells a bigger story.

> … Now I want a toaster that sings 'Viva Las Vegas'.

The punchline could relate to the topic in some way.

> … Now I want a toaster that sings 'A Hunka-Hunka Burning Bread'.

On the other hand, the comic juxtaposition could emerge from an examination of the whistle rather than the kettle. What happens when we hear humans whistling?

> The kettle's driving me crazy. Once I hear it I've got the tune in my head all day.

Virtually anything commonplace to the audience can be turned to comic effect through deconstruction, or a change of perspective or context.

A change of perspective or context can be enhanced when the teller themselves seems at one remove from the mainstream. Many successful observation comedians have, or play characters who have, strong regional accents (e.g. Billy Connolly, Jimeoin, Chris Rock, Jeff Foxworthy). Others have an offbeat appearance (Elliot Goblet, Steven Wright, Bill Bailey) or exhibit a personal quality that sets them apart from the herd (Eddie Izzard wears dresses, Julian Clary is deliciously camp, Emo Phillips sounds like a deranged cartoon animal).

Creating a distinctive on-stage persona enhances the 'otherness' of the comedian, commanding attention by holding out the prospect of a fresh perspective on familiar things. Even a ventriloquist's dummy is in essence a character disjointed or removed from the ordinary, and therefore capable of saying anything.

In other words, looking and sounding funny can be half the battle. If you intend to perform an observation routine, a good place to start is by devising a distinctive on-stage persona, based perhaps on an aspect of yourself that is already a little different.

EXERCISE

Deconstruct, change perspective on, or the context of, the following rituals of courtship in order to reveal comic insights.

For example, French kissing can be deconstructed into lips, tongues, teeth, saliva and heavy breathing. It involves an approach and meeting of mouths, the choosing of sides to tilt one's head, one kisser's adaptation to the other's technique, nibbling, sucking and tongues revolving around tongues. It doesn't take much scrutiny before each of these on their own begin to seem silly and a little disgusting. Even the name itself is odd: the French didn't invent passionate kissing any more than they invented etiquette—though they might have been the first to do it shamelessly.

A perspective change to a tongue's point of view will reveal this romantic pastime in a new light. A tongue might see kissing as a tiresome exercise for little reward—'I work and work but in the end I can't taste a thing, except sometimes a little stale tobacco'. Or the tongue might make a comparison to something incongruous like mining: 'It's hard work in the dark, but even if you find a gold tooth, you don't have anything to drill it with'.

Giving one of the kissers an archetypal personality yields other results: a toothless pensioner, a teenager with braces or Robin Williams' Scotsman will each have their own view on the art of pashing. And if a germ-o-phobe or someone with a blocked nose is asked to French kiss, how do they go about it?

Changing the context of French kissing prompts other questions: why don't newlyweds French kiss at the altar? Do the French always kiss like that? Wouldn't it make kissing goodbye to their grandmothers a little awkward?

Under this kind of scrutiny it doesn't take long before the act of French kissing seems ludicrous, pointless, embarrassing and un-sexy.

Examine each of the topics below in the same way:

Proposing marriage

Wooing a potential lover

Dumping a lover

Truth and Humorists

Many comedians and wise-cracking sitcom characters can get a laugh simply by voicing insights that their audience accepts have a grain of truth.

There is no formula to making insights funny beyond keeping them brief. The best comic lines of this type tend to imply a lot more than is said.

Sharp-witted comic characters can put their views in a nutshell. The right-wing radio talkback host, Neville Roach in *Shock Jock*, sums up his defence of gun ownership with the declaration 'Guns don't kill people—God kills people' ('Heaven Must Be There' by Steve Myhill).

Comedians who rely principally on this kind of material, such as the brilliant US reactionary Mort Sahl, sometimes call themselves 'humorists'. They don't do 'gags' *per se*. Instead, they make observations about the real world, typically politics, prejudice, relationships and the sexes. They are not exactly universal truths, but they express a perspective born of the comedian's own experience and shared by their fans.

Because a humorist's polemic is not gag-based, there is no guarantee it will work for every audience. A well-made, well-delivered gag will always have a degree of success: we can laugh at a joke even when we don't agree with its message. But the insights of Rod Quantock, the acerbic Australian left-winger, probably won't play in the gun clubs of Northern Queensland. Likewise, Friends of the Earth are unlikely to book the US Republican humorist PJ O'Rourke for any porpoise-kissing jamboree. While gags are, more or less, universally accessible, hard-won pearls of wisdom are not. If stand-up comedy is the performance vehicle of the brave, these people are at the foolhardy end of it.

All good humorists share one characteristic: an archetypal onstage persona, be it ethnic, regional, sexual or social. Performers like Rachel Berger, Richard Pryor, Woody Allen, Sarah Silverman, Lea DeLaria, Dave Chappelle and O'Rourke are all larger than life. They are 'character comics', but their character is a caricature of themselves.

Sometimes, the observations of humorists are not intrinsically funny. They're designed to confound their targets and comfort the converted. Janeane Garofalo made the following observation about conservative talkback-radio hosts: they 'have conned the American people into thinking there is such a thing as a pro-life, pro-war, pro-gun, pro-death-penalty Christian' (*Left of the Dial*, 2005). There is no 'gag' here beyond the negation inherent in hypocrisy. The statement could be regarded as simply an opinion, particularly if you happen to be a pro-life, pro-war, pro-gun, pro-death-penalty Christian. The thing that makes audiences laugh at Garofalo's observation is that she dares to say it. And her audience (as broad as Greenwich Village is wide) agrees with her. Likewise, PJ O'Rourke's views on nature will get cheers from his pals but boos from bushwalkers: 'Any person who has spent time outdoors actually doing something, such as hunting and fishing as opposed to standing there with a doobie in his mouth, knows nature is not intrinsically healthy'.

Understanding the comic intent in both lines requires the audience to know who is saying them. Out of context, read by someone with an opposing view, they could be seen simply as opinions.

Of course, all comedians infuse their humour with their personal beliefs, but humorists do nothing but tell the truth, the whole truth and nothing but what they reckon is the truth.

Truth, however, comes in many forms.

TRUISMS

Humorists and comedians all have truisms derived from their experience or identity:

> You can't buy love. But you can pay heavily for it.
> —Henny Youngman

> Australia has a history of male failures that became heroes ... Ned Kelly put a bucket over his head—hero. Burke and Wills got lost—heroes. Jews wandered in the desert for forty years, nobody called them a hero.
> —Rachel Berger

> That's right, 'Tell your Mama!', 'Tell your Mama!', 'Tell your Mama!'...
> Nobody tells Daddy shit!
> —Chris Rock

Comic characters can offer truisms that stem from their particular prejudices.

> The ship of state, Bernard, is the only ship that leaks from the top.
> —Sir Humphrey Appleby (*Yes Minister*, Antony Jay and
> Jonathan Lynn)

Green and green should never be seen, except with a dickhead in between.
—Bob Downe (Mark Trevorrow)

Never follow a hippy to a second location.
—Jack Donaghy ('Rosemary's Baby' by Jack Burditt and Tina Fey, *30 Rock*)

ASSERTIONS WITH A GRAIN OF TRUTH

Something doesn't have to be self-evident to contain an insight. These assertions often use metaphor or euphemism to make their point, and may be broadly accepted by their intended audience.

Liberals feel unworthy of their possessions. Conservatives feel they deserve everything they've stolen.
—Mort Sahl

A liberal is a conservative who hasn't been mugged yet.
—PJ O'Rourke

POINTED QUESTIONS

The truth can be left for the audience to infer. Sometimes the question itself pushes buttons that, in a different context, would be better left un-pushed.

Hitler was a bad man. Winston Churchill was a good man. But if you were in a balloon with Hitler and Churchill and you were losing altitude …
—Harry Hill

If money is the root of all evil, why does the Catholic Church have so much of it?
—Paul McDermott

DRAWING A LONG BOW

Some gags take an accepted fact and draw a conclusion that is absurd or does not necessarily follow.

If our founding fathers wanted us to care about the rest of the world, they wouldn't have declared independence from it.
—Stephen Colbert

If God didn't want us to eat beef, why'd he make cows so slow?
—Brothers Judd

Some comedians or comic characters use an audience's assumptions about them to build surprises. The bold and brazen Sarah Silverman repeatedly plays upon the audience's assumption that she is an archetypal razor-tongued beauty. They expect such a self-possessed modern woman to react angrily, or at least sassily, to a lewd approach at the entrance to a liquor store. However …

So I'm walking into the door, and standing, loitering outside the door
is a man. And I walk by him to.go in, and he says, 'I want pussy!' Now,
I don't want to seem conceited or anything, but (*getting excited*) he was
talking about me!
—Sarah Silverman

It's sarcasm, of course, which she sells as a genuine response.

The material of minority comedians will often focus upon the bigotry they face:

What do you mean you 'don't believe in homosexuality'? It's not like
the Easter Bunny; your belief isn't necessary.
—Lea DeLaria

… What would upset the Taliban more than a gay woman wearing a
suit in front of a room full of Jews?
—Ellen DeGeneres at the 2001 Emmy Awards

They're free to apply stereotypes to their own social group that could be viewed as offensive coming from others:

Terrorists don't take black hostages … I have yet to see one of us on
the news reading a hostage letter. Like, 'Uh … they is treatin' us good.
Uh, we are chillin' and shit. I'd like to give a shout out to Ray-Ray an'
Big Steve and, uh, send some Newports!'
—Dave Chappelle

Fat people are brilliant in bed. If I'm sitting on top of you, who's going
to argue?
—Jo Brand

And even though they can be the targets of bigotry, they're not beyond dishing out some of their own stereotypes:

I could be the first black President. I mean, I don't think anyone would
hurt me … because my vice president would be Mexican, for a little

'insurance'. I mean, you can shoot me, but you're just gunna open up the border.

—Dave Chappelle

Men lie the most. Women tell the *biggest* lies. A man lie is 'I was at Kevin's house'. A woman lie is, 'It's your baby!'

—Chris Rock

Is this fair? Or, as Daniel Tosh puts it:

Whaddya think of these faggots getting married? I can say that: I'm black. Here's a social experiment: figure out why the second statement softens the first.

There are Anglo-Saxon character comics who get away with material that could be regarded as offensive because the final laugh is aimed at the character themselves. Even within a predominantly Anglo-Saxon culture, an Anglo-Saxon comic can, like Rock and Chappelle, use self-satire to deliver jokes that ignore propriety.

Al Murray's masterful portrayal of a pissed British 'non-bigoted' bigot allows him to get away with things a non-character comedian would find difficult to sell.

When a Frenchman is in trouble, he doesn't do what you or I would do, does he? No, when a Frenchman is in trouble, he does something very strange. He doesn't shout 'Help'. The international word for 'Help', coming from the English word 'Help', meaning help. Used in times of stress requiring help.

You see, the thing about xenophobia is, it's a Greek word.

Catherine Deveny, a fearless left-wing columnist, shows she is capable of humour that may mildly offend its ethnic targets.

The first thing I saw when I got off the plane in London was a sign that read, 'Do you want to complain?' It was like landing in Germany to 'Do you want to engineer something with precision?'

All comedy writers are free to use ethnic and regional humour against white Anglo-Saxons because their culture is so dominant. Irishmen, Americans and blondes will just have to cop it.

Q: What did the white guy do before his blood test?
A: He studied.

—Unattrib.

Canada is like a loft apartment over a really great party.
—Robin Williams

EXERCISE

1. Choose an opinion held by one of your characters that stems from their prejudice or world view.

For example: the conservative Barbara takes a dim view of those who claim to be liberal. Her unpolished opinion is, 'People who believe they have "open minds" on social, sexual and political issues like to feel morally superior to those who favour personal responsibility, hetero monogamy and traditional institutions. In effect, their minds are closed to a broad range of viewpoints and the people who hold them'.

2. Reduce the opinion to its core assertion.

For example: '"Open" minds are in fact closed to a lot of conservative views.'

3. Use a metaphor, comparison, scenario or wordplay that presents the opinion simply. Dramatic irony or sarcasm can also be used to show the character's own limitations or hypocrisy on this issue. (In most cases it's best to express the viewpoint without greatly extending the length of the compressed statement.)

For example: There's nothing so narrow as an open mind.

Self-Referential Gags

Self-referential gags are like the mythical serpent, Ouroboros, coiled and biting his own tail. He may swallow the length of his own body right up to his neck or even consume himself entirely.

They're self-enclosed jokes that set up an archetypal quality (e.g. shyness or pedantry) or persona (e.g. a soccer mum or terrorist), then play on the audience's preconception. While the comedy in narrative gags derives from character traits established through the course of the story, in self-referential gags the audience doesn't need to know anything about the character in the joke beyond what is set up in the joke itself.

Once an archetype or characteristic is established, the punchline presents an affirmation, negation or exaggeration of that archetype or characteristic.

Self-referential gags often appear in narrative comedy. Like one-line gags, they set up a personal quality or role, then play upon it.

CONFIRMATION

The punchline is a direct confirmation of the premise.

> I enjoy using the comedy of self-deprecation … but I'm not very good at it.
> —Arnold Brown

> I used to be indecisive, but now I'm not quite sure.
> —Tommy Cooper

> I forgot something once. Buggered if I know what it was …
> —Flacco (Paul Livingston)

> JEMAINE: I can't believe you got that job and I didn't.
> BRET: You know, you've got to work on your people skills.
> JEMAINE: Yeah, shut up, Bret.
> —*Flight of the Conchords* ('Bret Gives up the Dream' by James Bobin, Jemaine Clement and Bret McKenzie)

NEGATION

The premise is undermined or absurdly negated by the punchline.

> I want to join the Optimist's Club, but they probably won't accept me.
> —David Cervera

> Nobody goes there anymore, it's too crowded.
> —Yogi Berra

> I don't like meeting strangers, which is why I try to get to know everyone.
> —Author

BARRY: I told you, Clive, never explain, never apologise.
CLIVE: Well, I didn't hear you ... sorry.
—*Shock Jock* ('Vive Le Difference' by the Author)

EXAGGERATION

The punchline takes the premise to a nonsensical extreme.

Yes, I like my coffee hot and strong ... like I like my women: hot and strong ... with a spoon in them.

—Eddie Izzard

I read *Fat is a Feminist Issue*. But I ate that as well.

—Jo Brand

I was a vegetarian until I started leaning toward the sunlight.

—Rita Rudner

There are countless examples (usually found on car stickers) of jokes that play on the qualities of a given archetype. These gags are typically confirmations of the archetype in the form of a pun:

Butchers do it in the raw.

—Unattrib.

Old professors never die; they just lose their faculties.

—Stephen Fry

You know you're a redneck if your gene pool has no deep end.

—Unattrib.

Blackadder is seeking an eligible princess. He dismisses most of the candidates as being too old or too young. The last thirty-nine princesses, he says, are mad ...

BALDRICK: They sound ideal.
BLACKADDER: They would be if they hadn't all got married last week in Munich to the same horse.
—*The Black Adder* ('Amy and Amiability' by Richard Curtis and Ben Elton)

COMBINATIONS

Some narrative self-referential gags perform two functions at once:

BRIAN: You're all individuals.
CROWD: Yes! We're all individuals!
BRIAN: You're all different.
CROWD: Yes, we are all different!
MAN IN CROWD: I'm not.

—Life of Brian (Monty Python)

In the space of five lines the crowd negates the premise 'We are all individuals' by trying to confirm it, and the crowd member confirms it by trying to negate it.

EXERCISE

1. Choose an archetype or characteristic, e.g., 'peace activists' who challenge institutions, chain themselves to trees and public monuments, start riots, meditate, smoke dope and get naked as a form of eye-catching protest.

2. List lines that affirm, negate or exaggerate that archetype or characteristic.

Affirm—'I want to be a peace activist so I can smoke joints, strip off and chain myself to the Statue of Liberty. World peace would be a bonus, too.'

Negate—'I want to be a peace activist and I'll kill anyone who tries to stop me.'

Exaggerate—'Being a peace activist at home is about setting priorities—do I chain myself to the fridge or the toilet?'

3. Pick your favourite.

Build self-referential gags using these examples:

Archetype:

Pessimist

Sex addict

Crisis counsellor

Animal psychologist

Jockey

Archetypal characteristic:

Bad memory

Political correctness

Fear of public speaking

Easily bored

Everything is predictable

Devise punchlines that confirm, negate or exaggerate the following:

'I forget things all the time'

'I get lonely at parties'

'I'm easily shocked'

'I don't believe in ghosts'

Working backwards from the punchline to the set-up can be easier, as it opens up a logical path:

1. Devise a punchline. This might be a simple sentence, but it should be short and conclusive, e.g.'I lost interest in it'. While this is not intrinsically funny, it opens up possibilities.

2. Define the emotion, sensibility or intention behind the punchline, e.g. 'I lost interest in it' suggests apathy or aimlessness.

3. Identify archetypes that experience the opposite or extreme of the quality you've identified, e.g. someone who *never* experiences apathy might include drill sergeants, Olympic athletes and motivational speakers, while those who are *always* apathetic might include roadside workers, teenagers at school or people with attention deficit disorder (ADD).

4. Identify situations in which the punchline would be positive or negative, e.g. losing interest could be positive when the subject is murder, or when the speaker is someone who (absurdly) prides themselves on their ability to lose interest. Losing interest would be negative when the speaker's livelihood or relationships depend on their continuing interest.

5. Identify possible causes for the sentiment behind the punchline, e.g. a loss of interest might be a response to a boring person, a boring subject or simply an inability to concentrate.

6. From the archetypes, situations and causes you've identified, mix and match until you come across a satisfying lead-in to the punchline, e.g. as motivational speakers are meant to inspire tenacity in others,

they're the people least likely to lose interest in things, making them a strong contender for a lead-in that the punchline negates: 'I used to be a motivational speaker, but I lost interest in it'. Alternately, attention deficit disorder by definition leads to a loss of interest. A lead-in based upon ADD suggests a confirmation of the punchline: 'I used to study ADD, but I lost interest in it'.

Devise other set-ups that will confirm, negate of exaggerate the following punchlines:

> … but nobody noticed.

> … but I thought it had some positive qualities.

> … but you have to see it my way.

> … but I'm not going to tell you.

> … but I guess you had to be there.

Flawed Logic

Flawed logic is the idiot brother of negation. Unsound reasoning undermines even the loftiest plans.

Flawed logic is grist for character comedians and sitcom's more clownish characters. Despite misplaced confidence, left to their own devices they can't think their way out of a plastic bag.

> Now they're saying cigarettes can cause cancer of the cervix, I'm always very careful to put them in my mouth.
> —Fiona O'Loughlin

> Why do people in ship mutinies always ask for 'better treatment'? I'd ask for a pinball machine, because with all that rocking back and forth you'd probably be able to get a lot of free games.
> —Jack Handey

> A man sits on a train throwing biscuits out the window. A woman asks him, 'Why are you throwing biscuits out the window?' 'To keep the tigers away,' the man replies. The woman frowns. 'But there aren't any tigers in Australia.' 'See?' says the man, 'It works!'
> —Unattrib.

Absolutes and extremes are regular elements in flawed-logic gags because they are immutable. A negation, reduction, exaggeration or irony that appears to contradict this can yield comic results. Death, for example, is an absolute, yet in the hands of a comic intelligence it can be changeable as the wind.

> You kill me and I'll see that you never work in this town again.
> —*The Man with Two Brains*, (George Gipe and Steve Martin)

> You realise that suicide's a criminal offence. In less enlightened times, they'd have hung you for it.
> —*Bedazzled*, (Peter Cook and Dudley Moore)

> MIKE: And say hello to Father Stephenson for me.
> STUDENT: He's dead.
> MIKE: Oh, that's terrible. Uh, well, tell him I'm sorry to hear that.
> —*Frontline* ('Playing the Ego Card' by Santo Cilauro, Tom Gleisner, Jane Kennedy and Rob Sitch)

But any absolute will do:

> Sterility is hereditary.
>
> —Alexandre Bouthors

EXERCISE

Devise simple twists on the following absolutes and extremes:

Hideousness

Deafness

Secret

Suicide

Virginity

Chapter Two:
Gag Categories

There is a fine line between fishing and standing on the shore like an idiot.

—Steven Wright

All categories, or genres, of humour (deadpan, smutty, feminist, musical, rhyming, satire, farce, topical etcetera) follow the same structure. Smutty humour, for example, no matter how filthy, derives from the same principles that govern family-friendly comedy. A gag is a gag, even with the C-bomb in the middle of it. Sexual and scatological jokes, for example, frequently observe the juxtaposition principle because there are so many euphemisms for sex. 'Banging like a dunny door', 'knob-polishing' and 'second base' all have literal meanings with which a gag-writer can play. These double-meanings can also be used to create narrative gags such as misinterpretations, distortions and cover-ups. And juxtapositions occur, although perhaps not as frequently, in all genres of humour.

Even innocent terms can be twisted into sexual positions. No word is safe—'going', 'coming', 'doing', 'having' and 'it' each have ribald applications. Guys named 'Roger', 'Dick' or 'Rod' also have a hard time, as does the phrase 'hard time'.

There are five types of straight-up gags:

- Incongruous juxtapositions
- Malapropisms and misinterpretations
- The obvious
- The absurd
- Wordplay

A joke may combine types. For example, Jane Ace, co-star of the ground-breaking U.S. radio domestic comedy *Easy Aces* (1930–1945), was renowned for malapropisms such as, 'I always wanted to see my name up in tights', which juxtaposes the incongruous images of her name in lights with her name spelt out in tights. Such hybrids don't make new principles. They merely confirm that there are a limited number of gag ingredients in the world. Combining meat and potatoes doesn't make a whole new substance.

Although the jokes below are broken down into categories and sub-categories, they are not a definitive or comprehensive list. The principles below do not cover narrative gags (gags that move a comic story). These are covered later in 'Narrative Comedy Principles and Exercises'.

Don't be put off if you don't laugh as you write your gags—it's hard to enjoy a sausage once you've seen what goes into it. If you do laugh it's likely to be at the more offensive gags you devise: their riskiness sparks a twinge of guilt or apprehension in the writer. (A table of professional joke-writers, for example, will simply nod at great gags in much the same way as a bricklayer admires a well-built house. But an offensive joke, or alternately a joke that's just not funny, can have them in stitches.)

In fact, a satirical, profane or sexual element is more or less essential to adult humour. Innocuous gags, such as knock-knock jokes, while technically humorous, are often only really funny to a five-year-old. Adults use humour to deal with things that cause genuine fear or anxiety, whereas kids' jokes tend to deal with an aspect of the world that, as adults, we've already figured out.

Incongruous Juxtapositions

'Incongruous juxtapositions' is a fancy name for gags that draw a connection between things that appear to have little in common.

PUNS

The simplest juxtaposition gag is the pun. They 'happun' all the time.

Puns are often seen as trite but the truth is, everybody uses them, from children to nuns to the world's greatest comedians. Puns are as sophisticated as the writers who create them. Some comedians may even get a perverse laugh by highlighting the lameness of a pun.

Puns include any humorous use of a word suggesting another meaning of the word:

> I was asked by a waitress ... 'Would you care for an orange juice?' I said, 'If it needed me.'
> —Carl Barron

> How long was I in the Army? Five foot eleven.
> —Spike Milligan

> My parents are from Glasgow, which means they're incredibly hard, but I was never smacked as a child ... well maybe one or two grams to get me to sleep at night.
> —Susan Murray

A pun can also use a word or phrase similar in sound to another word or phrase with a different but apposite meaning:

I will not be deterred. *You* will be deterred.
>—Flacco (Paul Livingston)
>(Sounds like 'You will be the turd')

The poet had written better poems, but he'd also written verse.
>—Unattrib.

When the cannibal showed up late to lunch, they gave him the cold-shoulder.
>—Unattrib.

An obvious, one-step punchline may provoke a groan and a slap to the forehead rather than a laugh; we think, 'Ah, I should've seen that one'.

Q: How do trees get on the internet?
A: They log in.
>—Unattrib.

As trees lack both a brain and fingers, they are unlikely ever to want to go on the internet, so the basic scenario of the joke lacks conviction. There is little to misdirect us and the joke feels lame. However, putting a group of not-so-hot associations together can have better results because it creates a rapid sequence of connections that the audience couldn't devise on the spot.

Q: What do politicians and pigs have in common?
A: They have thick skin, their snouts in the trough and they provide a lot of pork.

Okay, it's not a piece of comic genius, but it illustrates the principle. (There's a 'red oink' joke in there somewhere too, but let's quit while we're ahead.)

Even though a pun does not require a context to be understood, sitcoms regularly use them to display character as well as get a laugh:

SAFFIE: Where are you going?
EDDIE: New York.
SAFFIE: I don't think they let people with drug convictions in.
EDDIE: Darling, it's not a conviction.
PATSY: Just a firm belief.
EDDIE: Yes.
>—*Absolutely Fabulous* ('Fish Farm' by Jennifer Saunders)

Another form of incongruous juxtaposition relies upon the audience's common knowledge. This might be a frequently quoted text or song, or the life circumstances of a public figure. If it's a quote, the audience will run it in their heads as they listen, and when the punchline departs from the quote in a way that creates an unexpected juxtaposition, the result can be humorous.

> Sticks and stones may break my bones, but names will only cause permanent psychological damage.
>
> —Frank Woodley

This line relies for its impact on our familiarity with the childhood chant. For the second half of the chant, it substitutes something perhaps closer to the truth.

> I'm so tough my Rice Bubbles don't go 'snap, crackle and pop'. They just sit in the packet and say, 'Shhh, here he comes.'
>
> —George Smilovici

We're familiar with Snap, Crackle and Pop from the advertising campaign, so their suddenly hushed tone is a surprise.

> Tori Spelling walks into a bar. The barman says, 'Why the long face?'
>
> —Unattrib.

This is a joke on a joke, playing upon a well-known gag in which the protagonist is a horse. Horses have long faces. The actress Tori Spelling also has a long face.

The most straightforward technique for devising juxtapositions is as follows:

1. Choose two concepts you intend to juxtapose.
2. For each concept, draw up a list of associations. Words, names, songs, phrases, euphemisms, similes, people and organisations may all be included. The list can be as long as you like.
3. Look for connections between both lists. For example, a word that appears in both lists or sounds similar to a word in the other list. Or find phrases, songs or quotations that contain key words that relate your central concepts in some way, or can be manipulated to do so.
4. Devise a simple scenario or question, or make an observation that brings the two concepts together.

   For example, if you want to write a joke that connects horses and newlyweds, the two lists might include:

HORSES	NEWLYWEDS
Saddle	'Just married'
Hoof	Parents-in-law
Racing	'I do'
Jockeys	Honeymoon
Stallion	'Going To The Chapel'
Thoroughbreds	Virginity lost
Bridle	Bridal gown
Giddy up!	Bridal suite
Melbourne Cup	Groom
Theme from Black Beauty	Best man
Spurs	Down the aisle
Grooming	Altar
Horse-whispering	Church steeple
Steeplechase	Breeding
Breeding	Mister and Missus
Bloodlines	To honour and obey
Phar Lap	Civil ceremony
Stud	Confetti

In this case, the lists share a homophone: 'bridle' and 'bridal'. It's not difficult to imagine a scenario in which one of these words might be used. After some experimentation, a joke may emerge. For example:

> A honeymooning bride approaches a hotel reception desk and asks for a suite. The hotel manager asks, 'Bridal?' 'No thanks,' replies the bride, 'I'll break him in gently'.

There are also three homonyms:

HORSES	NEWLYWEDS
Steeple(chase)	(Church) steeple
Groom	Groom
Breeding	Breeding

Simply posing the question 'What do brides and horses have in common?' provokes the following answers:

> They both like a groom.
> They both run to steeples.
> They both need good breeding.

The bow can be stretched as far as you like so long as there's a recognisable connection for the audience. Note however that the former scenario is funnier because it reveals character and introduces an element of implied danger. We instantly identify with the poor groom.

EXERCISE

Devise punchlines for the following questions:

What do cats and porn have in common?

What's the difference between cats and porn?

What do lawyers and cannibals have in common?

What's the difference between lawyers and cannibals?

What do dwarves and blondes have in common?

What's the difference between dwarves and blondes?

CONVENIENT JUXTAPOSITIONS

A convenient juxtaposition starts with an observation on a particular topic or situation, then finds another topic or situation of which the same observation is true. For example, Phyllis Diller's gag below is about the futility of cleaning a house where children are continually making new mess.

> Cleaning your house while your kids are still growing is like shovelling the sidewalk before it stops snowing.
> —Phyllis Diller

> Giving birth is like taking your lower lip and forcing it over your head.
> —Carol Burnett

> Paying alimony is like feeding hay to a dead horse.
> —Groucho Marx

To create a convenient juxtaposition gag:

- Make a list of other actions that illustrate your observation.
- Choose the most appropriate and draw the parallel.
- It's possible to construct another joke on the same topic as Phyllis Diller's by finding a new scenario that also illustrates the idea, 'Actions that are immediately undone'.
- Make a list of actions that are immediately undone, e.g. windscreen-wipers clearing raindrops from a windscreen, jumping up high, blowing your nose when you have a bad cold.

- Selecting the latter, it's possible to draw a direct comparison: 'Cleaning up after kids is like blowing your nose when you have the flu: as soon as you're done you feel like starting again'. Or, more obliquely, 'I'd rather have a cold than clean up after kids. At least when I blow my nose I have something to show for it'.

TWO-MEANINGS

Comedian Ronnie Barker said, 'The marvellous thing about a joke with a double meaning is that it can only have one meaning'. As some of the gags above show, words with two meanings can be useful for clear and simple joke building. But 'two-meanings' gags can go a lot further than puns. They can comprise a play on a phrase, euphemism or name with two or more meanings.

> Last week, I flew into New York; the usual way, not like terrorists do it.
> —Author

The double meaning of the phrase 'flew into' is the key to this joke.

Euphemisms provide a bountiful world of joke components. In most cases their implied meaning is so commonly understood that it has overtaken their literal meaning. And that's where the fun begins.

> I heard that my dentist bit the bullet. You'd think he'd know better.
> —Author

> My girlfriend sent me a 'Dear John' letter. But my name's Kevin, so I dumped her.
> —Author

> We declared war on terror—it's not even a noun. After we defeat it, I'm sure we'll take on that bastard, ennui.
> —Jon Stewart

Inverting words to create a new meaning can also provide a gag:

> Q: What's the difference between a pickpocket and a peeping Tom?
> A: A pickpocket snatches watches.
> —Unattrib.

Note that in designing the joke it's necessary to begin with the punchline phrase ('snatches watches' versus 'watches snatches') and build the joke around it.

Gordon R. Dickson's collection of three novellas, *The Right To Arm Bears* (published in 1961) are a tidy play on the U.S. Constitution's second amendment, 'the right to bear arms'. The humour plays on the double-meanings of 'bear' and 'arm' depending on whether used as a verb or a noun.

Some people are cursed with a name that is a pun in itself:

Peter Abbott
Sean Hedges
Miles Long
Ophelia Cox

EXERCISE

Devise jokes using the literal meaning of some common euphemisms:

Example: 'drop-dead gorgeous': 'I went out with a guy who was drop-dead gorgeous. Which is funny because when he was alive he was nothing special'.

To be beside yourself

To drop off the perch

To drive someone up the wall

To go down for the third time

To fall off the back of a truck

Of course, euphemisms are in themselves convenient juxtapositions that have endured because of the quality of their comic observation. To create your own euphemisms, try this 'leap-frog' technique:

1. Think up as many associations with the subject as you can.

For an example, let's use everybody's favourite comic event—farting. Common associations might include:

Vapour

Smelly

Invisible

Unpopular

Embarrassing

Noisy

Release

Arse

2. 'Leap-frog' each of these associations to secondary associations. Cast your imagination as broadly as possible, e.g. roles in life, active words, songs, phrases etcetera.

For example:

VAPOUR

    Steam

    Clouds

    Menthol Vapour Ointment

    Storm front

SMELLY

    Bad breath

    Sewerage treatment facility

    Garbage collectors

    Pig-Pen from the comic strip Peanuts

INVISIBLE

    Vanishing cream

    Ghosts

    Snipers

    Ninja warriors

UNPOPULAR

    Politicians

    Parking inspectors

    Phone-marketers

    Offensive opinions

EMBARRASSING

    Faux pas

    Red-faced

    Public shame

    Eric Carmen's song 'All By Myself'

NOISY

    Marshall amplifier

AC/DC

Crisp packets

Noisy neighbours

RELEASE

Set free

On parole

The Humperdink–Charles song 'Release Me'

The prophet Moses, 'Let my people go'

ARSE

Back passage

Doorway

One-eyed

Freckle

As you can see, some of the new associations can be comic references to the subject in themselves. By massaging the secondary associations into suitable phrases, euphemisms for farting emerge:

Airing an unwelcome opinion

Putting out the garbage

A noisy neighbour moving out

Seeing the Minister to the door

Parking a ghost

If the subject of an intended gag is made up of more than one element, such as Phyllis Diller's premise, 'Cleaning your house while your kids are still growing', identify the essential idea in the premise. In Diller's case, the essential idea was 'Actions that are immediately undone', which provided the first step in the leap-frog to the punchline.

SYNECDOCHES

A synecdoche (pronounced 'sin-ek-doh-key') is a cousin to the euphemism and metaphor. (It's worth learning this term for the intellectual cache alone.)

There are four kinds of synecdoche open to exploitation by the humorist.

1. A part is named but the whole is understood:
'Eyeballs' meaning TV viewers.

'Bums on seats' meaning audience numbers.

Example: 'The boss said we need more bums on seats. I'll sit down while you go to the park and get the bums.'

2. The whole is named but a part is understood:

'9-11' meaning September 9, 2001.

'India beat England' meaning eleven cricketers beat eleven other cricketers.

Example: 'If India had known they could beat England with a cricket bat, they wouldn't have bothered with Gandhi's independence movement'.

3. The general is named but the specific is understood:

'Grog' meaning beer rather than beer, wine and spirits.

'Cats' meaning domestic cats rather than the genus that includes lions, tigers, cougars and so forth.

Example: 'They say cats don't like their owners. But I saw a tiger eat a zookeeper'.

4. The specific is named but the general is understood:

'Hands' meaning sailors ('All hands on deck')

'Football' meaning the game, the players and fans as well as the ball itself.

For example, 'I used to like a bit of football at lunchtime, but it gave me indigestion. Too leathery'.

Malapropisms and Misinterpretations

These gags are the pun's mad aunties. They play upon a character's misuse or misunderstanding of a word or phrase due to its similarity or connection to the intended word or phrase. Malapropisms, however, are always unintentional. An intentional malapropism is simply a pun—for instance, an architect remarking archly, 'This house is like the Taj Banal'. Malapropisms derive their humour in part from the assumed ignorance of the speaker. The same line 'This house is like the Taj Banal' becomes funnier when delivered sincerely by a character who genuinely wants to compliment the owner.

Malapropisms and misinterpretations work best when the meaning of the misused word or phrase is markedly at odds with that of the intended word or phrase. The actual meaning can be used to illuminate an aspect of situation or character.

In narrative comedy malapropisms and misinterpretations are usually the territory of dim-witted, clownish characters. Comic Freudian slips however are malapropisms that can expose even intelligent characters (e.g. 'I need to coerce, uh, I mean converse with you').

MALAPROPISMS

These involve the misuse of a word, usually because it sounds similar to the intended word. Malapropisms often point to a higher truth about the character uttering them or the intended subject matter itself.

> KIM: I want to be effluent, Mum, effluent!
> —*Kath and Kim* ('Sex' by Gina Riley and Jane Turner)

Malapropisms from radio comedienne Jane Ace include:

> I'm completely uninhabited.
> I don't drink. I'm a totalitarian.
> You could have knocked me down with a fender.
>
> —Jane Ace

> (Headline): Cheap Carpet Manufacturer Accused of Being Underlying Bastard
>
> —Paul Livingston

EXERCISE

A malapropism requires a word that bears some phonetic similarity, even tenuously, to the word intended by your character. Changing one word only, find a malapropism for the following expressions:

> 'One percent inspiration, ninety-nine percent perspiration—'
>
> 'Going at it hammer and tongs—'
>
> 'Pecuniary fund—'
>
> 'Struck by cupid's arrow—'
>
> 'To move with alacrity'

The first malapropism that comes to mind is often the best, as it tends to draw a clear connection for the audience.

MISINTERPRETATIONS

Misinterpretations occur when a character shows by their response that they've misunderstood the meaning of a word or phrase.

> MONICA: Hey Joey, what would you do if you were omnipotent?
> JOEY: Probably kill myself.
> MONICA: Excuse me?
> JOEY: (*indicating his penis*) If little Joey's dead, then I've got no reason to live.
> ROSS: Joey, *om*-nipotent.
> JOEY: You are? I'm so sorry.
> > —*Friends* ('The One With George Stephanopoulos' by
> > Alexa Junge)

> VIDEO STORE GUY: What about *Silence of the Lambs?*
> COLIN: Nah, I'm not really into nature films.
> > —*The Adventures of Lano and Woodley* (Colin Lane and
> > Frank Woodley)

> KIM *reveals a statue of baby Edam cheeses.*
> KIM: Here's your statue, Mum.
> KATH: Oh, what in the love of God is that?
> KIM: It's the statue you wanted.
> KATH: No, it's not, Kim!
> KIM: Yes it is, it's a statue of little baby cheeses.
> KATH: Little baby cheeses? Little Baby Jesus, Kim—Jesus!
> —*Kath and Kim* ('The Wedding' by Gina Riley and Jane Turner)

Unlike malapropisms, a character can deliberately misinterpret a line. In the following, Andy has just spoken to Ben Stiller, playing himself, out of turn.

> STILLER: Who are you?
> ANDY: (*meekly*) Nobody.
> STILLER: ... And who am I?
> ANDY: It's either Starsky or Hutch, I can never remember.
> STILLER: (*angrily*) Was that supposed to be funny?
> ANDY: You tell me, you were in it.
> —*Extras* ('Episode 2' by Ricky Gervais and Stephen Merchant)

Andy deliberately and rudely misinterprets what it was that was 'supposed to be funny'.

Misinterpretations can be targeted by others to make a specific point:

(Football coach) Ally McLeod thinks tactics are a new kind of mint.
—Billy Connolly

She's so dumb she thinks colic is a kind of sheep dog.
—Unattrib.

EXERCISE

Given the characteristic mentioned, complete each line with a misinterpretation:

Example: She's so innocent, she thinks a 'dildo' is a hobbit.

He's so dumb he thinks an 'IQ' is …

She's so lascivious she thinks a 'square root' is …

He's so out of touch he thinks 'J-Lo' is …

She's so selfish she thinks the 'Poor Box' is …

He's so square he thinks the 'Lambada' is …

Filtering misinterpretations through the broadly accepted characteristics of an archetype (a stereotypical character—see 'Archetypes') can generate deliberate misinterpretation gags.

1. List terms, beliefs, names, songs or phrases associated with the archetype.

2. Drawing on the common traits you've listed, write misinterpretations the character or archetype might deliberately employ for each.

Try it with the biggest 'kick me' target of all: lawyers. Their archetypical traits include greed, deceitfulness, heartlessness, soullessness, private-schooling, cocaine, amorality and wig-wearing. These qualities make them worthy of playful misrepresentation (see 'merciless ridicule').

Below is a selective list of terms and phrases associated with lawyers and the law. Write misinterpretations for each, e.g. 'pro bono' to a lawyer could mean 'free publicity'. When you're finished, write down and then 're-interpret' a few more lawyer-based terms of your own.

When lawyers say:	They mean:
Hostile witness	
Memorandum	

Criminal lawyer

The Bar exam

BMW

Misinterpretation gags can also derive from a character's flawed view of events:

> In my local paper, they had this advert: 'Please look after your neighbours in the cold weather'. I live next door to this 84-year-old woman and, do you know, not once has she come round to see if I'm alright. The lazy cow hasn't even taken her milk in for a fortnight.
>
> —Jack Dee

> Smartness runs in my family. When I went to school I was so smart my teacher was in my class for five years.
>
> —Gracie Allen

Documentarist Michael Moore, accepting an Academy Award for his film *Bowling for Columbine*, took the opportunity to criticise President George W. Bush for taking America into the Iraq War. This provoked the following comment from Steve Martin:

> It was so sweet backstage, you should've seen it—the Teamsters were helping Michael Moore into the trunk of his limo.

The Completely Obvious

This principle is so obvious—why didn't we see it before?

It's not that we immediately crack up at all obvious things—if we did, we'd never get out of the shower—but humans are clever creatures; when presented with a scenario, our minds can devise any number of rationales that might support it. As is often the case in real life, we can think too hard about things. Standing back for a clearer perspective is not as easy or natural as it sounds. While we wrestle with the details and possibilities of a scenario, an obvious gag slaps us in the face.

Obvious gags can have punchlines that are true but subvert our expectation of something more elaborate. Perhaps the best example is the first joke many people can remember:

> Q: Why did the chicken cross the road?
> A: To get to the other side.
>
> —Unattrib.

But an obvious gag doesn't have to be a childish one.

> My dad is Irish and my mum is Iranian, which meant that we spent most of our family holidays in customs.
>
> —Patrick Monahan

> A sure cure for seasickness is to sit under a tree.
>
> —Spike Milligan

> I saw that show, *50 Things To Do Before You Die*. I would have thought the obvious one was 'Shout for help'.
>
> —Mark Watson

There are jokes in this category known as 'anti-comedy'. Their punchlines, though salient, are darker than expected. The comedy derives in part from sheer daring. To write these gags, simply think of a question or premise and provide a response that's accurate, awful and blunt:

> Q: Why do kittens go to heaven?
> A: Because they're dead.
>
> —Unattrib.

EXERCISE

Here are some set-ups that suggest elaborate detail is to come. Tag them with simple, obvious-once-you-think-about-it observations, for example: There are ten ways to start a Russian motor vehicle ... but none of them work.

> The secret to a happy life is ...
>
> Married people have the best sex ...
>
> The best way to get off a deserted island is ...

Obvious punchlines identify anomalies that are plain once we notice them.

The conclusion drawn in the punchline of such a gag is usually nonsense or built upon incomplete logic. Often, these gags will take the form of a question to which there is no short or accurate answer.

> If Barbie is so popular, why do you have to buy her friends?
>
> —Unattrib.

> If you choke a Smurf, what colour would he turn into?
>
> —Unattrib.

Vegetarians tend to be the same touchy-feely bunch who go on about the environment. Well, maybe there'd be more environment if you lot weren't eating all the plants.

—Harry Hill

To generate these gags, think of terms, phrases or concepts that imply an assumption (e.g. 'We are here to help others'). Then examine this premise from all angles until you can kick the legs out from under it (e.g. 'So, what are the others here for?') Sometimes this means taking an idea (e.g. 'invisible ink') to its illogical conclusion (e.g. 'How can you tell when you've run out of it?')

Knock-knock jokes are obvious gags. The answer is under our noses, only appearing when the context of the key word is changed.

Knock knock.
Who's there?
Isabel.
Isabel who?
Isabel necessary on a bicycle?

—Unattrib.

Knock-knocks usually fail to get much of a laugh because there's only one element that is transformed, reducing the surprise to a blip. In the post-modern world, knock-knock jokes have a better chance when the form of knock-knocks themselves is being played with:

Knock knock.
Who's there?
Interrupting cow.
Interrup-
Moo!

—Unattrib.

As discussed in the introduction to the 'Gag Categories' chapter, knock-knocks work better for adults when they take on a darker hue:

Knock knock.
Who's there?
Fuck off.
Fuck off who?
Don't make me tell you twice.

Now, that's much more adult, isn't it?

Other obvious gags may be logically sound but morally dark, unfair or politically incorrect:

I'm sick and tired of seeing streakers at sporting events. I believe the true punishment for streakers at the cricket is to make them stay on the ground and bat.

—Elliot Goblet

Short people make better astronauts because if they die, there's less to be sad about.

—Author

Is it fair to say that there'd be less litter in Britain if blind people were given pointed sticks?

—Adam Bloom

To write these jokes:
1. Begin with a premise.
2. Examine the premise for double-meanings, associations and similarities, or contexts in which the premise could be in/appropriate.
3. Take the premise to a logical or nonsensical extreme. What is the implied assumption of the premise? What are the limitations of the premise? What are the repercussions of the premise? What would happen if anyone, everyone or no-one acted on the premise?
4. Based on the logical or nonsensical extreme, devise a punchline that is morally dark or politically incorrect.

EXERCISE

Using this technique, devise your own joke based on the premises below:

Example: The best thing about only having one testicle is … you can only get someone half-pregnant.

Cats use their tongues to clean themselves …

John Lennon said, 'All you need is love' …

Terrorist martyrs spend eternity with seventy-six virgins …

Once you've had a shot at the set-ups above, devise some of your own. The most useful set-ups tend to have two or more elements (e.g. 'guns' and 'killing people') because this gives you more to play with. Figures of speech, platitudes and axioms are often good material.

Identifiable social groups, however unfairly, are fertile soil for these gags. For example, short people are a perfect target for comedy, if only because so many take their height deficiency so seriously. (If you're short, and you're rankled at this suggestion, then … case in point.)

Not every set-up will present a punchline for every writer. And sometimes the punchlines that come to mind may be too distasteful for you or your intended audience. If you get stuck, move on to your next set-up.

More possible jokes will appear when you add to the set-up line (e.g. 'A recent survey said …', 'I hate the fact that …', 'My Mum always warned me that …'), pose it as a question or even turn it into an equation (e.g. 'If "x" is so, then "y" must be …') The more you play with it, the more the possibilities open up.

Simply using the contradictions in the premise can be enough in itself. As in 'Self-referential Gags' (see Chapter One), a statement can be taken to a logical conclusion, whereupon it negates or absurdly confirms itself.

> An original idea. That can't be too hard. The library must be full of them.
>
> —Stephen Fry

> The world is a dark, depressing place. See? I just made it worse.
> —Author

> I've decided to give up being a comedian. (Pause.) What are you waiting for? There's no punchline.
> —Author

> I saw a sign saying 'Question everything!' Or did I?
> —Author

To write an obvious gag that negates its own premise:

1. Devise a simple statement, preferably an observation, personal prejudice or declaration of intent, e.g. 'I don't like Mondays'.

2. Taking the statement at face value, try to establish the reasoning behind the statement and all its direct consequences, e.g. What are the possible reasons for, or consequences of, not liking Mondays? A reason might be their regularity. A consequence might be that Mondays don't like you either.

3. Write a tag that exploits the exposed contradictions. The more absurd the better, e.g. 'I used to like Mondays, but then they started coming round all the time. I need space!' Or, 'I don't like Mondays. And they're not talking to me either.'

Tangential thinking is required. In the examples above Monday takes on human characteristics.

EXERCISE

Here are some set-ups to get you started:

The best marriages are arranged marriages …

I bought a sawn-off shotgun …

Let me offer a word to the wise …

Obvious punchlines can be consistent with the premise, but still inadequate or absurd:

To stop global warming, leave your refrigerator door open at all times.
—Author

If a small child is choking on an ice-cube, don't panic. Simply pour a jug of boiling water down its throat and, hey presto! The blockage is almost instantly removed.
—Dava Krause

A lot of people are afraid of heights. Not me, I'm afraid of widths.
—Steven Wright

The steps to whip up consistent-but-absurd gags:

1. Take a simple proposition. It might be:

- A truism (e.g. 'The bigger they are, the harder they fall')
- A common event (e.g. a christening, the full moon)
- A popular belief (e.g. Honesty is the best policy)
- A law (e.g. regulations governing vagrancy or traffic violations)

Example: Take the popular belief, 'God is everywhere'.

2. Accepting the truth of the proposition, how should the world therefore behave? For example, If you're God, there's nothing new. Ever.

3. Follow the question to its logical or extreme conclusion. For example, If He's everywhere, where does He go to get away from it all? And how does He look down at us if He's under us too?

4. Look for ideas associated with the proposition. For example, God created the universe, so why not live there? And where does Satan live? Everywhere else?

5. Look for inconsistencies and gaps in the proposition. For example, If He's everywhere, why do people spend years trying to find Him? If He's in my house, He should help with the rent. If God is everywhere, how did He get there?

6. Look at the components of the proposition separately and in reverse order. For example, 'God' and 'everywhere'. Hence, 'Everywhere is where God is'. So, 'Where exactly is everywhere?'

7. Look for exceptions to the statement. For example, God is not in Parliament. And He had better not be at the Playboy Mansion.

8. Look for connecting ideas. For example, What's next to everywhere? Does 'everywhere' include Wagga Wagga? Can't He make up his mind and pick somewhere to live? Is He in my eyeballs? Why?

9. Link the proposition with the funniest or quirkiest result of your searches.

EXERCISE

Here are some party starters:

Bad people go to Hell …

0.02% of grandmothers are convicted of murder …

Life is like a box of chocolates. You never know what you're going to get—

Absurd Humour

Absurd humour mocks detailed analysis. Typically, each absurd joke or scenario is a world unto itself and has few specifics in common with other jokes in the genre. But there are some general guidelines to the art. It's arguable that all comedy is absurd. All humour points to the absurd in life, in that it generally turns on a logical contradiction or defies a logical expectation. But absurd humour seems to ignore contradiction and neutralising expectation in favour of a kind of negation—an entirely distinct concept.

Absurd comedy such as appears in the work of Monty Python portrays largely intelligent and rational characters reacting in realistic ways. It's simply the situation that's absurd. In *Monty Python and the Holy Grail*, the Black Knight believes he can still put up a fight, even though his arms and legs have been hacked off. Once we accept that he genuinely believes it, we accept that he's behaving rationally.

Absurd or nonsense humour pushes accepted norms to nonsense extremes, presenting the audience with a fresh perspective. In Monty Python's *The Meaning of Life* a Catholic mother and father have followed the dictates of the Vatican by breeding dozens of children. They have bred so many that when a baby plops out of the mother she is completely indifferent. The Vatican's view that 'every sperm is sacred' is taken to its logical extreme and then given a nudge: the parents have so many children that they are forced to sell them for scientific experimentation.

Through the juxtaposition of incongruous entities, personalities, values or behaviours, absurd humour creates scenarios in which the characters have nonsensical manifestations, aims or perspectives. In Monty Python and the Holy Grail, the Knights of Ni shout the word 'Ni!' to dominate their foes. Before the terrified King Arthur can pass them, they demand he bring them, of all things, a shrubbery.

The use of random elements like 'a shrubbery' pervades this type of humour. Yet absurd comedy can make a reasonable point. In each of the examples of absurd humour above, even though the action is absurd, something is being satirised. It might be the ideal of valour and the impossible quests in medieval epics, or the dictates of the Catholic Church. The target isn't random.

Anthropomorphism is common in absurd humour. And it's not just animals that can have human characteristics. In the absurd world, even a lunchbox can have a personality and a driver's licence, and a human being can think they're a lunchbox.

Absurd humour can play upon the absurdity within a joke itself, either reversing, neutralising or furthering that absurdity for a laugh.

Absurd humour has been around at least since the Middle Ages. In 'The Nun's Priest's Tale' from *The Canterbury Tales*, Geoffrey Chaucer (1343–1400) tells of a fox chasing a rooster round a barnyard, but describes it in lofty, heroic language more suited to a grand epic. This absurd technique raises animals to the level of humans, but also implies that the feats of man may not be as grand as we like to think.

Lewis Carroll's *Alice In Wonderland* is similarly anthropomorphic—the animals in Wonderland talk and have largely human concerns.

Absurdism as we know it came to prominence during World War I, when 'Dada' artists began seriously questioning institutions, language and culture. Perhaps the most famous example from the period is Duchamp's inverted urinal ('Fountain' by 'R. Mutt'). The art world and society at large were rocked by the idea that anything could be art if the artist said it was.

The Dada influence remains in absurdist TV sketch humour today. A Dada literary technique was to throw words inscribed on scraps of paper into a hat. The Dadaists would randomly remove some of the words and devise poems based on them. Some modern British sketch shows (e.g. *Big Train*) preserve the spirit of this apparent randomness in sketches such as Ming the Merciless vacuuming his suburban home, or a dozen jockeys trying to put out a house-fire.

Randomness is a component of much absurd humour:

Q: How many absurdists does it take to change a light bulb?
A: An orange.

—Unattrib.

This joke defies our expectation of a logical connection to the punchline. Once the key element 'absurdists' is mentioned, the substance of the punchline is almost irrelevant. It could be 'An elephant' or indeed 'A urinal'. The choice of a seemingly random punchline or element is typical in absurd comedy.

Haikus are easy.
But sometimes they don't make sense.
Refrigerator.

—Unattrib.

All the final line of the haiku needs is the traditional five syllables.

For ten years, Caesar ruled with an iron hand. Then with a wooden foot, and finally with a piece of string.

—Spike Milligan

Milligan's punchline satirises the grand language used by historians.

Having posed an absurd reality, some jokes extend and develop that reality:

A dog goes into a hardware store and says: 'I'd like a job, please'.
The hardware store owner says: 'We don't hire dogs; why don't you go join the circus?'
The dog replies: 'What would the circus want with a plumber?'

—Steven Alan Green

Once we accept that the dog can talk and that it needs a job, the gag goes a step further. A pattern is established by the first two propositions, but the absurd punchline still takes us by surprise even though it's consistent with the reality of the joke.

Other absurd gags extrapolate from their premise to an absurd conclusion:

My friend George is a radio announcer. When he walks under a bridge, you can't hear him talk.

—Steven Wright

Absurd jokes can rely on a punchline that plays with absurdity itself:

Two racehorses are in the stables. One horse says, 'The strangest thing happened in my last race. I was coming around the bend and heard a buzzing in my head. I got such a shock, I ran like mad and won the race'.

60

The other horse is amazed. 'The same thing happened to me—I was coming around the bend and heard a buzzing in my head. I ran like mad and won my race.'

A greyhound approaches them. 'I couldn't help overhearing you. I must say that I, too, was coming around the bend and heard a buzzing in my head. I ran like mad and won my race.'

The first horse looks at the other and says, 'Bugger me—a talking dog!'

—Unattrib.

Here, the absurd premise itself, talking horses, subtly establishes a convention: in this joke, animals can talk. It goes on to create an expectation that the substance of the joke is to do with buzzing heads, and we're blindsided by a punchline that instead simply violates the talking-animal convention. The premise is used against itself.

Shifting perspective from the absurd to the realistic is a good way to throw an audience off-balance. The following obvious-absurd two-part joke is an example:

Q: How do you fit two elephants into a Mini Minor?
A: One in the front and one in the back.

Q: How do you fit four elephants into a Mini Minor?
A: Look, you've already got two elephants in there. There's no way a Mini is going to seat another two.

—Unattrib.

The laugh in the second joke comes from the absurd premise of the first. In the second joke the absurd premise is first accepted ('You've already got two elephants in there') and then contradicted ('There's no way a Mini is going to seat another two').

Like most jokes, the absurd premise is initially accepted as part of the joke's 'reality' by the characters in the joke. In a joke, when a man walks into a bar with a crocodile, the barman sees it as a nuisance, not a sudden and shocking threat.

Absurdity can highlight everyday human concerns: in the *Monty Python* 'Argument Sketch', a customer has paid a professional arguer for an argument. The arguer, however, proceeds by simply rejecting everything the customer says. The customer feels ripped off.

MAN: …This isn't an argument.
MR VIBRATING: Yes it is.
MAN: No it isn't. It's just contradiction.
MR VIBRATING: No it isn't.

The customer's frustration at the intransigent arguer reflects that of all customers who feel they haven't received what they paid for.

Wordplay

English is organic, and is subject to all the breaches, redundancies, inadequacies, anomalies, paradoxes, contradictions and oddities found in any system that has grown through practice rather than design. Thankfully, this leaves the English language wide open to comic exploitation. Rather than exploiting the meaning of words, wordplay exploits the words themselves.

RHYTHM

You can create funny, tongue-twisting lines simply by exploiting rhythm and alliteration.

> HAWKINS: Did you put the pellet with the poison in the vessel with the pestle?
>
> GRISELDA: No! The pellet with the poison's in the flagon with the dragon. The vessel with the pestle has the brew that is true.
>
> HAWKINS: The pellet with the poison's in the flagon with the dragon; the vessel with the pestle has the brew that is true.
>
> GRISELDA: Just remember that.
> —*The Court Jester*, (Norman Panama and Melvin Frank)

> The dodo died. Then Dodi died, Di died and Dando died … Dido must be shitting herself.
> —Colin and Fergus

Nonsense words can bring a smile to any face. Try singing this classic Goons' song with gravitas:

> Ying-tong ying-tong ying-tong ying-tong ying-tong tiddle-i-po,
> Ying-tong ying-tong ying-tong ying-tong ying-tong tiddle-i-po!

The more serious your delivery, the sillier it becomes.

Lewis Carroll's poem, 'Jabberwocky' (*Through the Looking-Glass*), plunges us into a world of nonsense words that nonetheless seem to convey meaning.

> 'Twas brillig, and the slithy toves
> Did gyre and gimble in the wabe:
> All mimsy were the borogoves,
> And the mome raths outgrabe.

'Jabberwocky' seems meaningless, but its outgrabe mome raths spark the reader's imagination.

Repeating and shuffling key words can obfuscate a simple truth. In the following soliloquy from *Yes Minister*, Sir Humphrey Appleby explains an administrative quandary to a hostile committee. He makes sense and tells the truth but lays bare the tendency of bureaucracy towards pointless complexity:

> There is a real dilemma here, in that while it has been government policy to regard policy as the responsibility of ministers and administration as the responsibility of officials, the questions of administrative policy can cause confusion between the policy of administration and the administration of policy, especially when the responsibility for the administration of the policy of administration conflicts or overlaps with responsibility for the policy of administration of policy.
>
> —'A Question of Loyalty', (Antony Jay and Jonathan Lynn)

As you might imagine, Sir Humphrey baffles the committee into submission.

> It is a cliché that most clichés are true, but then like most clichés, that cliché is untrue.
>
> —Stephen Fry

> If you've noticed this notice, you'll notice this notice is not worth noticing.
>
> —Unattrib.

> HAWKEYE: I had a dream last night that I was asleep and I dreamed it while I was awake.
>
> —*M*A*S*H* ('Bananas, Crackers and Nuts' by Burt Styler)

Offensive language has a power that comedy can exploit. As comedian Lenny Bruce said, 'It's the suppression of the word that gives it the power, the violence, the viciousness'. This suppression of usually familiar terms and expressions allows a comedian to flirt with danger:

> The word 'blow' is fine by itself. The word 'job' is okay too. But put them together and you get … 'job-blow', which is still okay.
>
> —Ben Elton

The lyrics below are derived from dialogue in *The Sound of Music*.

> What is it you can't face? What is it yo-o-o-ou can't face?
>
> —The Doug Anthony All Stars

TRANSPOSITIONS

Transpositions can make for revealing gags:

> I'm not as think as you drunk I am.
>
> —Unattrib.

Splitting up words can reveal linguistic anomalies:

> I've been overwhelmed and underwhelmed. When do I get to be just whelmed?
>
> —Michael Scott

> All men are not homeless, but some men are home less than others.
>
> —Henny Youngman

> Freebase? What's free about it?
>
> —Richard Pryor

There are many words we use every day that, if bisected, reveal amusing anomalies, e.g. 'I felt discombobulated earlier, but I'm totally combobulated now; I'm in a state of total combobulism'.

EXERCISE

Here are some words to play with:

Fundamental

Postmodern

Respond

Decapitate

Henchmen

LIMERICKS

These five-line joke poems are the most popular humorous rhyming pattern. The oldest limerick on record was written by Thomas Aquinas (1225–1274), but they achieved broad popularity when the English absurdist writer Edward Lear, recognising that a rhyme can make a so-so punchline more satisfying, produced his *Book of Nonsense* in 1845.

> There was an old man who supposed,
> That the street door was partially closed;

But some very large rats,
Ate his coats and his hats
While that futile old gentleman dozed.

—Edward Lear

Many popular limericks are ribald.

In the Garden of Eden lay Adam
Complacently stroking his madam
And great was his mirth
For in all of the Earth
There were only two balls and he had 'em.

—Unattrib.

The limerick pattern is so well known that in itself it offers an opportunity to subvert audience expectation:

There was an old lady from Pucker,
And that's all I'll say about that.

—Richard Fidler

There was a young man from Japan
Whose limericks never would scan.
When asked why this was
He answered 'Because
I always try to fit as many syllables into the last line as I possibly can'.

—Unattrib.

ANAGRAMS

I realised I was dyslexic when I went to a toga party dressed as a goat.
—Marcus Brigstocke

Is it true that dyslexic atheists believe that there is no Dog?
—Unattrib.

These gags should be built around simple words that the audience can easily reassemble. A joke about being grabbed by a poltergeist at an anagram convention by saying, 'Let go, sprite!' will leave the audience scratching their heads.

ACRONYMS

For the best examples of humorous (i.e. rude) acronyms, contact the Defamation And Mortgage Negotiation Lawyers In Associated Repossession Settlements.

SPOONERISMS

The Oxford Don, Reverend William Spooner (1844–1930), was prone to transposing vowels and consonants in a most unfortunate way.

Let us glaze our asses to the queer old Dean!
'Let us raise our glasses to the dear old Queen!'
The Lord is a shoving leopard.
That may be, but He probably prefers to be known as a 'loving shepherd'.

A simple reference to Spooner invites the audience to apply a new meaning to an otherwise innocuous remark:

As the Reverend Spooner would say, you are a shining wit.

—Unattrib.

REPETITION

Repetition by itself can have comic value.

A customer asks a waitress what's on the menu.
WAITRESS: Well, there's eggs and bacon; eggs, sausage and bacon; egg and Spam; egg, bacon and Spam; egg, bacon, sausage and Spam; Spam, bacon, sausage and Spam; Spam, egg, Spam, Spam, bacon and Spam; Spam, sausage, Spam, Spam, bacon Spam, tomato and Spam.
VIKINGS: (*singing*) Spam, Spam, Spam, Spam, Spam …

—Monty Python

You realise you're an alcoholic when you repeat yourself. You realise you're an alcoholic when you repeat yourself. You realise you're an alcoholic when you repeat yourself.

—Robin Williams

Concepts, rather than words, can also be repeated to comic effect. Dogberry is a watch constable prone to verbosity and malapropisms:

DOGBERRY: Marry, sir, they have committed false report; moreover,

they have spoken untruths; secondarily, they are slanders; sixth and lastly, they have belied a lady; thirdly, they have verified unjust things; and, to conclude, they are lying knaves.
—*Much Ado About Nothing* (William Shakespeare)

In Shakespeare's time, a comic actor named Will Kemp was famous for his portrayal of Dogberry. Kemp was a renowned comic improviser so it's possible he stretched the above list further than six. Who knows how long Kemp could have continued to say the same thing? How long could Robin Williams or Billy Connolly continue?

Today, bumbling cops are still prone to officialese, preferring 'The suspect is proceeding at speed in a north-north-easterly direction and I am rendering pursuit' instead of 'I'm chasing him north'.

Chapter Three: Designing a Sitcom

Humour is the only test of gravity, and gravity of humour; for a subject which will not bear raillery is suspicious, and a jest which will not bear serious examination is false wit.

—Aristotle

Comedy Versus Drama

Narrative comedy is a not for the faint-hearted. Dramatic writers can explore the human heart at a measured pace, confronting their characters with choices that progressively force them to learn and change. A sound understanding of genre, story structure, character development, dialogue and narrative movement, plus native insight, comprise the dramatist's toolkit. Their craft is not easily mastered and their technique requires constant re-appraisal and refreshment. Worse, with all its wandering through the dim corridors of the human soul, a drama writer's life can be awfully depressing. It's a wonder anyone does it, but we're grateful they do.

Narrative comedy demands a firm grasp of dramatic technique—and much more. The comic storyteller must know how to *compress* drama, increasing pace, pressure, surprise, multiplying reversals of character and objective, heightening reality and intensifying action with successive tangential narrative changes. It requires a commonsense understanding of the absurd and the ability and inclination to expose human weakness and prejudice ruthlessly—beginning with one's own.

Drama presents fiction as reality, but comedy presents reality through fiction. Dramatic heroes are heroic despite their flaws. Fitzwilliam Darcy in Jane Austen's *Pride and Prejudice* is the perfect dramatic hero: stoic yet passionate, rude yet shy, flippant yet deadly serious. He's arrogant but irresistible, capable of the deepest love and the cruellest distaste. Raffishly handsome, this lord of the manor is capable, enigmatic and filthy rich. In short, Darcy is as far removed from reality as any character could possibly be. Though Austen's genius persuades us he is a real and complete human being, we'll never meet a Darcy in real life.

Likewise, well-written villains in drama are never wholly evil. A villain who appears wholly evil at the beginning of a drama should reveal themselves as a flawed human being as the story unfolds. Even Darth Vader, in *Star Wars*, finds himself through his love for his son.

70

Most comic 'heroes' by contrast are not heroic at all. They are hapless victims without the social skills or material resources to deal with their situation. When they do act heroically, it is often for selfish reasons. Basil Fawlty in *Fawlty Towers* is a classical example of the comic hero: bullying, inconsiderate, self-obsessed, paranoid, vindictive, lonely, lost, needy, greedy, spiteful, manipulative, egotistical, self-hating, overbearing, pussy-whipped, lazy, lascivious and a compulsive liar. Basil Fawlty is Mr Darcy stripped of the bullshit. We see in Darcy the person we would like to be. In Basil we see who we are.

Comic villains are typically evil from the get-go, and don't change much. Their flaws are immediately apparent and inspire neither sympathy nor empathy. For example, when we first meet Doctor Evil in *Austin Powers: International Man of Mystery* (Mike Myers), he's sending a henchman to a grisly death and is so behind the times he thinks a million dollars is a lot of money. Though Evil is powerful and equipped with awesome 'laser' weapons, he's bald, scarred and deeply flawed in both personality and outlook. And it's all downhill from there.

Drama writers may think they're showing life as it is, but if that were the case they would be making documentaries. Drama explores contemporary but universal issues with gritty, well-drawn characters in an intricately constructed narrative, performed by actors, backed up by stirring music and edited for dramatic effect. Drama's subject matter may be real but the vehicle in which it's presented is an artifice.

Comedy makes no pretence at 'reality'. The moment the audience starts to lose themselves in the action, their laughter snaps them out of it. By accepting the audience's distance from the characters (though that distance may be wafer-thin) comedy writers accept the demand that their stories must be more than real. They must represent the *truth*.

Where dramatists can leave the audience arguing over the moral questions in their story, comedy writers must deliver their message by flaming arrow. Their characters are unalloyed constructs and—unlike drama—the disengagement this causes is not necessarily a problem. There is no real emotional engagement, for example, in the satirical feature film *Wag the Dog* (by Larry Beinhart, Hilary Henkin and David Mamet). We dislike them all. Even when the film's most charming character, Stanley Motss is taken to his death, the audience's heart doesn't skip a beat. We may love watching Motss, but we are never asked to love him.

Unconstrained by verisimilitude, comic stories can move at a pace and intensity beyond anything we'd expect from the real world. This freedom from fakery is both a boon and a burden for comedy writers. It's a boon because it allows us to cut to the chase, pushing our characters and stories in ways that are openly concocted. It's a burden because we cannot hide behind a fantasy.

But comedy and drama do have one thing in common: they must tell the truth about life. In either genre, the moment the audience senses a lack of authenticity in the writing they switch to a sports channel and never return.

Steps to a Sitcom

There are many ways to build a comedy—everybody has their own method. Good ideas, be they for a film, sitcom or play, start with some kind of inspired leap when you're daydreaming, chatting or even thinking about another project. All of a sudden, an irresistible idea for a character, series or even just a joke pops into your head, and the process of building the concept begins.

The following principles and processes allow you to test and modify your comedy concept regardless of the stage of development. They will help you identify strengths, neutralise weaknesses, discover new possibilities and streamline each aspect of your concept. They can also help you determine whether, ultimately, the idea has 'legs'.

Though every writer has their own approach, this book lays out in a systematic way the essential elements of any sitcom, and with them, a logical method of proceeding.

- Theme: Choose your primary message for the series.
- World: Identify the world your characters will inhabit, including your major locations.
- Genre: Identify the kind of comedy (satire, farce or domestic comedy) that best suits your style and inclination, and choose your target audience.
- Characters: Build a combination of characters that will be a reliable source of conflict.
- Structure: Establish conflict, raise the stakes, increase pressure upon your characters and resolve your stories in an interesting way.
- Dialogue: Explore rhythms, dialectics, jargon and patterns of comic dialogue that suit your characters.
- Presentation and Pitch: Prepare your concept for pitching to a producer or network.

Choosing a Theme

Every TV comedy needs a theme, or what is known in feature-film development as a 'controlling idea'. This inspires a show's moral framework, the subtextual message that drives the show. Once you've had some initial thoughts about a project, take the time to identify its overarching theme. Often this is implicit in the show's premise.

For example, the controlling idea of *Kath and Kim*, 'Love of family ain't much but it's all we've got' is a message we draw from watching a dysfunctional family coping with their troubles. For *Gilligan's Island*, a show where seven castaways wait for rescue on a deserted isle, the theme is 'We survive together or perish alone'.

Both these themes contain an implicit grain of hope, but at heart they are serious and concern universal human issues. A light theme, such as 'Happy is as happy does', is not necessary for humour to thrive. The TV series *Kingswood Country* deals with racism, sexism and cultural wars. The show's main character, Ted Bullpit, faces isolation in every episode and the theme is that tolerance unites us while *in*tolerance divides us. Many a serious political speech has been made on the same topic—yet the show is a comedy classic.

A TV show represents months or years of work, so you need to say something to the world that's important to you. There is a difference, however, between 'serious' and 'dark'. A cynical theme like 'Dishonesty works', 'Greed is good' or 'A life without love is a life without hassles' presents three problems for the writer.

The first is personal. Though you might feel it is both important and true, will you still feel the same way after you've spent years of your creative life promulgating a cynical, joyless or empty message? (Or, if you think you will, maybe you should look at a career in law.)

The other two reasons are practical. Entertaining permutations on a cynical theme quickly run dry. For example, if 'Dishonesty works' is your theme, once your hero has become rich and comfortable, what else is there to do but teach him a moral lesson? Satires may depict their central characters winning the day through deceit, selfishness, heartlessness and villainy (see *Yes Minister*), but they are generally hollow victories. What positive qualities they may have are due to the extent that they thwart an even greater evil. Even the darkest satire has a moral rudder, using stories of dire treachery to highlight the shortcomings of our world rather than celebrating treachery itself. A satire's message might simply be 'The evils of this world are intractable', but even this message implies the ideal of a better and fairer society, impossible though it may be. The dismal daily horrors depicted in *The Fall and Rise of Reginald Perrin* simply underline the idea that the world would be a happier place if people were less ignorant, self-centred and petty.

Third, viewers are turned off by cynicism because ultimately it is unrewarding. They will simply find your show too depressing.

The characters in your show, on the other hand, can be cynical—it's just the controlling idea that cannot. Even the exquisitely painful *The Office* has a positive, if cautionary, theme: 'Be honest with yourself'. The antagonist,

David Brent, must learn to face his inadequacies or he will never discover his strengths. The protagonist, Tim, must embrace his ambition and act on his potential or lose Dawn, the love of his life, and spend his remaining days in lonely torpor.

You'll find richer soil for your episode ideas if your theme is more than an attack on the world you've chosen to explore. The theme of *The Larry Sanders Show* boils down to more than 'Network television is populated by bastards', though that message is clear throughout. By series end, Larry Sanders learns a grander, more challenging lesson: 'To thine own self be true'. And throughout the series we're on Larry's side, even though he's a selfish and scheming celebrity. We don't engage with his faults, but with how he acts in his world.

Your controlling idea might be in the form of a question. The theme of *The Nanny* is 'Do we deserve true love even though we are flawed?' The answer is subjective. To respond in the affirmative we must forgive Fran Drescher's nanny character all her faults.

To find a satisfying controlling idea, ask yourself what you are most curious about. The notion that writers should only write about what they know is misleading. Even in constructing a textbook the writer does more than jot down what they know on the first day. Writing is an act of exploration. Without learning as you go, the act of writing would be deathly dull—and the reading even worse. People write autobiographies because they want to make sense of their lives, not because they know everything that happened and what it means. Questions, not answers, keep us awake at night. So, what do you wonder about most? Love? Death? Identity? The true value of success? The price that others must pay so you can realise your dreams?

Be sure the theme, like the show's premise, is something you want to explore—otherwise you could waste years working on something you don't care about. And that is no laughing matter.

Choosing a World

The process of developing a sitcom usually begins with a 'Eureka' moment that involves, among other things, a setting, or 'world', for the show.

It's not necessary for a sitcom setting to be intrinsically funny. *The Librarians* is based in a suburban library, *Mother and Son* in a suburban home and *Cheers* in an average American bar. These places could just as easily be settings for tragedies. For instance, *Mother and Son* is a show about a middle-aged man, Arthur, and his aged mother, Maggie. The stakes and pressures are genuine and universal. Arthur faces losing any chance of a normal adult life as he cares for his ailing mother. Maggie, though she is shrewd and manipulative, is experiencing the first symptoms of dementia, a condition that fills her with terror. The show's apparent theme—love and frustration are inseparable—is not in itself comic.

What makes an ordinary setting funny are the characters, their conflicts, the trouble their natures lead them into and, of course, the self-contained or narrative jokes.

Don't be too concerned if the main setting for your sitcom is familiar territory. A family home is the staple environment for a domestic comedy (e.g. *Till Death Do Us Part*, *My Wife and Kids*). While the genre has expanded to include apartment blocks (*Friends*) and group houses (*Will & Grace*), the home is always dom-com's main arena.

Farce and satire settings have also been successfully reprised. For example, TV networks have been the settings for *The Jesters*, *Murphy Brown*, *Drop the Dead Donkey*, *The Larry Sanders Show*, *Frontline* and *30 Rock*.

The 'fish out of water' genre (*Mr Ed*, *Alf*, *The Addams Family*, *No Heroics* and *3rd Rock from the Sun*) features extraordinary characters in ordinary settings. *No Heroics*, for instance, follows a tribe of superheroes trying to get by without their special powers. It's the juxtaposition of these out-of-this-world characters with ordinary life that creates the show's comic conflict. The characters, not the premise, are what make a show truly original. *Mr Ed* and *My Favorite Martian* both have essentially the same outlandish premise: a single man living with a non-human character whose attributes must be kept secret. However, what makes the shows distinctive is that 'Mr Ed' is a smooth-talking troublemaker who understands human nature and 'Uncle Martin' is a curious and stubborn alien who often finds humans baffling.

Setting a sitcom on the moon will be attention-grabbing for the length of the opening credits. After that, the characters must do all the work.

Comedy and its Sub-Genres

Having chosen your theme, you're ready to decide on the genre that best serves the style, tone and perspective of your sitcom.

As a genre, comedy is generally considered to comprise three 'sub-genres'. These are defined by what can be called 'circles of engagement', or the level of affinity an audience has with the setting, characters, subject matter and theme.

DOMESTIC COMEDY

RAY: All three kids asleep. You thought I couldn't get Ally to take a nap.
DEBRA: Good job, honey.

RAY: Yeah. By the way, tomorrow we have to buy a pony.
—*Everybody Loves Raymond* ('Your Place or Mine?' by Jeremy
Stevens)

Domestic comedy tells the bittersweet truth.

This is the innermost ring of the circles of engagement. It offers the closest level of affinity and empathy with the characters. To achieve its emotional connection with the audience, 'dom-com' deals primarily with nuclear families, either conventional (e.g. *Everybody Loves Raymond, Home Improvement, The Cosbys*) or adoptive or single-parented (*Hey Dad..!, The Nanny, Diff'rent Strokes*).

As most people have come from one kind of family or another, such shows strike a chord. The subject matter of dom-com must be familiar territory for most of us: mothers and fathers struggling to find a work-life balance, marriage maintenance, interfering relatives, the difficulties of raising teenagers, paying the mortgage, getting fired, children learning life's lessons and so forth.

Since the 1980s, however, dom-com has expanded the definition of 'family' to reflect modern life. In some ways a family is now defined simply by the people who say they are in one: single parents with sibling flatmates (*Two and a Half Men*), a group of senior citizens (*The Golden Girls*), a group house with a hetero-gay mix (*Will & Grace*) or an apartment building (*Friends*). But no matter how far these shows stray from the original paradigm their subject matter remains familiar: the trials of single parenthood, the isolation of the aged, the single person's desire for a partner, the quest for love and commitment by young adults and so forth.

Dom-com generally generates the drama amongst the main family members—usually with a parent or parents as one side of the conflict. In *Everybody Loves Raymond*, Raymond's main problems stem from the rivalries between his mother, his wife and his brother. There are short-lived conflicts with characters outside the family (such as workmates) but mostly the family's immediate relationships provide enough trouble and strife. As a result most of the genre's action takes place in the family homes.

Dom-com's main characters are usually flawed but lovable. Poignancy is employed regularly, if sparingly. Loyalty, honesty (to one's self and to others), true love and courage are the meat and potatoes of domestic comedy. Dom-com stories typically deal with matters of the heart, inviting the viewer to engage emotionally in the dilemmas and choices of the characters. In the pilot episode of *Everybody Loves Raymond* (by Philip Rosenthal), Raymond is pressured by his wife to keep his meddling parents away from her birthday—for a change. Emotions run high. The parents' emotional pain at the rejection comprises the stakes with which Raymond must negotiate. The pressure on Raymond to decide where his loyalties lie goes to the heart of the series.

Emotional engagement is the hook that will catch the viewer. If your conflicts are commonplace, that hook becomes a net that will capture an entire demographic. If you've never been touched by a poignant scene from a sitcom, you should stay in more. You know you're truly in touch with your feelings when you tear up at *Mork and Mindy*.

In domestic sitcom, characters learn and change, but not fundamentally. Typically their life lessons deal with peripheral qualities that characters can reveal and resolve in one episode, such as a phobia about spiders. So long as the phobia isn't a running gag through the series (why fix a gag that ain't broken?) and the character hasn't dealt fearlessly with spiders elsewhere in the series, the phobia can form the axis of a learning curve without fundamentally changing the character.

Dom-com stories usually travel at a pace that feels natural rather than forced. The reversals may come more quickly as the story nears its climax, but not always.

- Dom-com protagonists are pre-occupied with their relationships.
- Dom-com explores the minutiae of emotional interaction.
- To achieve their desires, protagonists must learn and change—though not fundamentally.
- Poetic justice is always served.
- The viewer is 'inside' the story—that is, they must strongly identify with at least one character in the series.

In domestic comedy, human relationships are under the microscope.

FARCE

> BASIL: Do you remember when we were first 'manacled' together? We used to laugh a lot.
> SYBIL: Yes, but not at the same time, Basil.
> —*Fawlty Towers* ('Communication Problems' by Connie Booth and John Cleese)

Farce tells the painful truth.

Farce occupies the next circle of engagement. It keeps the viewer at arm's length—although only just. It does this in two ways. Firstly, although the characters in farce are recognisable, their relationships with one another hold little intrinsic interest. They do not strive for a genuine and mature emotional connection. For instance, Basil Fawlty in *Fawlty Towers*, arguably television's finest farce, is too self-obsessed to engage meaningfully with his wife, Sybil. He calls her 'the dragon'—and he means it. If the main character or characters cannot truly love, the viewer fails to establish an emotional bond with them. The relationships in farce may be familiar (husband and wife, boss and employee) but they are not explored dramatically.

Secondly, the settings for farce may be recognisable but, unlike the family home, need not be universally familiar. Farces have been set in large manor homes, hotels, home businesses, public buildings and offices. While many of us have been to these locations, we haven't necessarily stood in the shoes of those who inhabit them. In other words, we may have stayed at a bed-and-breakfast, but few of us have managed one.

Finally, and crucially, farce moves quickly. It pushes its characters through drastic, increasingly rapid and often increasingly unlikely story reversals. The suspense generated by these frantic and accelerating complications is the genre's main appeal. The emotions sparked by these goings-on may include excitement, frustration, annoyance and *Schadenfreude*, but sadness and empathy rarely get a look-in. (In a farce–dom-com hybrid such as *Frasier* pathos may be a regular element, but it's the dom-com strand of the stories that gets us choked-up.)

In this circle of engagement, though we may not regard the protagonist or protagonists as lovable, we do engage in their troubles. Nobody loves Basil Fawlty as a person, but he appeals to the disobedient child in all of us. Knowing him as we do, we look forward to the harsh treatment he metes out to other, generally more virtuous, characters that enter his world. We don't particularly care whether Basil is victorious or eviscerated by Sybil. We don't *feel* for him. The writers (Connie Booth and John Cleese) never ask us to shed a tear for any of their characters. We are engaged but not emotionally attached.

In essence, farce is the exploration of conflict between a protagonist and their world. This conflict is inevitable given their nature. For example, no matter who walks through Basil Fawlty's door, he's going to have a problem with them. Even Mother Teresa might find herself accused of a holier-than-thou attitude by the thin-skinned and self-aggrandising Basil. (How delicious it would be to see the saintly Mother Teresa being forced to clean the kitchen with a toothbrush as Basil shouts, 'Not so high-and-mighty *now* are you, you pontificating crone?!')

In farce, typically it's every man for himself. That is, the protagonist is self-absorbed and conflict is generated by the constant flow of guest characters from the outside world. Anyone can walk through the doors of Fawlty Towers.

Prejudice, selfishness, social eccentricities and status are the meat and hollandaise of farce.

Farce is often fast-paced and laden with wordplay and complications including misunderstandings and runaway lies. The already brisk plot gathers pace until the chaotic climax. There's a lot of running, hiding and lying through teeth. Mistaken identities, falsehoods and disguises abound. Doors (both literal and metaphorical) open and close as the characters strive with increasing desperation to achieve their aims. Unlikely or extreme behaviour is commonplace.

- Farce protagonists are preoccupied by their own status.
- To achieve their goal, farce protagonists may learn peripheral or tactical lessons, but they cannot change in any meaningful way.
- The characters are held at arms length by the viewer, but only just.
- Poetic justice may or may not be served.

In farce, human behaviour is under the microscope.

SATIRE

There's a place called a rainforest, it truly sucks ass.
Let's knock it all down and get rid of it fast.
You say, 'Save the rainforest,' but what would you know?
You've never been to the rainforest before.
>   —*South Park* ('Rainforest Schmainforest' by Trey Parker and
>   Matt Stone)

Satire tells the dark truth.

Sitting on the outermost circle of engagement, satire is unconcerned by most questions of character. Rather, it distils and inverts or exaggerates some aspect of our world in order to comment on society at large. One man becomes all men, a politician, all politicians. In a satirical world, moral values, worldly concerns and even commonsense may be upside-down. Just ask Gulliver.

Rather than exploring the nuances of individual behaviour, satire is preoccupied by the machinations of bureaucracies, communities, hierarchies and extended families. We may be entertained by a witty and sustained satirical attack on society, but the characters remain little more than pawns from which we are emotionally detached. Who ever shed a tear for *South Park*'s Kenny McCormick?

Even the noblest characters in a satire (often found in servile roles) don't earn the audience's empathy. We may pity them and even wish them success in their puny endeavours, but we never truly invest in characters who should know better than to passively maintain the status quo.

Consequently, as in farce, satirical characters do not change or grow in any fundamental way. Or, if they do, it's a sign the series is ending. (Only in the dying moments of the final episode of *Blackadder Goes Forth* does Edmund Blackadder become sombre as he dwells upon the madness of war.)

Its heartlessness makes it difficult for some viewers to enjoy TV satire, making it the hardest sub-genre to sell. The problem is not that it's too clever; some viewers simply can't see the point in watching often unlovable characters rattling around a bleak universe. The problems and conflicts of satirical characters are generally not those of the average viewer. *Yes Minister* explores the evils of political power. Unless you've worked in government, the immediate issues facing the minister, Jim Hacker, won't immediately resonate, and watching a sclerotic world at its worst can be very uncomfortable. Likewise, many viewers find the subject matter of *The Office*—the pointlessness and cruelty of the modern workplace—too painful to watch.

TV satire, no matter how funny, is rarely 'light'. Satire *deliberately* offends. Whether it's politics, sex or social commentary, satire takes no prisoners and makes no apologies. Satire challenges and often disparages our world view. The satirists place themselves above society and even religion (a satirist can, after all, cast the Lord as a finger-puppet). Broad appeal and digit deities rarely go together.

Satire illuminates by contrast, but in doing so it offers a dim view of the human condition. In *South Park* Kenny's customary death is never accompanied by a ray of sunshine or a worthy lesson well heard. Kenny dies. Those who killed him are 'bastards'. Move on.

Satirists tell us what is wrong with the world, not what is right. And yet, it's not a negative message. Implicit in satire is an appeal for change.

When a nobler character *does* offer a solution to the world's woes they are usually ignored. In *Yes Minister* Bernard Woolley is a junior public servant who generally offers sensible and morally correct advice that is wryly disregarded by those above him. It's a hard world.

The pace of a TV satire is dependent entirely on the world, issues or group of characters under scrutiny. Using its arsenal of metaphor and parody, satire can race like a Canterbury tale or plod like Don Quixote's nag.

- Satire's protagonists are often preoccupied with power, justice or social order.
- Common satire settings include homes, public institutions, businesses, factories and offices.
- Rigid hierarchies, social status and the *faux pas*, paradoxes or hypocrisies they engender are the meat and flies of satire.
- Satire explores human social behaviour.
- Satirical characters do not learn or change.
- The viewer is emotionally detached.
- Poetic justice is usually served—plus ten years' hard labour.

In satire, society is under the microscope.

CHOOSING A SUB-GENRE

Choosing a sub-genre can be a baffling and frustrating exercise. Baffling because the choice is filled with as many limitations as it is possibilities. Frustrating because, once you've chosen, the only way back is to scrap your idea and start again—not that you should ever be afraid of that.

The choice of sub-genre can however be made with more confidence if you begin by examining the theme of your show and your own sense of humour. If your theme encompasses love, belonging, forgiveness, friendship or family, you'll find a snug fit in domestic comedy. If your intention is to explore human fallibility, loyalty, tolerance and prejudice, farce may present the best field of play. If ambition, greed, systemic social sclerosis and dysfunctional families, groups or organisations tickle your fancy, you're leaning toward satire.

Your chosen theme will, by and large, dictate the choice of sub-genre. However, most writers are drawn to one sub-genre before another. (I find it hard to resist the allure of the satirist's godlike power.) If you have a strong affinity with one form, you may wish to re-examine your theme so that it better suits your taste. But beware: your theme or controlling idea must live up to its name. Think of it as your sock and the sub-genre as your shoe. Without the right sock for the right shoe, bushwalking is an uncomfortable business—and no fun to watch.

Let your own sense of humour be your guide. What you find funny is probably what you want to write.

Sub-Genre Hybrids

It's possible to create a genre hybrid, combining elements of one sub-genre with another. For instance, Shaun Micallef's *Welcher & Welcher* is a fine farce–satire hybrid that features a deeply flawed protagonist, complex and escalating stories and a deliciously scornful view of the legal world. There are however some challenges involved in a genre hybrid.

Firstly, the show cannot evolve from one sub-genre to another; it must be a hybrid from the get-go. Each of the sub-genres must be ever-present if only in the thinnest way. The show may lean towards one or the other, sometimes with one side taking the total weight, but the story must remain consistent for both. For example, if your show follows an everyday family who own a Cat that Rules the Galaxy with an Iron Paw, the audience must meet the cat in the first episode. If you introduce a feline inter-galactic tyrant halfway through the series you would bounce from one sub-genre to another. It would be like seeing a magical genie suddenly become a member of the Soprano family. The reality of the world your viewers have accepted is not just shaken by Darth Puss's arrival—it collapses altogether.

If the circle of engagement shifts and the reality of a show's world changes, the viewer asks, 'How am I meant to see this show?' A narrative that repeatedly jumps between one sub-genre and another is not a sitcom, it's a sketch show—with long sketches. This schizophrenia demands the viewer change their distance from the action while trying to follow a single narrative.

To work as a coherent entertainment, Darth Puss must be a character from day one, and he needs to remain throughout the series, even if only in the background, constantly conditioning the characters' lives. Viewers may only get hints of his true identity (a wheezing sound, a black mask, assertions of fatherhood) but as long as they know that the family home is also Imperial Headquarters then they're ready for the world you've created. (*3rd Rock from the Sun* establishes its alien family from the start and, though the issues they deal with are common and contemporary, the alien identity of the protagonists is never neglected or questioned.)

To combine sub-genres, and their inherent restrictions, remember the relationship between their respective circles of engagement. Those that sit next to one another are more easily hybridised, but dom-com, in the first circle of engagement, sits uncomfortably with satire, in the third. It's hard to ask the audience to peer down on the action from a God-like distance and at the same time pull on their heart strings.

Farce however sits relatively easily with both dom-com and satire. Its arms-length vantage point can be relaxed or extended to accommodate the demands of its fellow sub-genres. It's a balancing act.

Domestic comedy and farce blend most comfortably. Domestic comedy is primarily about touching our hearts and keeping us close to the characters, but it's not a huge stretch to place an antagonistic, bigoted granny in the mix. If the granny is at the centre of the show, the show is essentially farce: she's the star and her nature drives the conflict. But if granny is simply near, or shares, the centre of the show, her farcical nature can be a source of conflict without driving the major action, and the show is basically dom-com. A dom-com can incorporate farce's chaos so long as the viewer maintains empathy for one or more of the characters. Without that the show is simply a farce in a domestic setting.

One of the most successful dom-com–farce hybrids is *Frasier*. The characters pursue their everyday desires and we love them for it but Frasier also has a farcical aspect to his personality. Clever but self-absorbed, he manipulates others and lies his way into many complex situations, forcing him to take increasingly frantic action to put the toothpaste back in the tube.

Notwithstanding its proximity to farce, satire is the hardest sub-genre to hybridise. Satire keeps the viewer at a distance, and thus reduces both the bewilderment generated by farce and the emotional punch of domestic comedy.

The Librarians (by Robyn Butler and Wayne Hope) has the hallmarks of a farce–satire hybrid. The protagonist, Frances O'Brien is, like most farce protagonists, prone to conflict with virtually everyone she encounters. She is a highly-strung, passive-aggressive, devout Catholic librarian while her colleagues are masterfully drawn caricatures of the denizens of an urban community. We cringe at Frances' panicked shenanigans and sometimes pity her, but we feel no deep emotional attachment. Though her prevailing sentiment is 'poor me', Frances dominates her library, maintaining a fixed big-fish–small-pond hierarchy that is portrayed with satirical scorn.

In a dom-com–satire hybrid, viewers are asked to empathise with individual family members while accepting that the social structures around them, including perhaps the family itself, are the true problem. It's hard to feel for a group of people who have no insight into their most basic condition. For example, can we really care for a terrorist with girl troubles or a Nazi with an overbearing mother? Dom-com works because it touches our hearts. Satire works because it removes us from our empathies and engages our brains.

There are, nevertheless, successful examples of the dom-com–satire hybrid. *The Royle Family*, for instance, explores the sclerosis of the modern family. We love the characters and can be engrossed by their emotional struggles, but we are always aware of the overall bankruptcy of the modern family—at least as it's presented in the show. To achieve this, however, the writers largely restrict themselves to stories that can be told in the family lounge room. The workplace, the dole office or the neighbour's kitchen can never be visited without threatening the shallow illusion of the *Royle Family* world. Of course, the concept of a lounge-room show may have come first, but the genre hybrid certainly forces this restriction upon the show. Once the writers (Caroline Aherne and Craig Cash) committed to this hybrid they couldn't break out of that lounge room without losing the show's laser-like focus. Aherne and Cash turned this restriction into a virtue. Genius—pure and simple.

If you're still learning the ropes of TV comedy, however, you might be wise to walk before you can run. Pick one sub-genre and make it work for you. You can re-invent the wheel later.

The Power of Three

The number three is perhaps the most useful number in communication. For human beings, a pattern of three is a readily appreciated rhythm. Our brains are geared to recognise, comprehend and find satisfaction in a pattern of three. In sitcoms, the 'principle of three' is a technique that will get structure and dialogue humming.

The number three is everywhere in human culture. All around the world people count to three to co-ordinate a group lifting a heavy object. Firing squads follow three steps: ready, aim, fire. Meals are comprised of three courses: entrée, main, dessert. Christian Churches recognise a Father, Son and Holy Spirit. Stories are comprised of three acts that each consist of three steps: harmony, disturbance and resolution.

And, importantly, jokes often work with three steps:

Set-up
Confirmation
Resolution/Reversal/Revelation

When an Englishman, a Scotsman and an Irishman get together the Englishman sets up the scenario, the Scotsman confirms the scenario and the Irishman provides the resolution, turns the scenario on its head or reveals an aspect of the scenario that casts it in a new light.

A pattern of three resonates more strongly with more people than any other. Tripartite structures apply to arguments, jokes, stories, advertisements—in fact, to pretty much any form of communication. When Aristotle divided story into a 'beginning, middle and end' (see *The Poetics*) he was not inventing the three-act story structure, he was identifying it. Our bodies know the pattern well. Even sneezes and orgasms observe the pattern: (1) A stable but undeniable tickle of indeterminate length evolves into (2) a growing and inexorable wave of energy, (3) culminating in a short and sharp explosion. A story comprised of the first two steps only leaves the audience on tenterhooks, as though they have taken a breath but haven't sneezed.

Why is it so? Well, maybe it's something that's evolved with us from the sea. Waves are comprised of, you guessed it, three stages: pulse, build and crash. First comes the pulse of the wave, an invisible but powerful vibration that surges through the sea until it meets the rising ocean floor whereupon it begins to form a wave. Next, the wave builds and ploughs toward the shore, growing higher and higher until its peak teeters precariously. And crash! The wave topples upon itself in a thunderous tumult. Its journey ends as it laps gently at the shore and recedes.

The three acts of a story resemble these three stages, not only in number but because of the length and shape of them.

Consider a typical Act One (the pulse). It's normally a short act showing the story's world in normal balance. The hero is doing what he always does until the arrival of a catalyst. The hero gets moving.

Act Two (the build) is normally the longest of the three acts. It shows the hero struggling against forces beyond his control as he reacts to the complications deriving from the catalyst and his own actions. Events spiral out of control and a reckoning between the hero and the opposing forces is inevitable.

Then Act Three (the crash) hits with brief, irresistible and tumultuous power as the elements of the story collide. Chaos reigns, then settles as the hero overcomes or is defeated by the opposing forces. A new equilibrium is established. If he survives, the protagonist returns to his world, changed somehow but still recognisable as the hero we met in Act One.

If you consider films that you have found troubling or unsatisfying, it's often because they violate the three-part structure or do not execute it properly. This dissonance doesn't necessarily mean that the film is crap. It might be a deliberate challenge to the audience, leaving us with an uneasy feeling long after a film has ended. The audience might be provoked or disturbed. But *Star Wars* it ain't. Only the rhythm of the wave, the classic three-act structure, gives a general audience a satisfying sense of catharsis and completion.

Tripartite patterns even occur in limericks. These are rhymes that, although traditionally laid out in five lines, when recited to a constant beat take four sets of four beats to complete. In the example below the stressed syllables are underlined:

> The <u>Lim</u>'rick comes <u>in</u> from <u>sea</u>,
> A <u>slow</u> moving <u>ripple</u> is <u>she</u>.
> The <u>ripple</u> gains <u>pace</u>
> 'Til <u>all</u> is mis<u>placed</u>
> 'N' goes <u>back</u> where <u>she</u> used to <u>be</u>.

The stressed syllables combine with a silent beat at the end of each of the first, second and fifth lines to make up four sets of four beats. However we *perceive* the lines with silent beats as only three beats each. Thus, the first two lines of the limerick comprise 'Act One', with a total of six beats. The second two lines are 'Act Two', with four beats. The final line, 'Act Three', has three beats. Consequently, each 'Act' gains pace, a basic principle of drama.

'So what?', you say? Here's what …

Screenwriters can trust the Principle of Three to work with any audience, anywhere, any time. Humans are primally geared to respond to it.

Using patterns of three in dialogue can communicate and re-enforce the issues and topics at play while paying off in terms of laughs. Where one example may be funny, a triple-headed example or a group of three examples can be funnier. The writers of *Blackadder* use patterns of three regularly and to great effect.

BALDRICK: My name is Baldrick, my lord.
EDMUND: Then I shall call you 'Baldrick', Baldrick.
BALDRICK: And I shall call you 'my lord', my lord.
—('The Foretelling' by Rowan Atkinson and Richard Curtis)

As the example above shows, enacting the Principle of Three doesn't mean a character says the same thing three times. The way the line is phrased can change throughout the sequence.

The following is my own analysis based on a lecture given by Stephen Cleary.

The scene below, from *The Larry Sanders Show*, illustrates the tripartite pattern used by sitcoms the world over, showing that everything ancient can be cool again. Because the patterns overlap, the scene is both numbered (1,2,3) and lettered (A,B,C).

> HANK *is in his office.*
>
> HANK: (*into the phone*) My God, three hundred dollars for a water pump? (A)
>
> > BRIAN *comes rushing in, bursting with important news.*
>
> BRIAN Hank! (1)
>
> HANK: (*into the phone*) … But I still smell gas. (B)
>
> BRIAN: Hank! (2)
>
> HANK: (*into the phone*) … Yes, I do realise the water pump is not connected to the fuel system. (C) (*Raising his voice*) But I just had the mistaken impression that you had a nose. Tally-ho, fuckface.
>
> BRIAN: Hank! Hank! (3)
>
> HANK: Haven't you ever heard of knocking before you enter?
>
> BRIAN: Sorry …
>
> HANK: Now calm down. (1)
>
> BRIAN: Okay.
>
> HANK: Calm down. (2)
>
> BRIAN: Okay!
>
> HANK: Now, are you calm? (3)
>
> > BRIAN *tries to be calm.*
>
> BRIAN: Uh huh.
>
> HANK: (*slowly*) Now. (1) What is it? (2)
>
> BRIAN: Your car's on fire. (3)
>
> > HANK, *horrified, jumps up and races to the door.*
>
> HANK: Godammit! When were you going to tell me?
>
> > —('Everybody Loves Larry' by John Vitti)

There are several ways to apply the principle:

- *Simple repetition.* Brian cries out for Hank's attention three times—'Hank!' The double 'Hank! Hank!' only counts as one: it's Brian's *intention* that is at issue.

- *Tripartite development of an idea.* Hank uses three sentences to describe his frustration with his water pump before he turns to abuse.
- *Rhythmic exchange.* ('Now. / What is it?' / 'Your car's on fire.')

The scene structure also follows a three-beat pattern:

- Set-up (Hank is on the phone, Brian has a problem.)
- Confirmation (Hank calms Brian down.)
- Resolution (Brian reveals the truth, Hank reacts.)

Tripartite structures keep the story, theme and characters moving at an apparently natural pace despite unusual or complex activity. It also allows the actors to perform the scene briskly, confident that each beat is registering with the audience.

Tripartite patterns aren't hard to find once you look for them. In fact, like many of the other principles outlined in this book, they are so pervasive that it's a wonder audiences don't notice them.

SITCOM AND THE THREE-ACT STRUCTURE

In sitcoms, as in all stories, the three-act structure uses the power of three:

Act One: Set-up
The world and characters are introduced.
The central conflict of the story is initiated.
The act climaxes in the first turning point.

Act Two: Complication
A complication raises the stakes.
Conflict intensifies, climaxing in a second turning point.

Act Three: Climax and Resolution
The rising conflict climaxes in the third turning point or story climax.
The conflict is resolved, either for the better or, irreparably, for the worse.

Public broadcasters, such as the BBC and Australia's ABC which have no commercial breaks, frequently take a minute to establish the characters and the show's normal world in balance. Any elements that will cause trouble appear in a benign state. The comedy here is found in the characters themselves, engaged in the everyday conflicts of their imagined lives.

The first act of a commercial television sitcom is, however, often rudimentary. Commercial TV generally allocates about 21-minutes for its 'half-hour' shows, allowing for three three-minute ad breaks. The episode also loses time for its opening titles (ranging from five to thirty seconds) and closing credits (approximately thirty seconds). Even the 'breakers' leading into or out of the ad breaks (three to five seconds each) take valuable time. With as little as nineteen and a half minutes to tell a story, there's little room for a detailed 'getting to know you' Act One. The audience's knowledge of the series' premise and characters must be largely assumed so the stories can get underway.

Nonetheless, a first act that establishes the normal world must exist to provide a platform for the change created by conflict, and to establish ground rules for new viewers. Opening titles can aid in the set-up. *The Brady Bunch*'s titles swiftly sketch in the setting, main characters and overall series conflict. We are told that a man with three sons has married a woman with three daughters, and we see their maid join them all in a split-screen gathering. The opening titles to *The Nanny* tell the story of a glitzy door-to-door beautician from Queens who is accidentally hired as a nanny for the children of a millionaire widower. And *The Simpsons*' opening depicts Homer, the father, being slapdash at his nuclear power-station workplace, Marge, the mother, shopping with Maggie, the baby, while Lisa, the daughter, is thrown out of band class for being too talented and Bart, the son, causes chaos throughout the town. There's even a panning shot across a field that, if played in slow motion, shows virtually every character in the series. The titles end with the Simpson family jumping onto their couch, whereupon they fall prey to an outlandish twist, different for each episode, that only an animated world could allow. Say no more.

Opening titles don't have to be didactic to set up their show's world. The titles to Australia's finest domestic comedy, *Hey Dad..!*, simply shows snapshots of the characters at work and play around the family home, with the name of the show and the absence of a mother figure implying that Mum is not around.

Some opening titles merely suggest the sensibility of a show. *Frasier*'s five-second graphic of the show's name is accompanied by a sophisticated piano flourish. This is enough to signal that the show will involve urbane, adult characters. A new viewer will not expect to see a tractor in the first scene.

Once the opening titles have broadly established the rules of the game, the concerns of the story should be established as swiftly as possible. Even the first exchange, such as Will and Grace's below, can become a serviceable set-up. It's common for the characters to be placed under stress in the first scene and begin their journey to the first act's turning point:

GRACE: Good morning.
WILL: Bad morning. I just found a grey chest hair. So depressing.
—*Will & Grace* ('Will On Ice' by Michael Patrick King)

No matter the length of an episode, all of the main and secondary story strands should be up and running in the first five minutes. (In the commercial format, this means every story must be established before the first ad break.) Introducing a new strand after this time is confusing and breaks the momentum of the stories underway. Before the fat lady sings, the viewer needs to hear her clearing her throat early in the episode.

The third act of a sitcom is usually very short, and the resolution can happen in one line. The birds come home to roost and the show is over— although subsequent action can be implied off screen. In Act One of 'May The Force Be With You' (*Only Fools And Horses* by John Sullivan), Del's sidekick, Rodney, is accused of stealing a microwave by Del's nemesis, DCI Roy Slater. The cop is bent on sending poor Rodney to jail by any means. After much slipping and sliding, Del demands immunity from prosecution in exchange for giving Slater the name of the thief. Slater agrees and the immunity document is signed. Rodney watching his friend's apparent betrayal of the thief's code provides the episode's climax. The resolution is short and sweet. Slater asks who stole the microwave and Del replies with a smile—'I did'. Roll credits.

Ad breaks impose four segments on a commercial half-hour TV sitcom. It's common for each of the three turning points in a story to occur immediately before an ad break, acting as cliff-hangers to keep the audience tuned in. The climax can come before the third ad break, with a quick resolution that can be as short as a minute following the ad break. But given the second act is usually the longest, it's also common to put the third ad break just prior to the climactic scene.

In many domestic comedies the resolution is a brief lesson, followed by a lighter, character-based gag that shows all is back to normal. Farces are often resolved by a new round of chaos, or when the situation is irreparably worsened and recriminations are inevitable. Satires frequently end when both the protagonist and antagonist fail to achieve their goals and surrender to the inevitable.

Chapter Four: Designing Ongoing Characters

They say, best men are moulded out of faults,
And for the most, become much more the better
For being a little bad.

—*Measure For Measure* (William Shakespeare)

Character Building

The primary purpose of a comic character is to make us laugh. To do this, they must poke at us in clever but ultimately simple ways. We can't be sitting around after a punchline, reversal or stakes-raise trying to work out the reasons behind it.

A punchline punches.

A comic reversal spins on a dime.

Stakes rise in swift, clear increments.

This is not to suggest that a comic character can't survive an element of mystery, even to themselves. Complexity and nuance have a place, but they operate best when they stem from clearly drawn character qualities.

Creating a character demands not only the invention of their characterisation (the observable, external qualities of the character) but also of the things that drive them, their deep character. Their desires, fears and view of the world are the things that get them out of bed in the morning.

Characteristics (the qualities that constitute characterisation) fall broadly into four categories: role/s in life, physical attributes, status and home life. Thus a character might be defined in the following way:

- Role/s in life: police officer and father
- Physical attributes: tall, dark and handsome
- Status: a sergeant
- Home life: married to a capable woman who loves him

Comic characters, however, benefit from a juxtaposition of unlikely or incompatible characteristics. The cop above sounds like a perfect fellow—and for the purposes of a sitcom he might stay as he is just to irritate the less perfect males in the show. But in this guise he could only ever be a cameo. As a major character he's not going to last long.

To make him funny *in himself* the characteristics above need to contradict eachother. Sometimes a single incompatible quality can revolutionise a character. If, for example, the cop above is tall, dark and *cross-eyed*, his superhuman perfection is immediately undermined. A comic version of this character might look like this:

- Role/s in life: police officer and kleptomaniac
- Physical attributes: tall, dark and mono-browed
- Status: a former police commissioner who chose to become a sergeant
- Home life: married to a nymphomaniac he can never satisfy

The character may not need *all* these characteristics—any one of them is certain to make his life tougher—but the tougher his life is, the funnier it can be. When he is facing *insurmountable odds* at home (from his insatiable wife) and at work (from his partner, who may catch him stealing, and from his mono-brow which intimidates the innocent and guilty alike), then the hope principle comes into play in the poor cop's life.

Having selected comic characteristics for all your characters, the next step is to plot their general history. One short paragraph is enough to get a handle on them: the character's life in a nutshell. They need room to grow and change in the writing, so don't get bogged down in details. Fiddle with minutiae and you'll end up in the yoga position known as 'the swan inspects its own colon'.

Though it's no walk in the park, devising characterisation is the easiest part of the character-building process. The real work comes next and involves balancing characterisation with core drives, strengths, weaknesses and world-views that can be relied upon to regularly drive a character to action.

In the romantic comedy *Tootsie* (by Larry Gelbart, Don McGuire and Murray Schisgal), Michael Dorsey finds himself pulled in several directions as he struggles to maintain a false front as a female soap star. Dorsey is a well-rounded character. He has all the ego, self-doubt, wits, talent, insight, determination and fear of irrelevance many actors possess. If we met Michael Dorsey on 42nd Street he would come across as real and not particularly comic. The things that drive him to comic action are his core drives.

At the start of his story, Dorsey wants to be a famous actor but his unconscious *need* is for something more important and ultimately more fulfilling: love. The complications begin when he meets the woman of his dreams but she only knows him as his female alter-ego, 'Dorothy Michaels'. Caught between his desire for fame and his burgeoning love, an avalanche of weaknesses are exposed: self-deception (he thinks he can have it all), desire for affirmation (everyone wants a piece of him/her) and identity confusion (is he Michael or Dorothy or both?). Dorsey engages in a complex farcical dance as he tries to juggle both his identities, his true love, her amorous father, his agent, the TV network and his suspicious friends.

For all the complexity of his character, Dorsey's core drives (fame and love) are the primary catalysts for his actions throughout the story. His core drives explain *why* he acts. His characteristics (ego, self-doubt, wits etc) show *how* he goes about his actions.

The characteristics of Michael Dorsey's life are:

- Role/s in life—an amorous but underconfident heterosexual male actor and female soap star.
- Physical attributes—short, slight, not traditionally handsome.
- Status—poor and unknown at home but rich and famous at work.
- Home life—lives in a cheap flat with a male buddy.

Only when he reaches the film's climax does he choose between them. Love wins and his desire for fame is relinquished. Some of his characteristics—self-doubt and fear of irrelevance—are neutralised. The audience never loses sight of these drives. The choice Dorsey must make is always clear.

Unlike a film, a typical sitcom episode doesn't allow much time for a thorough exploration of a character's core drives. Sitcoms may have characters as complex as Michael Dorsey, but their journeys throughout an episode tend to cover a limited amount of ground. Usually, only one or two core qualities of the characters in a given episode are tested and explored. For example, in the episode 'Zing' of *Cybill* (by Lee Aronsohn), when Cybill finds there's no 'zing' with a man she's dating, she's torn by the 'zing' she feels when she meets his father. Cybill goes on a journey that reveals a range of her own qualities and prejudices as she discovers the various pitfalls of middle-aged dating. Her journey is complex and reveals her well-guarded fragility, but it's driven by simple catalysts: her desire for love and her suspicion that she will never find it. Having finished her journey with her date and his father, there is still plenty of mileage left in Cybill's desire for love and her personal doubts. In fact, there are many episodes of *Cybill* in which she wrestles with the same issue in different ways. In contrast, at the end of *Tootsie*, Michael Dorsey resolves his lust for fame and need of love.

Though all of a sitcom character's useful traits may have been explored by a series' end, those traits are dealt with step by step, episode by episode. Those qualities, like Cybill's and Michael Dorsey's, need to be simple and clear so the audience can see exactly which qualities and themes are being explored. This is even more important for archetypal or cameo characters who tend to be vehicles that test the more rounded regular characters. In the *Seinfeld* episode 'The Library' (Larry Charles), the library fine collector, Lt. Bookman is an archetypal cameo with one quality: suspicion. His sceptical disregard for Jerry Seinfeld tests Jerry's belief in his own respect for the law.

So, the principle for character-building is: 'From simplicity, complexity'. Once a character is built with big mud bricks we can fiddle with the curtains.

The next step in character building is to answer the following deceptively simple questions. (These were first revealed to me by the legend at whose feet the world's screenwriters sit, the glistening Jimmy Thomson.)

1. What do they *want?*
2. What do they *need?*
3. What is their *strength?*
4. What is their *weakness?*
5. What do they *fear?*
6. What or who do they *love?*
7. How does the *character generally see the world?*
8. How does the *world generally see the character?*

Answering these questions can drive you mad. They are unforgiving in their demand for clear and concise answers. These answers cannot be lists. They must be comprised of one element only.

Don't be glib or slapdash about this. It's important to be absolutely clear (and right) because the answers you devise will be the strings of your comic-character puppet. For example, if 'Bob' wants 'a peaceful life', this is the string the writer jerks when Bob is faced with his battle-axe mother-in-law's decision to move into Bob's home. To achieve his want, Bob may throw many things overboard, such as his mates, his beer-can collection and what is left of his pride.

Clarity and precision concerning these deep-character questions helps you both to portray the character and to talk about the character. If a producer asks you what your character needs and you have no answer, or forty different answers, you'll look lazy or ignorant of the forces shaping your characters. (Of course, the producer might be a beginner or a nong, in which case they won't ask and you'll get along just fine—for a while.)

WHAT DO THEY WANT?

A 'want' is the conscious objective of a character. It's expressed in some way by the character and is concrete. The viewer is aware when it's been achieved.

A character's want can be:

- *Temporal* (e.g. 'I want a hundred million dollars before I'm thirty')
- *A physical thing, animate or inanimate* (e.g. 'I want a lover', 'I want my grandma's ashes')
- *Outward-looking* (e.g. 'I want a promotion')
- *Inward-looking* (e.g. 'I want to learn to read')
- *Lifestyle-based* (e.g. 'I want to spend weekends with my family')
- *Moral* (e.g. 'I want to stand up to my bullying boss')

Our want can consume us to our detriment. John Lennon said 'Life is what happens when you're doing other things'. He was talking about how the relentless pursuit of our want clouds our vision of what we truly need. We race about the world, chasing our immediate goals, heedless of the inner voice that cries out for true sustenance.

WHAT DO THEY NEED?

A character's 'need' is their *un*conscious objective. Its outcome is qualitative, not concrete. It might be 'success' or 'confidence' or 'admiration'. It's a quality that can't be measured and therefore can never be completely or permanently achieved.

In *Whatever Happened To That Guy* (by Brendan Luno and Peter Moon) the former television superstar Peter wants success but he needs to be less selfish, and in the TV industry those two things don't go together. Characters are aware of their own want. The writer and the audience are aware of their need.

A character's want and need *must* be in conflict for them to interesting. For example, David Brent in *The Office* wants popularity but needs respect. The more he seeks the former, the further he'll get from the latter. Likewise, Minister Jim Hacker in *Yes Minister* wants to make a difference but needs to feel secure in his position. His want (to make a difference) puts his need (security) at risk. In *Liar Liar* (by Paul Guay and Stephen Mazur) Jim Carey's character Fletcher Reede wants to be a rich and successful lawyer but he needs to be honest, and in the legal industry those two things don't go together.

A contradictory want and need creates an inner conflict that ensures the character is always on a journey towards self-knowledge. Even if they achieve their want they cannot satisfy their need, and vice versa. Their search is flawed in the viewer's eyes, leading the character into strife whatever happens.

Without this conflict, a character's journey has no inner life. For example, a female character who wants to find a man but needs true love is not in conflict. Watching her chase a man is not interesting because we know that, when she gets him, there is no natural conflict that will undo her. Her want is not in conflict with her true nature. (Mind you, her want and need would be in conflict if she was attracted to cads. But in that case, her need wouldn't be 'true love' but rather something like 'social status' or 'security'. Even if she achieved these, the cad would ensure she remained unhappy and thus conflicted.)

WHAT IS THEIR STRENGTH?

A character's main strength might be emotional, such as resilient hope, fearlessness or moral conviction. In others it might be physical, such as Superman's main strength … which is, uh, strength.

Unlike wants and needs, a character's main strength and weakness can, ironically, be the same. Generosity, for example, can be a two-edged sword. It can gain them admiration and respect, but it can also see them exploited by others.

A character's main strength may not make them invincible or even lovable, but it's all they've got. Intelligence, knowledge or natural leadership can mark you for destruction by the less gifted. Weeds smother tall poppies. Or the character might use these qualities to achieve an evil end. A character may not even be aware of their strength: a beautiful character might see themselves as fat, furry and smelly. Who knows if the medicine cabinets of supermodels are bursting with appetite suppressants, back wax and odour potions?

Some strengths are neither benign nor desirable. Rat-cunning, ruthlessness or a psychopathic inability to emote can all help a character on their journey towards their main want.

Extrinsic strengths such as wealth or power aren't usually a character's main strength. Money and status can be won or lost but a person's nature dictates how they respond to that loss. For example, when Frances O'Brien in *The Librarians* loses her role as head librarian, she gets it back again pretty quickly. Her main strength is tenacity.

Whatever a comic character's main strength, however, it should compliment or contradict their main weakness.

WHAT IS THEIR WEAKNESS?

Just like personal strengths, weaknesses can be physical, emotional or psychological. They can also be two-edged, lovable, unacknowledged or suppressed.

As much as a strength can assist us in achieving our want, a weakness can actually drive us to action. Ugliness, compulsive deceitfulness or lust can motivate dangerous, slapdash or self-destructive behaviour.

Watch out for generalities, however. For example, choosing 'stupidity' as a character's weakness is too vague. We are all stupid in some way. (Having paved the way for the atom bomb, Einstein saw the stupidity of his actions and complained, 'I should have become a watchmaker'.) Rather than calling your character 'stupid', identify the quality that limits their intelligence or world-view. Ignorance? Naivety? Prejudice? Ill-founded egotism?

On the other hand, avoid a main weakness that is too specific. A weakness for cupcakes is unlikely to make a durable catalyst for a variety of actions in diverse situations. It might be a legitimate weakness but it won't be useful. Rather than being specific, try to be precise.

Like strengths, a character's weakness should relate to their nature and not to an extrinsic weakness such as a bad reputation or criminal record, which could be fixed by a good publicist or lawyer.

Strengths and weaknesses should relate in some way to a character's want, need, fear or love. A man whose want is to find a wife will have a strength such as 'persistence' or 'good looks' or a weakness such as 'lack of confidence' or 'ugliness' because these things will help or hinder on the way to the conscious goal.

WHAT IS THEIR FEAR?

Thankfully, many fears are shared by many people. As comedy is about getting under the skin of your audience, where better to stick your needle than in our common insecurities? They can be irrational. Agoraphobia or a fear of germs can be powerful catalysts.

The useful thing about common fears is that they *are* common. An audience will accept a character's extreme reaction to fear if the audience has also experienced that fear or know someone who has. By the same token, because it is a direct line into the soul of your character, it is often fruitful to base their fear on your own inadequacies. Do you think nobody truly loves you or, if they do, it's because they don't know the real you?

Pulling the 'fear' puppet string can narrow a character's focus, blinding them to the truth and to the consequences. A frightened animal will lash out at anything that approaches.

For a fear to consistently generate story material it needs to be broad. Cupcakes, again, aren't much use here. But a fear of commitment is a puppet string that can be yanked every week.

Common fears can be deadly weapons in your comic arsenal. They should be both intense and regularly exploited. Laughter, after all, is simply a sublimated fear response.

WHAT OR WHO DO THEY LOVE?

When they're down and defeated, what lifts your character's spirits? What will your character fight for, long for or die for? Identify this and you have the key to their soul.

Comic story structure can only advance through conflict between characters under pressure. Love, like wants, needs and fears, can make a character act against their nature, placing them in harm's way. They may suddenly make sacrifices that would normally be beyond them without hesitating.

When a penny-pinching boss gives everyone in her office a holiday so she can go to Paris with the man of her dreams, she's obeying love's demands. When a meek servant defends his true love against his master's bullying, love is in charge.

The resulting conflicts, both internal and external, and the potential repercussions are a devil's playground for the writer. Even the most wicked characters are not beyond love, though their love might be of themselves, money, power or winning. The more you pitch a character's love *against* their need, fear, weakness or role in life, the better. Love is often intertwined with all three. Loving someone is a daunting task. Even if they adore us back, the exposure inherent in love, particularly selfless love, places us at risk.

Because of this inherent risk, characters may suppress or deny their true love, but even this action leads inevitably to further pressure and conflict.

A comic character *must* have a love, no matter how humble or mean it may be. Without it, the character will be like anyone who lacks a passion—as interesting as cold sago. A character incapable of love, even of themselves, is without passion and cannot drive a story. Cut them and start again.

HOW DO THEY GENERALLY SEE THE WORLD?

Outlooks based upon optimism, opportunism and naivety can inspire trouble-making action. Parachutists, for example, are blessed with an unhealthy dose of optimism.

Juxtaposing a positive outlook with less likeable qualities can create ongoing comic strife. Corky in *Murphy Brown* assumes the best in those around her, but her habit of speaking her small-town mind annoys her urbane colleagues. Clive in *Shock Jock* is a gullible teenager who works in a radio station full of warring charlatans. He takes lies at face value, causing havoc when he diligently acts upon them.

The danger for characters with a pessimistic or cynical world-view is that they tend towards passivity. A character who sees the world as antagonistic and unbeatable might never leave the house. Yet obviously not every character can be optimistic. The secret to keeping them active is to make sure they have a powerful want, need, love or fear that will drive them to overcome their pessimism. This contradiction in their nature can make for an entertaining inner conflict. Artie in *The Larry Sanders Show* is a cynical TV producer. Though he expects the worst from his superiors, he loves making television and moves heaven and earth to protect Larry and keep the show on the air. It's the love that keeps this cynic coming back with hope in his heart. Bernard Black in *Black Books* is an agoraphobic cynic; he loathes the outside world and everyone in it. He's kept active, however, because his dark world-view is intense to the point of being pathological. He may not venture into the outside world but does his best to give hell to anyone who walks into his shop. (Besides, cynics are just failed idealists—and ideals are always worth fighting for.)

HOW DOES THE WORLD GENERALLY SEE THEM?

The answer to this may be implicit in your answers above. A bitter and cynical character, for example, may well be viewed as exactly that.

There's fun to be had, however, when the world grabs the wrong end of the donkey. The world can underestimate, aggrandise, condemn or celebrate a person unreasonably. The world can be wrong about a person as easily as a person can be wrong about themselves. For example, the idiotic newsreader Ted Baxter in *The Mary Tyler Moore Show* is viewed as a godlike genius by his wife,

Georgette. No matter how conceited, pompous and stupid he is, Georgette's benign view can't be shattered. Mary Tyler Moore's on-screen character Mary Richards suffers from self-doubt and bouts of emotional instability, but her colleagues see her as a rock-solid provider of personal advice.

More often the world sees the character as the audience does. For instance, Major Frank Burns in *M*A*S*H* sees himself as a capable leader, but his underlings view him as flaky, dopey and petulant.

Most importantly, the world the characters inhabit tends to condition how they are seen by that world. *The Larry Sanders Show* inhabits the competitive and cynical world of network television. This taints the cast's view of outsiders and each other. At the other end of the spectrum is *The Brady Bunch*, a series that follows a blended family of six siblings and two parents as they strive to live in harmony. Outsiders and family members are given the benefit of the doubt until events prove otherwise.

A world view of a character that is at odds with the audience's view can open up possibilities for dramatic irony. See what happens when an incompetent character is admired, a repulsive character is loved and a beautiful character is loathed.

Character Graph

Using your answers to the questions above, create a character graph for your characters like the one below. These graphs can help you:

- Compare the qualities you've chosen for each individual character in terms of inner-conflict.
- Gauge the mix of your characters, checking for replications or overlaps.
- Judge the balance of character qualities. Are there too many with the same general personality problems?
- Measure the range of outer and inner conflicts (moral, status, temporal, emotional, sexual, psychological) that a character's traits present. (Bear in mind that some characters can be effective with only a couple of strong conflict areas and minor roles can be useful on one level of conflict only.)

To illustrate how these questions and answers work, let's take shot at answering the questions for comedy characters 'Bob and Barbara' and their friends, 'Dick and Deborah'. These four people will be the guinea pigs for the rest of the book.

BOB is a middle-aged real estate agent. A conflict-averse fellow, he's beaten by life at every turn. Worse, he's bullied by his domineering wife and business partner, BARBARA. (Fellow feminists, relax. Swapping their roles would surely be a less pleasing gender-balance, no?) They're both in their third marriage—to each other.

DICK is a carpenter with permanently bandaged thumbs. He is Bob's best friend. Dopey and lovable, Dick worships Bob whom he sees as a smart businessman. DEBORAH is a lightweight, flaky dreamer.

	BOB	BARBARA	DICK	DEBORAH
WANTS	A peaceful life	To be right always	To be Bob	Happy-happy joy-joy
NEEDS	To stand up for himself	To be valued	Respect	Acceptance
STRENGTH	He can be sneaky	Forcefulness	Enthusiasm	Easy-going
WEAKNESS	Gutlessness	She's thin-skinned	Gullibility	Too forgiving
FEAR	Conflict	Embarrassment	Disappointing Bob	Hurting others' feelings
LOVES	Barbara	Herself	Bob and Deborah	Everyone
SEES WORLD	As against him	As full of morons, weaklings and liars	As a complicated puzzle	Heaven
WORLD SEES HIM/HER	A hopeless loser	A scary woman	A lovable idiot	A nice lady

BOB AND BARBARA

Bob's greatest inner-conflict is that he wants 'a peaceful life' but he'll never get one until he 'stands up for himself' and establishes a proper balance with Barbara. Standing up for himself against Barbara is bound to cause a ruckus.

Barbara's inner-conflict lies in her weakness, 'she's thin-skinned'. Sensitivity to criticism is a sure sign that her ego, boisterous and bold as it is, has an Achilles' heel. A thin-skin suggests conscious or unconscious self-doubt. This weakness makes Barbara less archetypal than a classic battle-axe. It allows for moments of poignancy and reflection, making Bob's love more believable.

However, to stay on top, Barbara must suppress her doubt, deny it and guard it from 'embarrassing' exposure. Pushed to the extreme, Barbara is a titan standing on eggshells, a common condition.

Throw Bob and Barbara together and a world of potential conflict unfolds.

Their *moral* conflicts chiefly stem from dishonesty. Bob avoids conflict with Barbara by biting his tongue and being 'sneaky' in achieving his aims. Sneakiness is not a positive quality and, when Barbara (inevitably) catches him out, there's little doubt she'll make him aware of the fact—with a brick. Barbara fears embarrassment, a condition that stems from the exposure of weakness, and there's no-one more capable of causing her embarrassment than the bumbling Bob. His dishonesty (seen whenever he agrees to things he doesn't believe in) can only lead to greater dishonesty. Public exposure is likely to follow, placing Barbara in the position she most dreads.

Bob and Barbara's *status* differential is completely out of balance due to Bob's weakness and Barbara's overbearing nature. Bob *could* be her equal if he manned-up. But any effort he makes to correct their power balance is sure to run into everything in her list.

With such imbalances, emotional conflict will arise. Frustration and self-doubt curse them both, albeit for different reasons.

Bob loves Barbara. She's a force of nature—indomitable and passionate (albeit for her own causes). Barbara may love Bob *because* he meekly surrenders to her will and not despite it. Like any romantic-comedy couple, they both need each other. Bob needs Barbara to help him make decisions and give him direction. Barbara needs the affirmation of Bob's love. Their natures, however, are not built to recognise these needs. Frustration abounds.

Sexual conflict is not immediately apparent in the graph above. But they're married, so sex, whether it happens or not, is a critical factor in their relationship. When sexuality rears its head, Bob and Barbara are geared to be out of balance, which is where we want them.

Psychological conflicts between Bob and Barbara arise from his 'Nemo' status (he has no self-regard or -awareness) and her 'ego' (she can't see past her own nose). One will always tread on the other's toes. Freedom versus control is another psychological area where they'll both struggle. Bob has neither freedom (Barbara's the boss) nor control (the boss is Barbara). Barbara has neither control (Bob is too bumbling to follow her orders to the letter) nor freedom (as she sees it, she cannot go AWOL lest Bob screw up their business).

Bob is not going to enjoy being controlled in all things. Barbara is going to be frustrated because she feels responsible for everything.

Bob fears conflict. Barbara will never give up until she is shown to be right.

Overall, Bob and Barbara's relationship seems to offer enough conflict and pressure to keep them in strife for a lifetime.

It's worth noting that, like the lovers in a romantic comedy, if Bob and Barbara were combined into one person, that person would be a complete adult, capable of great sensitivity and determination.

Sitcom is largely about locking opposite personalities together and watching them struggle. Comic duos tend to feature opposite personalities (e.g. flighty versus plodding, mousy versus domineering, easily-distracted versus single-minded) who can only achieve their goals when they temper each other's natures and work together. If we took the best of each and rounded out the extremes, a nigh-perfect human would result. For example, *Mother and Son* features a manipulative mother, Maggie and an easily-manipulated son, Arthur. If they were one person, they'd make a well-rounded person capable of cunning and thoughtfulness, strength of will and compassion.

NO-CONFLICT CONFLICT

One level of conflict that often goes unconsidered is the conflict a character has *with the audience*. When a domineering character goes unchallenged by those around them, it can be maddening to witness. Our blood boils when David Brent in *The Office* bullies his co-workers and no-one stands up to him. The conflict is with *us*. We squirm in frustration, yearning for a champion who will put him in his place. (In the second series of *The Office* the writers bring on our champion in the form of Brent's new boss, Neil Godwin, who eventually sacks him.)

In Bob and Barbara's case, Bob 'loves Barbara' but she 'loves herself'. The conflict here is desire versus disregard. When Bob's weakness meets Barbara's brutality, there's no competition. But the audience cringes as they witness it.

Conventional morality dictates that a character's moral actions will inevitably bring consequences, good or bad. If Barbara or David Brent continue to act badly, they'll eventually be caught in a net of their own making.

If no-one will challenge Barbara, the audience must wait for fate to do the job. The wait can be agonising. Meanwhile, with desire versus disregard as Bob and Barbara's running condition, the writers must invent further conflict between them and outside forces. These conflicts must play upon their essential dynamic without forcing them to resolve it. Once it's resolved, the series is over.

DICK AND DEBORAH

Moving on to Dick and Deborah, the same process as above will highlight the conflicts available to the writer.

Deborah is 'happy', 'easy-going', 'forgiving', sensitive to others and 'well-liked'. At best, Deborah is a bit dippy. Her marriage to Dick would appear to be conflict-free. Her qualities don't suggest any intrinsic conflict with the other three characters. And, as her Want and Fear both relate to maintaining a happy atmosphere, she's not in conflict with herself either.

Nor does she have a conflict with the audience. We might want her to snap out of her Martha Stewart daydream but that would stem from personal politics and not a contradiction of conventional morality on Deborah's part.

Lying, cheating, point-scoring or rumour-mongering go against Deborah's easy-going nature. She's more likely to let matters slide than confront them. For example, if Bob is trying to clinch a deal with an old-fashioned client who declares that a beautiful wife is the sign of a good businessman, Bob may decide that Barbara's homely appearance will jeopardise the deal. So he might ask Deborah to pretend that she's Barbara (without informing Barbara, of course). The ever-positive Deborah would probably tell Bob that Barbara is beautiful in her eyes, 'and she must be beautiful in yours or you wouldn't have married her three times!'

To force Deborah into dishonest action, Bob would have to concoct a once-off provocation that puts Deborah's happiness and home at risk. And he'll have to invent a new provocation each time he wants Deborah to become involved in mischief. Such goads spark storylines of their own, an unnecessary complication for the writer.

Characters should be built for independent action. If we want a fluffy character like Deborah to stay in the show, she'll need a quality or two that will get her into strife, either inadvertently or deliberately. For example, what happens if we intensify her fear of 'hurting others' feelings' to a more manic fear in the same vein? A woman who fears 'the slightest ripple in social equilibrium' will have more reason to act in the name of keeping the peace.

Deborah loves 'everyone'. Don't fall asleep! Let's add two words to that description: Deborah loves 'everyone *but Asians*'. Got your attention now? A sweet but stupid lady with a racist streak is not unknown in the Australian political scene. But even this nasty addition is not enough to keep Deborah in regular conflict unless we move the show to Hong Kong or make Bob Chinese.

Even if we did that, Deborah poses no threat to either Bob's or Dick's equilibrium. And Barbara needs, if not a worthy rival, someone who will question her dominance with a degree of impunity. Not only that, but the names 'Barbara' and 'Deborah' sound similar. Character names should be readily discernible or they risk causing confusion during production and for the viewers.

The quartet already has two softer characters (Bob and Dick) who are unable to challenge Barbara.

Hmmm … It's time to accept the fact that 'Deborah' must be pushed off a cliff. She must be replaced with someone who can challenge Barbara, the most antagonistic member of the cast so far, while rocking the boat with Bob and Dick.

Introducing 'Delores'. For maximum conflict potential, Dick's wife Delores should be built to compete with Barbara on psychological, temporal, status and physical levels—'My friends are closer, my diamonds are bigger, my marriage is stronger and my new breasts are a marvel!' Each of these claims will hit Barbara where it hurts, intensifying her dim view of the world and poking her thin skin.

Using Barbara's graph, we can instil Delores with qualities that'll vex Barbara in a variety of ways, opening up a broad range of story possibilities. For example, Barbara's need is 'to be valued'. By making the world see Delores as 'a desirable woman', we give her the admiration Barbara wants. This will provoke Barbara's envy, an emotion that can inspire dishonest or unfair actions.

To make this juxtaposition really sting Barbara, we can base the world's appreciation of Delores upon shaky ground. Barbara will be even more outraged at the attention Delores receives if Delores' weakness is that she's 'a compulsive (but careless) liar'. If Delores gets away with lies and distortions that Barbara can see through, it's doubtful Barbara will be able to contain herself.

Next, let's give Delores some ambition. A want and fear based around the achievement and maintenance of social status will make her strive for equality with, if not complete dominance over, the high-status Barbara. This ambition will drive Delores to lie (badly).

To match Barbara's strength ('forcefulness'), Delores can have a quality that works on a mind-over-muscle principle—Delores' Strength can be that she's dumb-like-a-shark. Cunning will make Delores capable of undermining Barbara's forcefulness. It will also enable Delores to devise schemes that manipulate Barbara's fear ('embarrassment') and re-enforce the world's view of Barbara as a 'scary woman'.

By elevating Delores' physical appearance, we can challenge Barbara's view of herself as master of all she surveys. So let's give Delores beauty plus Botox plus boobs. Beauty will give Delores an ace in her competition with the average-looking Barbara who can only match her with lashings of Botox and breast upgrades, procedures that Barbara will undergo in the name of dominance. This is a level of competition that has no end, a rivalry that can operate under the guise of being 'best-ever friends'—just ask middle-aged actresses. The fact that it's pathetic is all the more reason to exploit it—small-mindedness and weakness are both playgrounds of character comedy.

Beauty and the sexual power that comes with it are weapons Delores can use to dominate and manipulate dopey Dick and bumbling Bob. For Dick, Delores' beauty and fashion come at a hefty financial cost. For Bob, Delores' under-the-radar flirting will be frustrating and alarming. Bob's decent enough to prefer she desisted from flirting, but he's smart enough to know that raising the issue would surely be met by Delores' tearful denials—and there's no doubt she'd give her own version of events to Barbara …

Of course, Delores' flirting with Bob wouldn't be genuine. She'd never have sex with someone so plain, but she wants to hear him begging her for it. Stealing the heart of Barbara's husband would prove to Delores that she's Barbara's superior.

For a minimal back-story, let's make Delores come from a poor family. This can provide the basis for a world-view, that everyone is 'looking down on her because of her poor upbringing'. It's an insecurity that Barbara can play upon. (Poor Dick may not even know the truth.) Compensating for her original low social status will present a chronic problem for Delores. There's not enough money in the world to make her feel equal to those around her and no-one's reassurances can erase the fact that she's from the wrong side of the tracks.

So, where Barbara has too much self-regard, Delores hides the fact that she has none. They're both playing from the wrong ends of the field, with Bob and Dick as the indecisive linesmen.

Delores is now a living human inspired by the personality requirements of the show. She's been created through juxtapositions with others, but her weapons, tactics, goals and vulnerabilities are her own.

Importantly, Delores has a variety of inner- and outer-conflicts that stem from the answers to eight simple questions. Unlike 'Deborah', Delores would relish the idea of pretending to be Barbara so Bob could fool his sexist client (above). Delores would take Bob's request as an assurance of her physical superiority to Barbara, and the hoodwinking of the client would appeal to her manipulative streak. She'd throw herself into the role with gusto, and that's where the trouble would start.

Delores' graph reads as follows:

WANTS	Social status
NEEDS	Genuine reassurance
STRENGTH	A cunning manipulator
WEAKNESS	A compulsive (but careless) liar
FEAR	Losing status
LOVES	Jewellery
SEES WORLD	Looking down on her because of her poor upbringing
WORLD SEES HIM/HER	A desirable woman

INTERNAL AND INTERPERSONAL CONFLICTS

While there are several layers of conflict arising from the profile graph above, devising a graph detailing the internal and interpersonal conflicts of your characters can help pin down the intrinsic, ongoing conflicts within and between the characters.

A conflict graph will also show the balance of the basic conflicts between your characters according to their natures.

	BOB	BARBARA	DICK	DELORES
BOB	Bob wants a peaceful life but needs to fight his wife to get it	Bob is sneaky to avoid Barbara's wrath	Bob is frustrated by Dick's dopiness	Bob is frustrated and shaken by Delores' sly flirting
BARBARA	Barbara expects the worst of him	Barbara's weakness is that she's thin-skinned but she wants to be right all the time—an impossibility	Barbara hates how Dick takes Bob's side without question	Competition! Barbara must be better than Delores on every level
DICK	Dick's not smart enough to follow Bob's lead	Dick is hurt by Barbara's jibes	Dick wants to be Bob but he needs to be his own man	Dick is stressed-out by Delores' bottomless insecurities
DELORES	Delores is offended and annoyed by Bob's resistance to her flirting	Delores and Barbara compete over every little thing	Delores is frustrated by Dick's good nature and dim-wittedness	Delores wants social status at any cost, but needs genuine reassurance

Now that we've locked in the core qualities of the characters, there are two other questions. Warning: they can shatter any composure the previous questions haven't already destroyed.

WHY ARE THEY FUNNY?

Don't panic, there is a reliable answer to this question. By juxtaposing two or more of the qualities you've identified in your answers to the questions above, contradictions and tensions within a character should emerge. Like comic reversals and negations, the warring qualities within a character work to make them intrinsically funny.

For example, Larry in *Curb Your Enthusiasm*, *wants* society to be more civil but his *weakness* is insensitivity. In trying to correct the small breaches of etiquette that others commit, he's capable of appalling rudeness. For example, when a nurse gives higher priority to a young female patient over Larry because of petty adherence to an administrative guideline, Larry vows to correct this breach of commonsense and courtesy. On the way to his next appointment he races against and wrestles with the poor girl as he tries to get into the surgery before her ('Interior Decorator' by Larry David).

Another key to finding the funny aspects of a character is to identify how the character's qualities limit their world view. Cliff Clavin in *Cheers* is a know-it-all. His confidence that he has all the answers to life's mysteries blinds him to the fact that he doesn't have a life.

If we use the scenario of Bob's ruse to substitute Delores as his wife to impress a client, some comic carry-on emerges. Delores will take on the role of masquerading as Bob's beautiful wife with gusto. But she is prone to push things too far to cement her position as Most Desirable Wife. After exaggerating the joy of their 'marriage', she might even turn her guns on the client himself. Meanwhile, Bob will desperately try to contain Delores—an impossibility. As he's a fumbler, it's likely he'll make the situation worse by clumsily escalating the lies.

If Dick enters unexpectedly, Bob will have no choice but to warp the lies he and Delores have already told the client. Dick is prone to believe everything Bob says (though the sight of Delores in Bob's arms will take some quick thinking). Delores will also have to use her cunning to re-frame Dick's affection for her.

The real trouble starts when Barbara comes home. The threat of her recriminations will dramatically increase the stakes for Bob. (Losing the client will be the least of his problems.) Bob will be forced to apply panicked, elaborate cover-ups and distortions to save himself from exposure. Delores will use double meanings and her own distortions to both maintain the lie and injure Barbara. The naïve Dick will take everything at face value, becoming hopelessly confused. And Barbara, suspicious and forthright, will use sarcasm and tough questioning to discover the truth.

The four characters will make this bad situation worse through the combination of their natures.

WHY ARE THEY IN THE SHOW?

A character may have everything they need to be funny and interesting but still have no function in the dynamics of a given show. For example, a meddlesome cleaner with a bad memory might have made a funny regular character in *Fawlty Towers*, but the other major characters (Sybil, Polly and Manuel) already fulfil the three functions needed to lead Basil Fawlty into regular conflict: Sybil polices him, Polly reluctantly helps him and Manuel confounds him. The meddlesome cleaner might be a useful cameo but she has no place in this dynamic.

To justify a character's inclusion in a show, they must:

- *Be active.* They must have a personal purpose or habit that drives them to action. Even the layabout Simon Moon in *Frasier* is a *determined* layabout who will go to no end of trouble to spend a lazy hour on the couch.
- *Test the qualities of the other major characters.* Characters must be driven to actions and attitudes that cause conflict and pressure for those around them. In *Frasier* Simon Moon's opportunism and laziness drives the purposeful Frasier to distraction. His idleness makes him a burden to his sister, Daphne. And his hogging of the TV remote causes Frasier's sportscast-loving dad terrible angst.
- *Not duplicate the function of any other character.* There's little point in having two layabouts like Simon Moon in a series unless the duo's dynamic is the source of fresh conflicts with the other characters and each other.

THE CHARACTER TEST-DRIVE

Once you've built your characters, the process of development continues. (Remember, at any stage, right up to the moment the director shouts 'Action!', all your characters live under the axe. Don't hold onto a character attribute that, despite being interesting, doesn't contribute to the dynamic interaction of the character ensemble. No matter how much time and effort you've put into their creation, be prepared to change them or remove them entirely.)

The next step is to take them for a spin. Try them out in the situations below and see how they react.

Each character should react in different ways. Don't force their reaction. If they don't seem to be naturally geared towards a particular response, go back to their graph and see what is missing from their make-up.

Aim for clear and original choices based upon the level of your character's status, prejudices, fears, desires, self-confidence, self-awareness, social skills or guts.

Simply set up the situation and choose the 'puppet string' that offers the most interesting response. For example, if Bob knows that Barbara is making a bad business choice, the first string to pull is his 'fear of conflict'. How will Bob reconcile his fear with the commonsense aim of doing good business?

But Bob is not a robot. By cycling through his strengths, weaknesses and other qualities more possibilities emerge. For example, he loves Barbara. Faced with Barbara's bad business decision, perhaps he stands back and admires his indomitable wife's risk-taking: 'It's risky, but if anyone can make it work, darling, you can!' As Bob's fear of conflict is a regular obstacle to speaking his mind, pulling his 'love' string (pardon the French) will surprise the audience but remain consistent with Bob's character. And encouraging Barbara to make a bad business decision will inevitably backfire on Bob.

The test-drive may also reveal that a character is *not* living up to their comic potential if:

- The character's graph suggests no clear response to the given situation.
- There are no responses that would surprise an audience familiar with the character.
- None of the choices the character could make cause further trouble or raise the stakes.

First, try out your characters in a situation in which they appear to have the upper hand. The following examples involve Bob, Barbara, Dick and Delores.

'X' catches Bob trying on a dress he's bought for Barbara (to see if it will fit her):
- Barbara assumes the worst (in her eyes) and believes her husband is a cross-dresser.
- Delores vows to keep Bob's 'secret' (fat chance!) and is pleased that Bob appears to need more than Barbara to make him feel complete.
- Dick, not wanting Bob to feel uncomfortable, puts a dress on as well.

A character's reaction is likely to be different when confronted by a different person in the same situation:

'X' catches Dick trying on a dress he's bought for Delores (to see if it will fit her):
- Bob gently refuses to believe his friend's story, telling Dick cross-dressing is completely normal.
- Barbara orders Bob to stay away from his best friend, Dick.
- Delores (who knows Dick copies Bob in all things) assumes Bob put the idea into his head. She doesn't believe Dick's honest excuse because he never thinks for himself.

Next, try your characters in a situation in which a character does *not* appear to have the upper hand:

> Bob catches 'X' in a lie about his/her movements on the night when Barbara's cookie-jar was burgled:
> - Barbara bullies her way out of it, deepening the lie.
> - Delores bursts into tears immediately and hugs him—closely.
> - Dick confesses, kicks himself and *insists* on being punished.

Switch the roles so a different personal dynamic is at work:

> Delores catches 'X' in a lie about his/her movements on the night of Barbara's cookie-jar burglary:
> - Barbara tries to turn the tables on Delores—where was *she* the night of the cookie-jar burglary?
> - Dick tries to come clean, but he's so anxious that he ties himself in knots and inadvertently implicates Bob.
> - Bob desperately expands the lie, knowing Delores will use his theft of the cookies to undermine his relationship with Barbara.

Now try some open-ended scenarios for test-driving your characters. You can provide your own particulars according to the relationships and setting and likely events of your show. The main purpose of the exercise is to see how your characters react in situations that change or test their usual demeanour, status or outlook.

1. 'X' defies 'Y'.
2. 'X' obeys 'Y' without question.
3. 'X' accuses 'Y' of falsehood.
4. 'X' tells 'Y' s/he needs a thousand dollars but won't say why.
5. 'X' asks 'Y' to tell 'Z' a white lie.
6. 'X' discovers his/her sworn enemy, 'Y', in a compromising position.
7. 'X' is caught in a compromising position by sworn enemy 'Y'.
8. 'X' shares a saucy secret about 'Y' with 'Z'.
9. 'X' shares a *terrible* secret about 'Y' with 'Z'.
10. 'X' thinks that 'Y' is planning to murder him/her.

When you've explored these scenarios, devise your own.

Putting Words in Their Mouths

Another useful test-drive for your characters is to write a short speech or rant for them. With persistence, their tone and idiom will emerge. This exercise can also identify deficiencies in their make-up.

In order to make the rant dynamic, make sure it's about something that's about to happen rather than something in the past. The character can draw upon the past to explain the situation or argue their case, but they should be trying to persuade with their speech, not just relate a story or give information. Making the speech active brings out the inner qualities of the character.

The character needs more work if:

- you have to force their intentions or attitudes
- their intentions or attitudes are unclear
- their intentions or attitudes are inconsistent with their natures

Don't get carried away by these rants. Keep them to a maximum of 150 words and stick closely to the character you have devised. This exercise is about test-driving the characters you've built, not discovering new ones.

Here's an example with Dick talking to Bob about Delores' bossy ways:

> DICK: You're right again, Bob. Delores is always tricking me into doing things I don't wanna do. I gotta show her who's boss—or the *equal* boss. Or maybe the little-bit-less-than-equal boss. I have to use my words. I'll just stand tall and talk to her like a grown man, using my words. But hang on, I'm not tall, and my voice is pretty high—what if I sound like a grown woman? And what if I pick the wrong words? I might hurt her feelings. It'll be a disaster, a total disaster. New plan, Bob. I'm gunna do what she tells me and not say a word. That'll show her.

Dick (above) manages to completely reverse his position without anyone's help. The negation ('like a grown man, using my words') is consistent with Dick's guileless nature. His final position ('I'm gunna do what she tells me and not say a word') is consistent with his dim-witted nature. It's silly, sure, but credible given Dick's limitations.

Archetypes

> There are two kinds of people in the world; those who believe there are two kinds of people in the world and those who don't.
> —Robert Benchley

If you're not sure where to start with a certain character or combination of characters, comic archetypes may provide a base from which to build. An archetype is a model of a person, the essence of a particular identity. In the same way the principles underpinning jokes have ancient roots, there are archetypal comic characters that have been around, in countless guises, for millennia. Many of these tried-and-true characters populate contemporary comedies of all kinds.

Comic archetypes such as the Clever Slave and Braggart Soldier are characters in some the earliest surviving comedies in Latin literature, written by the Roman playwright, Titus Maccius Plautus (circa 254–184 BC). The Clever Slave is a witty and mischievous rascal who often tricks his master and considers himself superior to those around him. Blackadder is arguably a contemporary incarnation of this archetype. This acerbic and self-serving underling manipulates and steals from his master/s. Tony in *The Hollowmen* provides an example of the Braggart Soldier: bold in speech but a chicken in war. A boastful coward, Tony loudly promises to change the world but runs away from the conflict change demands.

Both of these archetypes are the ancestors of characters in *Commedia Dell'Arte* (the 'Comedy of Professional Artists') which came to prominence from the 16th to the 18th centuries. (The Clever Slave is ancestor to *Commedia*'s clever servant, *Harlequin*, the Braggart Soldier to the blustering buffoon, *Il Capitano*.)

Commedia is still regularly performed in Italy today, usually as street theatre. The wide variety of characters in *Commedia*'s short plays are all archetypes, recognisable by their caricatured masks.

The characters of *Commedia* include Columbine, a witty and attractive woman who is capable of lying or manipulation to achieve her aims, but is prone to panic. Another *Commedia* archetype is *Marinetta*, a tough-talking, battle-hardened and morally-sound lady whom no man can match. *Commedia* also offers sets of archetypes such as *Il Innamorati*, a pair of young lovers so smitten with each other they're incapable of rational thought. They are plagued by a range of obstructive male elders known as the *Vecchi*.

It's arguable that some modern sitcom characters have their roots, either deliberately or inadvertently, in these archetypes. Columbine could be said to reflect Grace in *Will & Grace* or Elaine in *Seinfeld*. The tough-talking title character in Murphy Brown and hard-nosed Brooke Vandenburg in *Frontline* both resemble *Marinetta*. When Kramer and the librarian Marion are madly in love in the *Seinfeld* episode 'The Library' (Larry Charles), their behaviour resembles the love-blind and melodramatic *Il Innamorati*. As in a typical *Commedia* comic romance, their love is placed at risk by Lt. Bookman, an older powerful man who behaves like a *Vecchi*.

The plays of *Commedia* are improvised interpretations of well-known stories and characters. The audience's familiarity with both stories and characters means the actors' chief task is to reinvent the tried and true, to impose their own meanings on the archetypes through metaphor, local references and topicality. The defining issues are the skill and originality with which the short plays are presented. Like comedian Charlie Ross, who performs the original

Star Wars trilogy solo live in *One Man Star Wars*, *Commedia* actors make the familiar new again.

Over time, other archetypes have developed. For example, the Nutty Neighbour is the model for benign characters who treat the protagonist's home as if it were their own. Like a stalker who's not so interested in them, they poke their noses into everyone's business without becoming too emotionally invested in it. Kramer in *Seinfeld* or Eldin Bernecky in *Murphy Brown* fit this role.

To avoid archetypes becoming clichéd, writers attach all kinds of bells and whistles. The world in which the characters live will have its own pressures and culture, creating fresh perspectives. Secondly, an archetypal character's role in life can be at variance with their nature. For example, the Idiot (also called the 'Clown' or 'Baby') archetype is a well-meaning and gullible innocent capable of misunderstandings, taking things literally and making inadvertent malapropisms (see Chapter Six, 'Narrative Gags'). Idiots are terrible liars, can't keep secrets and are honest to a fault—if there's something that shouldn't be said, the Idiot can be counted on to say it. Many sitcoms include characters with all the Idiot's characteristics, but the archetype's role in life, sex, age and status varies from show to show.

Rose Nyland in *The Golden Girls* is an example of the Idiot archetype. Rose is an older woman who is the 'baby' of her new family of retired women. Her friends regard her as a child though they treat her as a genuinely beloved equal. In contrast, the Idiot can be at the hub of knowledge and information: Corky Sherwood in *Murphy Brown* and Ted Baxter in *The Mary Tyler Moore Show* are newsreaders. Betty Wilson in *Hey Dad..!* is a secretary with classic Idiot characteristics who plays the role of daffy big sister to the children of the Kelly family. At the lowest end of the status scale is the servant's servant Baldrick in *Blackadder*. He's a classic Idiot who, unlike those above, is treated with scorn and disgust. Though audiences may not immediately recognise Rose, Corky, Ted, Betty and Baldrick as being related, the five characters share identical flaws and exhibit those flaws through the same gag types.

Archetypal characters can be given their own distinct desires, fears and ongoing problems. Betty Wilson wants to be taken seriously, fears screwing things up (she makes a mess of things *because of* her fear), and feels anguish for her boss, the widower Martin Kelly. Baldrick wants a turnip of his own, fears losing his job and suffers from a chronic lack of attractiveness and hygiene. While the Idiot's outlook tends to be rosy, each manifestation of the archetype can have their own prejudices or personality flaws. Corky Sherwood is proud of her beauty but fawns over her idol, Murphy Brown. The other newsreader Idiot, Ted Baxter, scorns his competition and believes his own hype.

Archetypal characters need not be clichéd. As stated above, an archetype can be placed in any role in life, age group, sex or social status. Lt. Bookman is an archetypal hard-nosed cop who avoids being a cliché because of his innovative role as a library fine collector. His deadly serious, bad-cop attitude is at odds with the relatively trivial late-book crimes he investigates, an imbalanced perspective that provides fresh humour.

Cameo or secondary roles can benefit from being based in archetypes. In the average sitcom, time is limited and viewers want to get a handle on a given character without having to work too hard. Archetypes are recognisable and accessible. For example, a character based on the Idiot (albeit with their own individual bells and whistles) can give viewers quick insight into the character. If you're stuck on a particular character, try breaking them down to an archetype they resemble, distilling their essential qualities, then building them up again.

ETHNIC, REGIONAL AND GAY STEREOTYPES

For the purposes of this book, we will consider 'stereotypes' as being simplified characters whose personal characteristics accord with their ethnicity, social group or role in life. For example, a court jester manifesting the Idiot archetype could be construed as stereotypical (or clichéd) because the pairing of their role in life and personality is not new or unexpected.

The writer's defence in using ethnic, regional or gay stereotypes is usually, 'Hey man, it's *ironic*'. And maybe it is. But, to be the wowser's advocate, these stereotypes are also a straight-up, in-your-face piss-take on another culture or social group, and the viewer's lack of prejudice cannot be assumed.

The ethnic stereotype has inspired some of the most popular characters in sitcom. Apu Nahasapeemapetilon in *The Simpsons* is a much-loved star, despite the racism in his stereotype.

The attraction of the ethnic stereotype is that it brings with it a range of unfair but well-recognised characteristics. We don't need to be told that Apu is an elephant-worshipping, bullet-riddled workaholic. One look tells us all that, and we can get on with the story.

Part of the reason why audiences laugh at the ethnic stereotype is that they know they shouldn't. This naughtiness inspires a twinge of fear of reprisal. Fear equals laughter. A few neat gags and you have a star.

Ethnic gags often appear in successful sitcoms without causing picket-lines at TV networks. *Blackadder*, for example, gets away with many an ethnic joke that, if quoted out of context, might cause offence.

MRS MIGGINS: 'Bonjour, Monsieur'. It's French!
BLACKADDER: So is eating frogs, cruelty to geese and urinating in the street.
—*Blackadder III* ('Nob and Nobility' by Richard Curtis and Ben Elton)

The regional stereotype plays upon the broadly-attributed qualities of regional or social groups of a given society. For Westerners, these stereotypes are based on English-speaking Caucasians. Like an Irish joke, these characters are a form of cultural, not racial, prejudice. Some examples are the suburban ocker Aussie Ted Bullpit in *Kingswood Country*, the snobby upper-class store assistants Trude and Prue in *Kath and Kim* and the horny Southern Belle Blanche Devereaux in *The Golden Girls*.

Regional archetype characters usually have exaggerated accents and are prone to malapropisms. Some accents can be so strong that the character is totally incomprehensible to the audience (though other characters may translate), as in the case of PC Bob Walker in *Hot Fuzz* by Simon Pegg and Edgar Wright.

'Regionalism' may become a no-no in a distant feudal future, but for now it's deemed okay. Be warned: it can rankle with those associated with the stereotype. New Zealanders are kinda over the sheep jokes. And frankly, so are the sheep.

The gay stereotype is typically razor-tongued, promiscuous, camp as an Army bivouac and often too clever for his own good. Examples include the department store menswear salesman, Mr Humphries in *Are You Being Served?*, Manhattan cabaret performer, Jack McFarland in *Will & Grace* and actor-turned-soldier, Gunner 'Gloria' Beaumont in *It Ain't Half Hot Mum*.

The Gay Stereotype's stock in trade is bawdy double entendres and sexual banter. He's a camp, highly emotional and vain person who is rarely, if ever, rewarded with meaningful sex or in a relationship for longer than an episode or two. (Sadly, the writers only *push* the boundaries—they don't change them.)

Catchphrases work effectively for ethnic, regional and gay stereotypes. The catchphrases are readily repeated and speak to the heart of the archetype. *The Simpsons'* Indian stereotype, Apu, shows his dogged insistence upon doing his humble duty by saying, 'Thank you, come again!' even when his store is a smoking ruin. These catchphrases can be used to make a broader, satirical point. In a lethal parody of wartime Germany's conscious ignorance of Hitler's evil, Sergeant Shultz (*Hogan's Heroes*) blocks his ears and insists, 'I know nussink!' *Team America* (by Pam Brady, Trey Parker and Matt Stone) defines the isolation of the despot when Kim Jong-il sings his signature song *I'm So Ronery ('lonely')*. And Jack (*Will & Grace*) often says his own name with a cabaret star's flourish that displays his self-obsessed personality.

Presenting the archetypes and stereotypes above in fresh ways is the challenge. Archetypes provide a *starting point only* for the true character-building. You might use the character profile graph to generate new attributes for an archetypal character. Your imagination is the only limit to the characteristics that will set them apart from their forbearers. The ingredient that makes an archetype your own is you.

Rejecting archetypes as 'too easy' is unwise. Nothing is 'too easy' in the sitcom business. Great sitcom writers, such as Mitchell Hurwitz (*The Golden Girls*, *Arrested Development*) and Gary Reilly (*Kingswood Country, Hey Dad..!*) have claimed to use archetypes as starting points for some of their characters. Reconcile yourself with the fact that, as soon as you decide your series will need a protagonist and an antagonist, or two antagonistic protagonists, you're already following tradition, entering territory where cliché and hackney-ism can run rife. Again, *you* are the factor that will make your characters original.

There's no room for a comprehensive list of comic archetypes here— it would fill a book. Should you wish to learn more, read *The Triumph of Pierrot: The Commedia Dell'Arte and the Modern Imagination* by Martin Green and John Swan (Macmillan), or *Lazzi: The Comic Routines of the Commedia Dell'Arte* by Mel Gordon (PAJ Books).

Chapter Five:
Creating an Episode

It's hard enough to write a good drama; it's much harder to write a good comedy; and it's hardest of all to write a drama with comedy, which is what life is.

—Jack Lemmon

The Hope Principle

There's an ancient principle that underpins many comic stories.

Ever since Homer (the writer of the *Odyssey*, not the bloke from *The Simpsons*), heroic stories have been comprised of some simple elements: a hero strives to overcome seemingly insurmountable obstacles between himself and his goal. He has weapons, tools, brains and skill. Throughout, his heart burns with an enduring hope that he will succeed.

If the story is a heroic drama, he'll triumph. If it's a tragedy, he'll fail and die.

Aristotle's *Poetics* states that 'Comedy aims at representing men as worse, Tragedy as better than in real life.' He takes the template above, applies it to comedy and identifies two differences. Aristotle says that comedy doesn't demand a noble, wise or heroic protagonist—quite the opposite. Secondly, the comic protagonist should *lack* the weapons, tools, brains or skill they need to achieve their goal.

There's a joke about a wide-mouthed African tree frog that illustrates Aristotle's principle nicely:

A wide-mouthed African tree frog (a tree frog with a very wide mouth), bounces through the jungle. He approaches a monkey.

'I'm doing a survey on animal diets', says the Treefrog. 'What do you eat, Mr Monkey?'

'Nuts and berries,' replies the monkey.

The wide-mouthed African tree frog thanks him and approaches an anteater.

'Mr Anteater, what do you eat?'

'Uh, ants,' replies the anteater pointedly.

The wide-mouthed African tree frog thanks him and bounces down to the river where he spots a crocodile.

'Mr Crocodile, what do you eat?'

'I eat wide-mouthed African tree frogs.'

The tree frog purses his lips tightly. 'Really? You don't see many of those around these days ...'

The wide-mouthed African tree frog has a goal—to survive. He faces a seemingly insurmountable obstacle (the crocodile is powerful, dangerous and likes eating tree frogs). The tree frog doesn't have the weapons, brains or skill to escape the crocodile, so he tries the only thing left to him—hiding his identity. His pathetic attempt is his only hope and he gives it all he's got.

When it comes to telling the joke, the punchline works best if the tree frog's eyes seem as innocent as a naughty schoolboy's. He thinks he might get away with his deception. The more hopeful the tree frog seems, the bigger the laugh.

We never find out what happens to the frog. The joke is over once the tree frog's goal, the obstacle he faces, his inadequacy and his enduring hope have been presented. The options for continuing the story (e.g. the frog and the crocodile become friends or the crocodile takes pity and releases the tree frog) are workable, but they're not comic.

The tree frog demonstrates the 'hope principle' that lies at the heart of cover-ups and distractions (see Chapter Six, 'Narrative Gags'). When Basil Fawlty is lying to Sybil in *Fawlty Towers*, his desperation is soothed only by the enduring hope that he will get away with his deception.

The more forlorn the hope, the more feeble the attempt, the funnier the situation becomes. Watching a character struggle on despite the odds touches something very human in all of us. When they maintain unfounded hope despite their pathetic inadequacy, the odds against them mount and so do the laughs.

In *Welcher & Welcher* by Shaun Micallef, Quentin Welcher's insurmountable obstacle is his own deficient personality. He wants to be a successful lawyer but lacks knowledge of his own failings, and thus doesn't see that success will never come until he learns and changes. So he resolutely struggles on, filled with a hope born of self-delusion.

This principle underpins the narrative arc of individual stories. In *Seinfeld* George Castanza is as inadequate as they come. He's short, fat, bald, insecure, petty, dishonest, miserly, angst-ridden, lazy and obsessive. No matter what he turns his hand to, he's doomed to fail. When George sucks up to his black boss by comparing him to Sugar Ray Leonard, his boss accuses him of racism. George doesn't believe himself to be racist, but realises he has no black friends. He strives vainly to make some so he can prove his progressiveness to his boss. Finally, George fakes a friendship with his exterminator, but his boss sees through the ruse and now believes George is racist *and* callously manipulative. The boss exits, furious. When a young waiter innocently remarks that George's departed boss looks like Sugar Ray Leonard, George races to catch him. But it's too late. George's behaviour throughout the episode has rendered the proof meaningless ('The Diplomat's Club' by Tom Gammill and Max Pross).

The hope principle is not underpinned by any moral imperative. It's completely unjust: it's not fair that someone should retain hope against all odds and still be frustrated. But comedy is truth. The hope principle recognises that if the worst can happen, it probably will—even if, most of the time, the worst is not too bad.

You might think a similar principle underpins certain serious narratives, such as the hobbit Frodo Baggins' journey into the dark land of Mordor in J. R. R. Tolkien's *The Lord of the Rings*. It doesn't.

Yes, Frodo faces seemingly insurmountable obstacles (the all-powerful magician Sauron) and he has enduring hope ('Where there is life', he says, 'there is hope.'). But Frodo's tools are more than sufficient for his task. His unbreakable sword can detect orcs and goblins. His vial of Elf cordial glows in the dark and blinds giant spiders. He's accompanied by the future king, the mightiest wizard in the land, three of the toughest warriors in Middle Earth and his manservant, Sam, who will lay down his life for Frodo without hesitation. Best of all, Frodo bears a magic ring that makes him invisible and has the power to destroy Sauron and his armies. Frankly, Frodo couldn't be better equipped if he had a Hummer with a machine-gun turret. As for his personal qualities, Frodo is brave and noble. For such a shorty, he has remarkably few insecurities.

The hope principle belongs to comedy alone. Dramatic heroes have it easy by comparison.

The principle however does not always apply to secondary characters, who often serve different purposes for the writer. George Castanza's parents, for instance, have one primary story function: to torture George. They're well-equipped for torturing, with cantankerous natures, sharp tongues and thick skins. And they certainly don't need any *hope* to rain misery upon their son, and each other. Most of the time, they effectively act as George's obstacles. But for a comic protagonist the hope principle is nearly always essential. The hope principle drives a comic hero far beyond rational limits in pursuit of their goal. To make this believable, the viewer must suspend their disbelief. Hope, no matter how slender or ill-founded, has the power to blind both the protagonist and the viewer to reality.

Comic stories tend to end in ironic failure. Shakespeare, whose comedies and tragedies follow Aristotle's model, allows his comic heroes to fail ironically—that is, by discovering they never really wanted what they were striving for. Only the purest of heart will achieve their goal, but even then the victory is hollow. For instance, Robin in *Robin Hood: Men In Tights* (by Mel

Brooks, Evan Chandler, J. D. Shapiro) marries Maid Marian, but can't get her chastity belt open.

Conventional morality dictates that characters must overcome their personal flaws before they're rewarded. Modern sitcoms often feature comic heroes who strive against obstacles and maintain an enduring hope of success, but because of their personal failings, they fail and end up where they started. For example, the main characters of *The Hollowmen* (by Santo Cilauro, Tom Gleisner and Rob Sitch), always end with the status quo or worse. Any victories they gain are, as the name suggests, hollow. And no matter how hard Gilligan and his shipmates (*Gilligan's Island*) try, they repeatedly fail to escape from the island. When at last they do escape (in the 1978 reunion special, *Rescue From Gilligan's Island* by David P. Harmon, Al Schwartz, Elroy Schwartz and Sherwood Schwartz), it's not long before they are stranded on the island once more.

APPLYING THE HOPE PRINCIPLE

If you're wrestling with a scene that is close to funny but not quite there, try standing back and looking at the way the characters are striving for their goals. It may lack a desperate 'any strategy is a good strategy' edge because:

- The obstacles your comic hero faces may be too small.
- Your comic hero may be too capable of winning because of his personal attributes or the tools he has at hand.
- Your comic hero's goal is not important enough to him or her.
- Your comic hero is pessimistic.

The No-Hoper Principle

The flipside to the hope principle relates to antagonists and is comprised of the following elements: a villain is impeded by a minor obstacle. He overreacts and is *doubly* punished as a result.

The no-hoper principle complies with the law of inverse significance: comic characters attribute vast importance to trivial things, and treat important things as trivial. When a comic villain is impeded only slightly, he reacts with all the force at his disposal. These characters never doubt that their bomb-to-kill-a-bug technique will succeed, even though, hidden in the bomb cloud, the bug frequently escapes to fight another day.

An example is the comic villain who slips on a freshly mopped floor. Rising to his feet, he notices a sign marked 'Caution—slippery floor'. Angry, he kicks the sign, loses his balance and falls again—harder.

At any stage, the villain could stop, think and consider the risks. He could choose to tread carefully over the wet floor, wait for it to dry or avoid it entirely. But he's a villain. Whether through self-importance, impatience, control-freakdom, anger management issues or any other evildoer shortcoming, the comic villain consistently defies and underestimates obstacles. This mindset is not based upon hope but upon ego. Comic villains cannot see their own deficiencies.

This principle can work in a broader narrative arc. In *Robin Hood: Men In Tights*, the villainous Sheriff of Rottingham is frustrated when his wooing of Maid Marian is interrupted by Robin Hood. In the real world, the sheriff would get the girl easily. He's rich, powerful, educated and handsome, while Robin is a penniless vagabond who lives in a tree. However, instead of adopting a more personable demeanour that might attract Marian, the Sheriff overreacts. He tries to slaughter Robin and his Merry Men In Tights. Fool! He not only loses Marian, but his life.

Like the hope principle, the no-hoper principle tends to define the story-driving characters. Secondary antagonists tend to act with more moderation. A villain's sidekick, for example, may advise caution. In Jay Roach and Mike Myers' *Goldmember*, Number Two initially advises against Dr Evil's scheme to produce sharks with lasers attached to their heads. As they are an endangered species he will have to make do with ill-tempered sea bass.

Because secondary antagonists tend to be more even-tempered they often escape the retribution visited upon their masters. Number Two never receives the punishment his master suffers. Perhaps his name is enough.

APPLYING THE NO-HOPER PRINCIPLE

If your villain isn't working, either in a scene or throughout the story, check them against the no-hoper principle. Your villain might be:

- Too wise. He should be blinded in some way by his ambition.
- Too patient. Though he may have waited calmly for his chance, when he does act he should do so without precision and with overwhelming force. Villains lash out with their eyes wide shut.

Despite this it should be clear that the villain is a credible threat and could with care and planning easily attain his goal. For example, Dr Evil in *Austin Powers: International Man of Mystery* (by Mike Myers) is a multi-millionaire with weapons of mass-destruction. Comic bad guys are undone as much by their personal flaws and limited world view as by the hapless protagonist.

The Victim's–Fault Principle

Comedy and tragedy essentially mirror one another. Both are driven by a sense of cosmic justice that punishes sin. In both, it's essential that the protagonist takes action that leads them, at first unconsciously, towards their own demise.

The difference between comedy and tragedy is the stakes and the importance the characters place on them.

In tragedy the protagonist sees the stakes in roughly the same light as the audience. When the Titanic is sinking in James Cameron's dramatic film of the same name, all the characters are fully aware of their plight. In comedy the protagonist and the audience see the stakes in completely different terms.

In conventional comedy, the protagonist sees the stakes as very high (and consequently struggles hard for them) when the audience knows they are not overwhelmingly important. Consequently, the protagonist's punishment is also not generally that severe, although to the protagonist, at the time, it feels like the end of the world. When Frances O'Brien in *The Librarians* is seen grasping the clothed breasts of an untroubled colleague, she faints from embarrassment. Though context is important, in the real world the incident probably would not cause such a severe reaction and remedying the matter wouldn't require drastic measures. ('Amnesty' by Robyn Butler and Wayne Hope).

Satire or black comedy reverses the formula: stakes that for the audience are terribly high are treated by the characters as of lesser importance. In *Frontline*, sensationalist reporter, Brooke Vandenburg, interviews the mother of a crazed gunman holding his children hostage. When the interview needs to be re-shot, she displays her total lack of appreciation of the mother's distress by asking 'Would you be able to cry again?' ('The Siege' by Santo Cilauro, Tom Gleisner, Jane Kennedy and Rob Sitch).

In some cases, a benign character's flaws, not their sins, can lead to comic events. For instance, a generous character who donates their time to fix a car, despite the fact they have little mechanical knowledge, can inspire laughter when the car runs them over. Though the character is trying to be helpful, they are too stupid or innocent to know the task is beyond them. Gilligan in *Gilligan's Island* is a well-meaning but naïve character who discovers some tree sap that he's confident can glue the castaways' boat back together. Of course, having raised everyone's hopes, Gilligan is scolded when the sap proves to be water soluble and the boat sinks. ('Goodbye Island' by Albert E. Lewin, Sherwood Schwartz and Burt Styler)

A high-status character's flaws can inspire other characters to inflict punishment upon him. In the comedy film *Trading Places* (by Timothy Harris and Herschel Weingrod), Dan Aykroyd plays 'Louis Winthorpe III', a wealthy stockbroker who's both arrogant and spoilt. Because of these qualities, his employers select him for a nasty lesson in humility. Watching Winthorpe unravel is funny because his negative qualities make his reduction to poverty seem deserved. (Once he's learnt humility, however, he becomes more heroic in the audience's eyes. He's then able to turn the tables upon his employers. Because of their callous manipulations, they suffer terrible—and humorous—losses.)

The own-fault principle keeps characters active in their own journey, as opposed to being innocent victims of something that could happen to any of us at any time.

If an event in a script lacks comic punch, it may be simply due to the fact that all of your characters have a sense of proportion that is reasonable.

Believability

No matter how outlandish comic stories become, they must nonetheless be 'believable'.

Given that a comic story could include, for example, an elephant juggler marrying his uncle to save the planet from a Tic-Tac invasion, the issue of believability may seem irrelevant. But the believability of any sitcom is based upon two criteria. Firstly:

- Once a reality is established, no matter how tenuous or far-fetched it may be, that reality must not change.

The physical laws of the show's world may be presented in a rudimentary way—the sets, special-effects and props may be crude—but once established, those laws must remain consistent.

For example, the alien Alf (*Alf*) is quite obviously a furry puppet. Nevertheless, he is always accepted by the other characters as a real alien. *The Ghost and Mrs. Muir* features a ghost who can only be seen by the widowed Mrs Muir, now living in his house. Although he loves her, love can only do so much and he is *never* able to kiss her. The action in *Bewitched* obeys the laws of magic as the characters present them: some spells can't be fixed with a twitch of the nose; certain procedures *must* be carried out. The astronaut in *I Dream of Jeannie* accepts that his flatmate is a genie with godlike powers. The world obeys Jeannie's commands, but even so she can be trapped helplessly in her bottle. The physics of this 'reality' never change throughout the series.

Secondly,

- Characters must always act and react according to their natures.

Whatever your characters think, feel or do must always be consistent with their true natures. A gay gerontophilic elephant juggler might agree to marry his ugly old uncle without batting an eyelid. However, if marrying his uncle is abhorrent to the juggler, there must be a credible external motivation to overcome this, such as saving the world, if his nature has a noble bent. Alternately, a gun to the head is a fine motivating tool. Stick a sawn-off shottie in the juggler's nostril and he'll be screaming 'I do! I do!' even though, clearly, he doesn't.

The scenario is far-fetched, but the juggler's choices remain consistent and credible. So long as the peculiar physics of your comic universe are observed, and the characters behave in a way that's consistent with their natures, the comedy writer is afforded considerable latitude in their portrayal of reality. The audience will accept a scenario that is outlandish, unlikely or heavily reliant on coincidence, so long as they feel they can believe in the characters. If characters act against their natures without proper motivation, even though this may suit the writer's purposes, the audience will reach for the remote control.

Comedy's audience suspends disbelief with an eagerness that dramatists must envy. The science fiction world of *Star Wars* may have been based in a galaxy far, far away, but that galaxy and its outlandish inhabitants are depicted meticulously. A comedy, however, can be performed with glove puppets (*Punch and Judy*) or crude animations (*South Park*) because the audience's enjoyment stems from the characters, not the illusion of reality. Most studio-based sitcom sets are fairly obviously studio sets, particularly when the action moves 'outside'. The backyard of *Home Improvement* could never be mistaken for a real backyard. The plants are plastic, the grass is fake, the sunshine is fluorescent. The viewers are given just enough information to accept that the characters are in a yard. After that, their imaginations fill in the blanks as their attention is directed to the action.

In terms of plotting, sitcom takes liberties that drama dare not. Events are compressed and stories can turn on a dime several times in a segment. Stakes rise quickly, moving the story at a breakneck pace that would beggar belief in real life.

In *Frasier* ('The New Friend' by Bob Daily), Frasier makes friends with Roz' new boyfriend, Luke. When Roz and Luke break up, she praises Frasier for comforting her during the split. However, Frasier and Luke maintain their friendship. They do so behind Roz' back because Frasier doesn't want her to think he is disloyal.

Next, Roz re-ignites her relationship with Luke and insists that they keep it a secret from Frasier. She feels Frasier has been a true friend by comforting her after the breakup and she doesn't want him to think she is weak and doesn't value his efforts.

From this point, Frasier and Roz each behave with the fevered secrecy of someone having a secret love affair.

Roz joins Frasier at Café Nervosa and invites him to dinner as a way of thanking him for his support during her breakup with Luke. Frasier accepts her invitation. Moving aside, Frasier quickly phones Luke and cancels their own secret engagement. In moments, Luke calls Roz to say he is suddenly free. He invites her on a date. Roz secretly accepts his invitation.

Roz then invents an excuse to Frasier and cancels her dinner with him. Frasier feigns disappointment and immediately phones Luke to tell him he is now free to see him. Luke, however, tells Frasier he has just accepted a surprise invitation and cannot meet him.

Frasier returns to Roz, prepared to go to dinner with her. She is so touched by a friendship bracelet Frasier has just given her that she moves aside to call Luke and cancel their date again.

Niles, sitting nearby, has overheard each of Frasier and Roz' phone conversations. He has said nothing but is clearly unimpressed. While Roz is on her phone cancelling with Luke, Niles heads for the exit. As he passes, Frasier tells him he's now available for the evening. To Frasier's bafflement, Niles assures him, 'No, you're not,' and walks out the door.

This series of reversals at Café Nervosa takes less than two minutes.

In reality, this situation would never occur. Frasier and Roz' friendship is strong and neither is genuinely dishonest. In the real world, Frasier would simply tell Roz that he wishes to maintain his friendships with her and with Luke. Roz might be rankled but she would accept that Frasier is free to spend his time with whoever he likes. Their friendship might be uneasy for a time, but not as bad as a marriage on the rocks.

In sitcom, however, once an object has been established as being of high sentimental or worldly value, the audience knows it will be smashed, stolen, proven a fake, lost, given to charity by an unknowing friend or thrown out the window in a fit of pique. The same goes for relationships. In Frasier's case, his honest friendship with Roz is threatened by his shenanigans with Luke, since his lies would hurt her far more than an open friendship with her ex.

Secondly, the pace is blatantly implausible. In sitcom a twist can happen within seconds of the stakes being established, but viewers don't object. Quite the opposite—swift escalation of the stakes is both expected and desired, and tenuous coincidences in the service of rapid plotting are forgiven by the audience and usually accepted by the characters.

Sitcom dialogue may bear little resemblance to actual conversation so long as it is clear and the characters pursue their objectives.

So, how does sitcom get away with this flimsy regard for the ebb and flow of real life? The answer is found in the actions and reactions of the characters. Though they may be exaggerated or compressed, they are nonetheless grounded in a credible response to the situation. In a drama, the characters' actions might be more nuanced and inhibited, but essentially they are the same.

We accept the convoluted scenario above because it's based in truth: we know Frasier is a psychologist who places a high value on protecting the feelings of others. His action is extreme but stems from a quality that Frasier is already known for. Roz is known for placing a high value on Frasier's friendship. Her secrecy stems from an appreciation of Frasier's apparent loyalty. The scene is comic because their disproportionate behaviour breaks the bond of empathy and allows us to laugh at the outcome.

In short, comedy occurs when characters attach exaggerated importance to something we can see is not that important—or alternately attach little importance to something we can see is crucial.

These extreme or disproportionate reactions are what the audience has tuned in for: they are what make the situation comedic. The audience will jack up only when characters act against their nature for no apparent reason.

Like everything in a sitcom, plot development is subject to one overriding priority: time. Comedy moves fast. Events that, in a film, might take ninety minutes to unfold, a sitcom may cover in as little as twenty-one minutes. There's no time to establish stakes or raise them at a realistic pace. Nor is there time to include more than a rudimentary introduction to the characters involved, or establish a series of events that might explain a coincidence, unless those events themselves comprise a story. Better to allow the coincidence and move directly on to how the characters deal with it. By and large sitcom writers must assume the audience is familiar with the regular characters' personal traits and go straight to getting those characters into trouble. This is often done by highlighting only the traits that will be challenged by events in the story.

When the grouchy doctor Becker (*Becker*, 'Point of Contact' by Michael Markowitz) saves the life of a choking woman, she starts to send him small gifts. Becker however has a well-established fear of meaningful bonds with others, so he finds the woman's attention threatening. His friends assure him she is merely being polite but Becker is convinced she is a 'psycho' stalker: 'Next she'll be dancing on my lawn wearing my skin for a hat!' By the time the woman explains she is a nun and her gifts were simply an expression of her Christian gratitude, Becker's fear of human connections has caused him enough anguish to fill the episode.

Typically, new or cameo sitcom characters enter the action at a run, generating story almost before they've been established. This is why so many sitcom cameos are archetypes or caricatures: the writers show only that which will push the story forward.

EXERCISE

Take a familiar sitcom character and see how swiftly you can put them in a position in which one of their qualities is challenged. For the sake of the exercise, allow yourself 150 words of action and/or dialogue to start the scene and throw a spanner in the works. Chances are, the quicker you can raise the stakes and threaten the character's equilibrium, the funnier those 150 words will be. If you can do it with fewer words, so much the better.

Make sure however that the character acts and reacts in a way that is true to their nature. Their actions may be extreme, but they must be justifiable in terms of their objective and personality traits.

An example of this almost-immediate challenging can be found on the first page of the first scene of 'The Barber' by Andy Robin, for *Seinfeld*. George Castanza is applying for a job with a small but prestigious company. The boss, Mr Tuttle, likes George and it's all going swimmingly. He praises George for his ability to grasp things quickly ('I don't have to explain every little thing to you') and George agrees.

Mr Tuttle hires George and continues, 'Of course—' but the interview is interrupted by a secretary who informs Mr Tuttle of a phone call he has to take. Mr Tuttle bids George farewell without qualifying his 'Of course—'

George is left on tenterhooks—'Of course' what?!

George's supposed ability to grasp things quickly is trashed. His pride and tendency to fawn to power are no sooner established than they're exploited: George decides that, in order to keep the job, he must maintain the façade that he knows every aspect of the job.

The rest of the episode is devoted to George's deceitfulness and tenacity as he chooses to lie instead of simply asking for a clarification. His reaction to the situation is disproportionate—in reality, we'd all point out to Mr Tuttle that he was interrupted before he could mention an important detail.

Comic Storytelling

The demands of a classic comedy story in structural terms are much the same as those of drama. There are three acts, comprising a set-up, complications and a resolution. Once the protagonist, their world and their goals have been established, the protagonist faces ever-increasing risk and conflict as they strive to achieve their goals. The obstacles inhibiting the quest grow in size, potency or number until, in a brief and climactic final act, the protagonist either overcomes the obstacles, reaches a stalemate or is defeated. In most cases, the resolution stems from the nature and actions of the characters. A comedy character's tools, status and moral backbone are usually inferior to those of drama characters but, experimental stories aside, comedy and drama stories tend to follow the same ancient pattern.

The difference is that comedy stories, particularly sitcom stories, compress the twists and turns of the classic three-act structure. Drama can present its stories in a natural flow, but a sitcom episode must distil its reversals and revelations to their essence. Most quality sitcom episodes could be stretched into a satisfying ninety-minute dramatic film narrative. This might require expanding the scope of the characters' emotional journeys, adding depth and detail (i.e. back stories) to their path towards lasting change and giving greater attention to character, including simply making them more competent, but the essential plot elements would remain unchanged. For instance, in *The Golden Girls* the elderly Sophia discovers her new beau, Alvin, has Alzheimer's disease. Her journey goes from the set-up (Sophia meets Alvin and likes him) to complications (Alvin's memory and mood become erratic, the relationship is endangered) and then to resolution (Sophia decides that she can't help Alvin and lets him leave her life forever). Meanwhile, Rose, the most childish of the four older women in the show, finds that her teddy bear is being held hostage by a ruthless gangster girl. Only when Rose changes her outlook and defies the terrifying girl does she get her bear back. ('Old Friends' by Terry Grossman, Susan Harris and Kathy Spear).

Sophia's story could easily fill a longer narrative. Alzheimer's disease, and the complications that go with it, is rich territory for any writer. The themes of such a story might include the loss of loved ones, the slow erasure of one's identity and the awful living death that the tragic condition can impose. More time could be spent exploring Sophia's character, her past and the elements of her life that are under threat if she chooses a lifelong relationship with Alvin. Her journey towards Alvin and her final surrender of him could underpin a heartbreaking feature film. Even Rose's story could be adjusted to provide the basis for a thrilling B-story; for instance, the teddy bear could become a human relative and the girl an adult kidnapper. Its theme (helplessness in the face of a lost loved one) reflects that of Sophia's story in a different context. There's no doubt the two tales could be interwoven, their emotional scope broadened and the characters' journeys given greater texture. Sophia relinquishes her love while Rose fights for hers … Yep, if you like a tear-jerker, this story could be your cup of tea.

The humour in Sophia's journey in this episode stems from the playfulness of her relationship with Alvin; we see her sarcastic wit juxtaposed with her schoolgirl's excitement at the romance. Having laughed with Sophia, the audience is vulnerable when the dark truth of Alvin's illness hits home (see Chapter Six, 'Sitcom Poignancy'). Rose's story is rendered comic by making the object of her affection a teddy bear rather than something the audience would consider more worthy, such as a person. Similarly, the threat to her great love is reduced in stature from a gangster to a little girl (who nevertheless retains many of the gangster's qualities). The unspoken sorrow of Rose's story is that, having lost her husband, she's reduced to loving a teddy bear.

When developing a comic storyline, begin by exploring its dramatic possibilities. (I won't go into this process: there are many books on the structure and substance of drama.) Once the events, stakes and emotional journey of the characters are worked out in a series of dramatic acts, focus on one or two of the characters' core personal qualities that are challenged by the story. Where a dramatic film narrative may challenge a protagonist in many ways, revealing layer upon layer of their character, sitcoms tend to focus on only one or two key character traits. Tugging only one of these 'puppet strings' (main desire, unconscious need, weakness, strength, love, fear, outlook or public perception) can produce the core of a sitcom story. In *Yes Minister*, Sir Humphrey's main fear—the loss of control—motivates his actions and is the basis of his anxiety. Remember, believability is rooted not in realism, but in the actions of characters in accordance with their natures. Whereas in drama characters learn progressively from the dramatised events of the story, in sitcom changes of objective must come swiftly. A perennial narrative gag is the 'reversal', in which characters suddenly change in response to pressure or a realisation. For instance, a man who claims to be courageous and firm of purpose, when threatened with a pocket knife, might immediately hand over his wallet. These swift reversals lay bare the weakness, hypocrisy and self-serving natures of the characters, but to get a laugh they *must* be set up and paid off instantly. With less than twenty-one minutes to tell a three-act story, there's no time to savour the emotional nuance. Just tell the damn story. Sitcom demands we deliver each step of a story clearly and simply, and then race to the next one.

FOLLOWING CHARACTERS

Characters drive stories, not the reverse. While apparently random and unexpected things occur in stories, most 'inciting incidents' (the event that gets the story moving) are not unique: the arrival of an unpopular relative, a tidal wave or a bag of money have all been done before. It's how characters respond to these events that makes a story original.

Selecting an appropriate response to a situation is best done from 'inside' the character. Being 'outside' a character means making value judgements about their behaviour by comparing it to what you might do in the same situation. Being 'inside' is to stand in their skin, think as they might think. Inhabiting a character imparts a more fluid sense of their possible responses to a given situation. You can come up with action that is quirky or surprising, but that action is more likely to be true to character if you're inhabiting them rather than imposing action from outside. After all, your characters stem from you and are a part of you. They each reflect some aspect of your personality and your experience of the world. Even an evil character should carry within them some quality you personally identify with. This is not to say that everything in your stories should be cut and pasted from your life. Writing is, after all, an act of the imagination. But you should always understand each character's point of view.

Your life can furnish you with inspiration, but rarely can it furnish a complete story. For example, you might devise a character based upon a school bully from your youth. You vividly recall his negative traits (e.g. cunning and physical strength), but to write that character convincingly requires the addition of a sympathetic quality that allows you to inhabit the character (e.g. he's lonely). Now you are 'inside' your created bully and better able to judge what he'll do in your imagined scenario. Who knows? The story may require that he turns out to be a good person who's merely misunderstood. Stubbornly adhering to your understanding of real-life characters and past events inhibits your imagination. If that's your aim, make a documentary.

Once you've built a character, confront them with a challenge or place them in jeopardy. How they react will set your story apart from any other. If a bag of money arrives on their doorstep, a swindler's response might be different to a detective's; but *your* swindler and *your* detective may surprise you again.

When you know your characters well, they take on a life of their own and lead you through your imaginary world.

KICK START A STORY

Once a setting is established, throw a spanner in the works. The 'spanner' can be a simple event, such as a man has an old school friend over for the weekend. But this event should be loaded with at least one complicating factor that is not easily resolved, for example the man's wife has always had a crush on the friend.

The purpose of any comic story, no matter how outlandish, is to reflect real and spontaneous human interactions. It's important to identify each character's motivation, emotional state, and their given circumstances at every step.

A powerful, clear desire can turn even an independent, strong-willed character into the writer's plaything. In the service of that desire they will do things they regard as repellent, terrifying, criminal or embarrassing. In fact, having done so, their investment in the object of their desire is even greater, leading them to perform acts even more drastic or heinous. The object itself may appear trivial to the viewer, but that's the fun of it.

Clear and imperative desires inspire strong, clear emotions, which are ideal material for building a scene. Identify an emotional arc (happy-to-worried, angry-to-forgiving etcetera) for every character in every scene, or even every exchange of dialogue of your script. Knowing a character's emotional state and motivation at all times helps the writer to select the appropriate joke.

In the case of the husband above, his initial motivation would be twofold: show his friend a good time, and keep his wife away from the friend. He may even have a third desire—to cast his friend in an unattractive light, without the friend being aware of it. At the outset, the husband's emotions will range from excitement at the prospect of seeing his friend and trepidation or jealousy that his wife's old flame will be rekindled. The wife and friend will also have their own emotional states and motivations. And it's possible that each of the three characters is not being open about their true feelings and desires when the story begins, fooling each other and the audience.

It's vital to know exactly what is happening in the hearts of your characters at every point in a story. Characters' motivations and emotions will change as their circumstances change. For example, the husband's priorities will change if his schemes to dampen his wife's desire for his friend are discovered by the friend. His new priority will be to save his friendship and his emotional state will be more panicked.

If you know your characters well, the range of their responses to a situation should be clear. No matter how an episode's events escalate, keep the essential question before you: 'How will each of these characters react now?' It's likely more than one option will present itself. Trace where each option leads and what complications arise from it. Then assess those complications based on how uncomfortable they'll be for the characters, and how they serve the theme of your story (which usually means whether they continue to play on the same character weaknesses). The most uncomfortable complication for your main story is usually the one to pick.

An episode's inciting incident should rub the show's characters up the wrong way. In the *Dad's Army* episode 'Branded' (by David Croft and Jimmy Perry), the gentle and lovable Godfrey, a private in a troop of World War II home guardsmen, announces to his comrades that he was a conscientious objector in World War I. Conscientious objection is bound to provoke a reaction from a band of weekend warriors, but each of the other characters reacts in their own way. Captain Mainwaring is outraged (his love of duty is challenged) and he condemns Godfrey as a coward. Private Walker, the troop's shady spiv, feels 'a bit sorry for the old boy' but doesn't defend him. Pike, the innocent young guardsman, has no understanding of conscientious objection beyond his mother's advice to her lover that 'men ought to be men'. Godfrey is ostracised by the other troop members, but this soon becomes emotionally unbearable for the old chums. As the third act unfolds, Godfrey is proven to be the opposite of cowardly when he saves Captain Mainwaring's life. He's also revealed as a hero of World War I: he objected and joined the medical corps, but went into no man's land to save several of his comrades. His fellow guardsmen have a unified response to this news that shows the values they share: they're all surprised that Godfrey could keep such heroism a secret, sheepish at their own behaviour and relieved to welcome the soft-hearted fellow back to their fold.

Private Godfrey's story is a touching and funny three-act tale that reminds us not to judge books by their covers. The characters each act and react in ways that accord with their natures. Conscientious objection to war is a 'spanner' that would create problems in any Home Guard unit, yet a surprising, funny and moving story develops from the original and believable reactions of these particular characters.

BUILDING SCENES

It's a rule of thumb for drama and comedy narratives that the state of things at the beginning of a scene should be changed in some way by the end of it. The more stark and swift the changes in each scene, the more interesting the story will be. While it might be amusing for a short time, a scene in which characters simply say witty or silly things to each other will soon lose the audience's interest. Sure, it works in stand-up comedy, but a comedy story must obey the ancient laws of storytelling or it will tread water until it drowns. Characters must be doing things, chasing their goals, reacting to situations, at war with each other, struggling against all odds and adapting to meet challenges.

Before writing a given scene, map out the basic events of the scene, the changes of fortune, the purpose of the scene in the story and the character qualities that are being challenged.

To keep a story moving, the three-act pattern (Set-up, Complication, Resolution) that provides a shape to stories on a macro level can also be applied to individual scenes (see Chapter Three, 'The Power of Three'). Whether a scene is at the beginning, middle or end of an episode, setting it up, complicating it and resolving it for better or worse will ensure it moves the story along, keeping the episode lively and interesting. Sometimes, a third act can include a false resolution, an occurrence that feels like a resolution but isn't. This is swiftly followed by a true resolution.

Dynamic scenes are often what could be called a 'dance of opposites' in that characters swap roles and perspectives. For example, a king might become the pawn of a servant if the servant is blackmailing him. Great scenes can be built by cycling through the possibilities that a situation or character offers. For example, in Scene 8 of an episode of *Will & Grace* entitled 'I Never Cheered For My Father' (by Adam Barr), Will's mother Marilyn reveals she's been having a secret affair with her ex-husband (and Will's father), George. The affair has been going on behind the back of George's former mistress (and now girlfriend), Tina.

Marilyn's been enjoying the tantalising secrecy of her affair and chastises Will for revealing it to Tina. Will's attempt to bring everything into the open has taken the excitement out of it. Because of this, Marilyn is considering ending the affair.

Tina, busty, brash and beautiful, arrives. She's appalled that Marilyn is the 'whore' who's seeing her boyfriend. Just when Tina was in a stable relationship (that she gained through wicked seduction), an interloper is stealing her man!

So, the ex-wife is acting like a seductress while the seductress is acting like a wronged wife.

The scene then cycles to a new position: Will orders Tina to leave his father and Marilyn to return to her husband. The two ladies reluctantly agree.

Next, the ladies privately agree upon a third and final position: they'll each take George on specific nights of the week. 'Oh, this is great!' exclaims Marilyn. 'And it's even more exciting now that we're lying to Will.'

Adam Barr, the writer, has both ladies at the beginning of the scene playing the opposite of their stereotype. Will, the son, then adopts the role of a disciplinarian 'father' ordering the women back to their stereotypical roles. Finally, the script cycles the roles again, returning the situation to its starting point, with a twist that will keep both ladies satisfied: Will is going to play the unknowing partner.

The scene follows a three-act pattern. The set-up is Marilyn's chastising of Will. The complications are the arrival of Tina, the swapping of roles and Will's negotiation. The third act of the scene first shows a false resolution where the two ladies agree to Will's demands, then moves to a true resolution where the ladies agree to deceive Will and share their time with George.

This three-act pattern involving the swift cycling of opposites creates a delightful farcical dance that takes less than five minutes to complete. Like the 'Old Friends' episode in *The Golden Girls*, it shows comedy's compression of narrative. The events of the scene could be stretched to comprise an entire episode or even a dramatic movie-length story.

COMIC DIALOGUE

Finally it's time to put words into the characters' mouths. At the first pass, however, none of them needs to be witty—only the bare essentials of what *must* be said are required. This part of the process could be regarded as listing the dialogue's 'bullet points'. Essentially, you are laying down the subtext: the message under the words or actions in a scene—what's *really* being said. The exchange might look like this:

> GAZZA: I'm standing my ground. My creative integrity is paramount.
> PRODUCER: I'll ruin your career.
> GAZZA: I surrender.

The exchange is so bald it lays bare the subtext: Gazza is a mouse who thinks he's a lion.

The next step is to see where and how a narrative gag or straight-up gag might support this. In the instance above, Gazza changes his mind under pressure from his producer, so the dialogue could take the form of a comic reversal: the character states their position firmly, pressure is placed on the character, the character changes their mind but tries to keep their dignity.

> GAZZA: I have my standards. That scene is the heart of the episode.
> There is *no way* I will cut it.
> PRODUCER: I guess I'll have to find another writer.
> GAZZA: Wait! I just needed time to think about your feedback. Let's
> cut the scene.

An allusion to an archetype can make the point even sharper. For instance, the exchange between Gazza and his producer could be framed as a slave versus his pharaoh. Gazza's ideals are useless against his Producer's power.

> GAZZA: (*as Moses*) Let my juices flow!
> PRODUCER: No.
> GAZZA: I demand creative *freedom.*
> PRODUCER: (*to a lackey*) Bring me another writer!
> GAZZA: … Uh, the creative freedom to do it *your* way, oh mighty one.

This process can be applied in reverse. The purpose of any line in a scene is to advance the story, change the characters' emotions, reveal character, offer a new (relevant) perspective or reflect the story's theme. To ensure every line of action or dialogue is performing one of these functions, write out the subtext of each line. If the subtext of a given line or exchange (or indeed the whole scene) doesn't do any of the above, it may need to be cut or altered so it serves a purpose.

You may find a gag-type or principle that can transform your dialogue bullet points into a humorous exchange. Remember a character can get a laugh simply by displaying their known qualities or by summing up the situation.

SITUATION CREATION

Amongst the many things required by situation comedy is (you guessed it) a situation. Devising a comic situation, however, can be a maddening process—particularly when the writer puts the cart before the horse. The horse, in this case, being character.

Characters drive stories, not the reverse. Any narrative demands active characters who respond to events in accordance with their own personalities, creating or causing further events. Consequently the place to start a story is *always* with your characters.

One of the easiest traps to fall into is 'Wouldn't it be cool if … ?' Having a vision of your characters dealing with a particular ludicrous event is fine, but it's possible to go mad building a sitcom situation that accommodates that event. Cause and effect are the building blocks of story development but working from effect to cause doubles your workload.

Let's imagine you want to include a pink pony in the climax of your script. For some reason, the pink pony appeals to you—it's new, original and could be a funny sight. Except, how does the pony get there? And why is it there? And what are the characters doing about it? Why? Why? Why? Before you know it, you're writing the story backwards, which is about as easy as *reading* one backwards.

The beginning is the best place to start. Bring in the pink pony at the start, either physically or as an issue that the characters must deal with. As a story element it might be enough to get your characters moving—but only if it creates a problem beyond feeding and dung-disposal. That is, it cannot simply be an amusing event. It must create a *situation*.

So, start with the pony, see if it tests your characters in some way. If the pony's cute and funny but doesn't spark an interesting chain of events, cut it.

The best situations challenge a character's true nature. For instance, a ruthless character who doesn't care what people think of him won't be too concerned at being exposed as a liar. But if this exposure will lead to the loss of his true love, then he will work hard to maintain the friendship and alliance of anyone who discovers the lie—even though it is his nature to hold them in contempt.

Start with a character, identify one or more of their qualities and build from there. You may find the following three-step process useful in building situations that place your characters under pressure.

Set-up (e.g. the insecure husband (protagonist) excitedly prepares for the arrival of his old friend visiting to watch the footy Grand Final on TV).

Complications (e.g. his wife reminds him she had the hots for his friend when they were all at school together. The friend arrives and is still very attractive and likable. And he's become rich! With the protagonist in a stew, the next step is to have them deepen the situation with an action).

Resolution for better or worse (e.g. the husband decides to lie that his friend is gay so his wife will lose interest).

The situation is now evolving, or 'active'. The husband's actions will cause complications that he will have to overcome as the story approaches the second turning point. Typically, the second turning point presents him with an opportunity or crisis that allows him (and us) to frame the terms of the climax, even though we don't know whether he will succeed. As he nears his goal, the third and final turning point brings him up against the thing he fears most—in this case, loss of his wife and friend due to their new-found romance or to his own dishonesty.

Usually, protagonists deepen their trouble by acting 'externally', making efforts to change the situation without changing their own outlook. External actions might include donning a disguise, telling a fib, cheating, hiding evidence, manipulating others, forcing others to do their will or obeying the will of others against their own better judgment. External actions tend to be improvised short-term fixes, for example, if the husband whispers to his wife that his old friend is gay.

Yet, protagonists can usually only resolve their troubles by acting 'internally', that is when their actions are based upon a change in outlook. Internal actions might include being honest, facing the music, standing up for themselves, overcoming a fear, doing the right thing, accepting the inevitable or surrendering a prize. Internal actions tend to provide lasting (albeit minimal) change in the protagonist. For example, the husband feels guilty, finds his lies can no longer be sustained and comes clean, revealing his fear of losing his wife to his handsome friend.

Internal action, when it finally comes, doesn't necessarily mean the protagonist will avoid punishment or that matters will have reached a stage where they're irreparably worsened. (In this example the husband may be given the chore of cooking dinner in the kitchen while the wife and friend watch his beloved footy match.)

RESOLVING STORIES

The climax and resolution of a story must directly answer the concerns raised early in the story. This may seem obvious, but many a first draft has failed to answer the primary question raised in the first act, e.g. 'Will Bob get his money back?' With this in mind, it generally pays to have an idea early on how the story will be resolved. That way, the stakes can go sky-high without causing the writer too much anxiety about where it's all leading. (This is not the same as planning the end before the beginning: the climax must emerge as an answer to the question posed by the first turning point.) For example, choosing a resolution in which the jealous husband decides to neutralise the situation by coming clean offers a general direction for the story. With this resolution in place, the process becomes one of escalating tensions and increasing the complications to a point where the husband finds them unsustainable and confesses.

Once you have settled on a resolution, the options for escalating events become clearer.

With the proviso that it must relate directly to their concerns, regularly ask yourself, 'What is the worst thing that can happen to the character now?' Don't just put your characters under pressure, squeeze them till they choke. Whether you take your characters around the world, to Hell or to jail, the beacon of your resolution guides you towards the climax.

MULTIPLE STORYLINES

Episodes with several storylines that resolve or complicate each other can be a delight for audiences. *Seinfeld* made a virtue of this technique and viewers revelled in the introduction of new storylines for Jerry and his friends to negotiate. The show's unlikely connections between characters and events, and the manner in which each storyline was paid-off by another, were surprising and satisfying. No coincidence seemed too outlandish.

Making multiple storylines resolve each other is a creative process with many difficulties but only one challenge—keep it simple! Ideally, the resolution should come in one story-beat only. This saves episode time, keeps the stories a step ahead of the viewer until the last instant and makes it easy for viewers to grasp.

Despite a reputation for cleverness, what the *Seinfeld* story resolutions had in common was simplicity. Though each episode appeared to be a complex web of story strands, with the last segment of each episode piling unexpected resolution upon resolution in an almost chaotic way, the impression was misleading. If you examine a *Seinfeld* episode, you'll find a delightful simplicity and clarity to each story's structure. If there is genius in *Seinfeld* (and there is) it is to be found here.

Given the time constraints, multi-plot episodes allow for only so many story beats per strand. The resolutions must be swift and easy to grasp.

Time is not the only consideration. If your show is designed for prime time then your audience will be of all ages, so your stories must be clear and resolve in a way that is satisfying for both kids and adults. Even if your show is aimed at adults, human beings come in all brains and sizes, so simplicity is crucial. Master screenwriter Simon van der Borgh says, 'Never be afraid of being understood'.

Simplicity however does not equal stupidity! Surprises, reversals, conflicts and resolutions all demonstrate a comedy writer's story-building skill, but when they're neat, clear and punchy he demonstrates his talent.

RAISING THE STAKES

The primary purpose of any scene, except the resolution, is to 'raise the stakes' or increase the pressure on the characters. 'Raising the stakes' however is a catch-all term for something that can be done in many ways. It is a common mistake to repeatedly raise the stakes at only one level.

Generally speaking, characters have something at stake in all the following areas:

Moral stakes are raised when a character makes a decision that by their own standards is immoral, confronts a moral issue or is forced to balance one moral priority against another. The pressure to make a decision can be external (e.g. another character can threaten, beguile, coerce or unknowingly direct them to make the choice) or entirely self-generated (e.g. the character is being compromised by a lie they have told to maintain appearances).

The most common moral problem facing sitcom characters is dishonesty. Though a lie may be told with the best of intentions, it tends to grow in detail, complexity and magnitude, increasing the moral pressure on the liar or liars until they are exposed. Lies create knowledge differentials which in turn create misunderstandings. Chaos and hand wringing are never far behind. In an episode of *The Games* when an International Olympic Committee (IOC) member dies in his office, Sydney Olympics official John and his cohorts pretend the dead man is still alive. To fool onlookers, they hold fake meetings with what seems to be a very quiet and passive IOC member. John even goes so far as to get the IOC member's 'approval' on some new planning measures. Anticipating the arrival of VIPs Nelson Mandela and Princess Margaret, John and co. resort to ever more desperate tactics to cover their subterfuge. They finally taking the extraordinary step of sending him off in a car while pretending he is alive to the other passengers ('Dead Man', John Clarke and Ross Stevenson).

Status stakes are raised when a character's status is threatened. A character's status is their position in any hierarchy, including their role in life. The threat may take the form of replacement, demotion or redundancy. Whether they're a doctor, a mother, a president or a pauper, everyone has a perception of their own status. Any event that forces an alteration of that perception can cause tremendous upheaval in a character's life.

In *Everybody Loves Raymond*, Debra finds her status as a mother is repeatedly threatened when her mother-in-law meddles in her family's affairs.

In *All in the Family*, Mike's status as a husband is threatened when Gloria demands an equal partnership in their marriage ('Gloria Discovers Women's Lib' by Norman Lear and Sandy Stern).

Status anxiety can lead characters to behave badly. In *Seinfeld* Jerry spends an episode worrying that his new girlfriend mistakenly thinks he picks his nose. He can't let the trivial misunderstanding ride lest he become known as a nose-picker. His dogged insistence that there was 'no pick' turns the girlfriend off him ('The Pick' by Larry David and Marc Jaffe).

Emotional stakes are raised by any threat to a character's strongest emotional bonds. The imminent loss of a mother, father, lover, friend, teddy bear or even a prized memento can goad a character into reckless, uncharacteristic action.

In *Diff'rent Strokes* the two adopted boys, Willis and Arnold, are sent into a spin when their adoptive father, Philip Drummond, falls for a woman who plans to send them away. The more love Mr Drummond feels for the woman, the greater the emotional stakes for the boys. Fear of abandonment, jealousy, disappointment and anger provoke Willis and Arnold to create problems for the interloper ('The Woman' by Ron Alexander).

A breach of trust, misplaced jealousy or a lack of consideration regularly raises the emotional stakes in sitcom. The relationships involved, particularly those of major characters, tend to be resistant to permanent breakdown—but the characters don't know that! Anger, emotional pain or the bruising of pride can place relationships under stress or cause a temporary rift. In *The Simpsons*, Marge feels so under-appreciated by her family that she abandons them and goes to the 'Rancho Relaxo' health farm to examine her options. Only by recognising and apologising for his shortcomings does her husband, Homer, win her back ('Homer Alone' by David M. Stern).

Another risk to comic relationships comes from one or more of the characters labouring under a misapprehension that leads them to be dishonest or unfairly punish others. For example, in *So I Married An Axe-Murderer*, Charlie is convinced his wife is … well, the title says it all. When he accuses her, she is heartbroken at his lack of trust and dumps him. (Turns out she was innocent of any crime.)

In domestic comedies, the greatest emotional threat is usually the departure of a 'family' member or the entire disbandment of the 'family'.

Temporal stakes are raised when a character is threatened with the loss of money or worldly possessions, or obstructed in acquiring more. Whether it's inheritance money, the family home or a pack of breadcrumbs, people will fight to gain or keep possessions, particularly if their livelihood or quality of life depend on them, or if they are connected with other stakes such as status anxiety or emotional stakes.

In *The Golden Girls* Blanche freaks out her housemates by considering an offer to buy the house, imperilling her 'family'. When her housemates accuse her of selfishness she takes offence. Her inclination to sell increases and her friends' anguish increases with it. Only when she weighs up the money against the loss of her imperfect but beloved 'family' does she refuse the offer. The stakes for her housemates are primarily emotional, but for Blanche they are purely temporal ('We're Outta Here Parts 1 and 2' by Barry Fanaro, Mort Nathan, Terry Grossman and Kathy Speer).

Physical stakes can attach to an actual stake—just ask a vampire. When a character's life and limb are threatened, or they face the prospect of significant pain, they can react in extreme or uncharacteristic ways. For instance, in *Gilligan's Island*, Gilligan and the Skipper discover a head-hunters' totem pole that bears a resemblance to Gilligan. When the pole is broken and the headhunters invade the Island, Gilligan is forced to pretend that *his* is the head on the totem pole. The headhunters are hoodwinked, but only because the normally chicken Gilligan overcomes his fears ('High man on the Totem Pole' by Brad Radnitz).

Stakes in any category can be real or imagined but either way, they'll have equal weight in a story.

All of the stakes above can be based on absurd foundations. In *Monty Python and the Holy Grail*, King Arthur is terrified when the Knights of Ni heighten Physical Stakes by threatening to send him mad with their annoying repetition of the word 'Ni'. Likewise, irrational phobias particular to a given character can be used to heighten the stakes for that character. *Seinfeld's* Kramer suffers Psychological Stakes when he experiences Coulrophobia, a fear of clowns.

The main thing is that the stakes are important to the characters and challenge their individual natures.

KNOWLEDGE DIFFERENTIALS

'Knowledge differentials' are perhaps the most common story tool in sitcom. A knowledge differential occurs when one or more characters know more than another character or characters. Usually neither character is aware that there is a misunderstanding until it's too late or until one of the characters clarifies the situation.

> INSPECTOR CLOUSEAU: (*indicating the hotel's dog*) Does your dog bite?
> HOTELIER: No.
> > CLOUSEAU *bends to pat the dog. It bites him.*
> INSPECTOR CLOUSEAU: I thought you said your dog did not bite.
> HOTELIER: That is not my dog.
> > —*The Pink Panther Strikes Again* (by Blake Edwards and Frank Waldman)

In Abbott and Costello's classic 'Who's On First?' sketch (without which no exploration of comedy is complete), the pair discuss Abbott's baseball team and which base each of the players are on. The team members have unlikely names such as 'What', 'Because', 'Tomorrow', 'I Don't Know', but Costello doesn't know that. In the extract below, the name of the player on first base is 'Who'.

COSTELLO: Well then, who's on first?
ABBOTT: Yes.
COSTELLO: I mean the fellow's name.
ABBOTT: Who.
COSTELLO: The guy on first!

… and so on. Throughout the sketch, Abbott has complete knowledge of the team members' peculiar names and is perfectly calm. He answers Costello's increasingly hysterical questions honestly and can't see what the fuss is about. And in fact he could easily resolve the confusion by saying, 'Listen, the player's actual name is "Who"', but instead we are treated to what is rightly regarded as some of the finest comic wordplay in the English language. The simplicity of the misunderstanding exposes a baffling range of linguistic possibilities. Just by bouncing between various applications of the word 'who', Abbott and Costello wrote themselves into comedy history.

Perhaps the most remarkable aspect of the sketch is that, at its heart, it's nonsense. In reality, nobody has a name like 'I Don't Know' or 'Because'. However, the audience accepts this absurdity because the knowledge differential and wordplay are the focus of the piece. It's enough that Abbott and Costello both act believably within the confines of their absurd premise— the players' nonsense names don't diminish the audience's enjoyment.

Beyond their usefulness in sketch comedy, knowledge differentials can also generate narrative. When one character gets the wrong end of the stick, the double meanings in another character's words or actions can drive action and cause complications. Mind you, any misunderstanding should be at least vaguely credible. The person labouring under the misapprehension should be able to justify their warped view to themselves.

Example:

BOB *reads a newspaper article detailing a rise in husband murders.* BOB *has just inherited money from a rich aunt. He notes that* BARBARA *has been strangely secretive lately. In fact she's planning a surprise birthday barbeque for him, but* BOB *wonders if she is plotting his murder.*
Later, BOB *overhears* BARBARA *telling her friend* DELORES *how to soften a steak,* BOB's *favourite, with a meat hammer.*
BARBARA: I just have to keep bashing with the hammer until the job is done.
DELORES: What about the blood?
BARBARA: I'm not squeamish. I may even enjoy it. Oh my, Bob's not going to see this coming!

The scenario exploits Bob's ongoing fear of his wife. Once the idea is in his head Barbara's most innocent actions take on a dire meaning for Bob. The sight of Barbara sharpening a knife or bringing home rolls of plastic gives him the horrors. Further, Barbara notices that Bob is suspicious and becomes more secretive about her party plans. She tells him white lies about her preparations that, when uncovered, apparently confirm Bob's fears.

Should Bob decide to follow his wife to the supermarket, he'll see her purchasing lighter fluid, a can of petrol (for the mower) and super-size garbage bags, all of which have sinister associations. Even if he later sees her buying streamers and champagne he can interpret this as covering her tracks. And so forth.

Sitcoms provide countless examples of this story-building technique. In *The Honeymooners*, Ralph's tendency to hypochondria and panic is exploited when he finds a letter from a doctor and believes the doctor has given him six months to live. Ralph is thrown onto an emotional roller-coaster—despair, sudden cherishing of his wife, fragile stoicism—until it's revealed that the 'doctor' is actually a vet. Alice's mother's dog is the one with six months to live ('A Matter of Life and Death' by Marvin Marx and Walter Stone).

Not all knowledge differentials involve death and disaster. Anything of importance to the characters can provide material for a knowledge differential. In *Fawlty Towers*, ('The Hotel Inspectors' by Connie Booth and John Cleese) Basil is warned that hotel inspectors are about. When Mr Hutchison mentions he comes into constant contact with hotels in his 'professional capacity', Basil mistakes him for one. Hutchison is actually a cutlery salesman, but Basil goes from his usual sarcastic sniping to sycophantic fawning, going so far as to say that Hutchison himself could do a better job of running the hotel. When Hutchison asks if the hotel has a table tennis table, Basil replies desperately, 'Indeed it does; it's not in absolutely mint condition but it could be used in an emergency'. (This is reportedly Cleese' favourite line in the series.) Finally, when Basil discovers the truth, he turns on Hutchison like a lazy susan, only to have Hutchison punch him on the nose—just in time for the *real* hotel inspectors to see the whole thing. The misunderstanding plays upon one of Basil's known qualities: he's only polite and professional when it serves his purposes.

The power of a simple misunderstanding to drive a story is limitless but there are a couple of essential elements. The first is obsession. Julius Caesar's assertion that 'men believe what they want to' is a regrettable truth. Once a character has an idea in their head and obsession blinds them to other explanations of the facts, they reject any attempt to clear the air as a trivialisation (e.g. if you think you're dying, a friend trying to convince you otherwise can be dismissed as well-meaning but deluded). Distortion is inevitable once obsession is in play and this allows the misapprehension to continue. So while a simple misreading of the facts can generate a story, the strong emotions that arise from the misunderstanding give the story its punch and make the obsession believable. Fear, jealousy, greed, desire, loathing—any of these can blind a person to the truth.

The second essential element is dishonesty. In the example above, if Bob would only speak openly to Barbara about his fears, she could quickly and easily put them to rest. But there's never a good time to say, 'Darling, are you planning to kill me?' There's also dishonesty, albeit benign, on Barbara's side. If she told Bob the truth about her secretive actions, the misunderstanding would be resolved, but that would ruin the surprise party.

While many knowledge-differential-based stories run on negative emotions (as in the example above), positive emotions can cause just as much single-minded obsession. Consider the flipside of the scenario above. What if Bob is convinced that Barbara is planning a surprise party for him, but in fact she *is* planning to kill her useless husband? Her scheming with Deborah, her knife-sharpening and petrol-purchasing as she prepares to murder her husband can all be misinterpreted by the lovesick Bob. 'She's planning me a surprise barbeque!' (This of course has story ramifications that, in an ongoing series, are probably impossible to reconcile, but let's leave that aside.)

Handled well, obsession-based knowledge differentials can lead a character to cling to their misapprehension even when other characters, fully aware of the situation, actively try to persuade him of the truth. For example, a man who believes his female workmate is hiding her love for him may distort anything she says or does to fit the picture in his mind. She slaps him? She's playing hard-to-get. She says 'I hate your guts' and puts him on a harassment charge? She's playing *very* hard-to-get. She sleeps with his best friend? She's trying to make him jealous …

The complications stemming from a simple misapprehension can lead to the most outrageous or uncharacteristic behaviour.

Knowledge differentials are often the main ingredient of a sitcom's main or 'A' story. (Subplots are often referred to as 'B' and 'C' stories.) Once the misunderstanding is established, most of the episode is spent increasing the 'evidence' that seems to support it, forcing or enticing that character into increasingly drastic action. Finally, the character is exposed or forced to confess their understanding of the events so far. The other characters reveal the truth, apologies are made or butts kicked, and the episode ends.

A knowledge-differential story may also involve a character realising that a misunderstanding has occurred and exploiting the situation rather than clarifying it. In *Three's Company*, the three housemates become convinced their depressed landlord, Mr Furley is suicidal when he's overheard asking someone on the phone whether 'gas is quicker … and painless'. While they do their best to cheer Mr Furley up with massages, Aspirin and pep-talks, Furley doesn't think to mention that he was in fact speaking to his dentist about a tooth removal. Once the crafty Mr Furley overhears the housemates discussing his impending suicide, he decides to exploit their kindness and fakes an even deeper depression. This sends the housemates into a frenzy of spoiling Mr Furley. Once they discover the truth, they decide to turn the tables and ... well, you get the idea ('The Goodbye Guy' by Howard Albrecht and Sol Weinstein).

In building a story based on a knowledge differential, you'll save time if you explore all plot permutations at the treatment stage, particularly if you plan to shift the differential during the story (as in Mr Furley's case, above). Starting with a solid plan allows you to commence work on the script itself in the confidence that you won't be retracing your steps when some enticing plot idea doesn't work out. (Of course, if, despite careful planning, a better idea occurs to you while scripting, see it through. But exhausting most possibilities before you've begun keeps these seismic Eureka moments to a minimum, and your schedule on track.)

Chapter Six:
Humour and Story

Gags die. Humour doesn't.

—Jack Benny

The driving force behind narrative comedy is character. Comedy deriving from character underpins all of the gag principles detailed in this chapter.

American playwright Neil Simon boasted that he wrote his comedies without ever writing one joke. Without starting a debate about his definition of a 'joke', Neil Simon's comedies rely for their humour on the antics of his characters rather than straight-up, self-contained gags.

Often, a character has only to act in accordance with their nature to get a laugh. For example, David Brent in *The Office* is a character well-known for his hypocrisy. When Brent discovers a pornographic picture with his face pasted onto one of the participants, he roundly condemns the pornographic images that have been discovered in the office. He downloads porn photos to show his boss how easy it is to access such images. But then he's distracted by the images and, as he continues condemning porn to his boss, views them with fascination ('Work Experience' by Ricky Gervais and Stephen Merchant).

This hypocritical behaviour is what the audience has come to expect from Brent and it provokes a cringing laugh. While the humour in this instance is a negation, there is no 'gag', no punchline or climax that culminates the negation. Instead, the entire scene is the joke, provoking laughter throughout. Brent acts in accordance with his nature. It's the phenomenon of Brent that makes us laugh more than any particular joke he unknowingly provides.

Character gags aren't all at the expense of their subject. In many cases, characters we love exhibit benign qualities that provoke affectionate laughs. Clownish characters like Chrissy in *Three's Company*, Betty in *Hey Dad..!* and 'Woody' Boyd in *Cheers* are all over-endowed with friendly innocence. They are adults with a childlike view of the world, a contradiction that is bound to provoke laughter. They don't need to provide a gag *per se*; their gullibility, naivety and general lack of life experience create the humour.

Benign qualities can cause as much trouble as malign ones. Clownish characters often fail to understand the jokes of others and misunderstand basic situations and concepts, (e.g. when Woody first arrives at Cheers, he expects to meet his pen-pal, Coach, with whom he's been exchanging pens). Even such minor misunderstandings, although sweet, can lead to dire consequences.

All comic situations should arise from characters acting in accordance with their natures (see Chapter Five, 'Creating an Episode'). Larry David (playing himself) in *Curb Your Enthusiasm* is a deeply flawed comic character with a petty streak. In 'The Corpse-Sniffing Dog' (by Larry David), he quibbles over whether he should thank a friend's wife for the dinner that the friend paid for. But then Larry finds he needs to retrieve a dog he gave them lest the dog's owner, after a complex turn of events, wreak a terrible revenge upon him. Larry visits his friend's wife and pretends he's apologetic for his pettiness. He claims that he now sees he was wrong not to thank her for dinner, even though her husband earnt the money that paid for it. Then he asks for the dog. The wife sees through his pretence, is appalled by his fraudulence and refuses to hand it over. Larry's left in the lurch. Like Neil Simons' plays, *Curb Your Enthusiasm* is relatively gag-free, relying instead upon Larry's active-but-negative qualities.

A laugh can be generated when a character simply confirms by their actions a personal quality that the audience recognises. Eldin Bernecky in *Murphy Brown* is a renovator who arrives in the first episode and continues to renovate Murphy's home throughout the series. Once Eldin's dithering work ethic is established, he gets a laugh by simply mentioning a renovation he did that 'lasted a year—it was a nightmare'. Because we know Eldin, this innocent observation is funny.

Characters' shortcomings can drive stories that have the audience in stitches. Watching the stakes rise despite, or because of, a character's frantic attempts to resolve their predicament is the force behind many a comic tale. A well-designed comic character, with well-chosen faults and blind spots, makes a strong launch pad for comedy. Sure control over who knows what when, and how characters react to the knowledge differential, can have us biting our nails with one hand and slapping our thigh with the other without ever hearing a witticism.

Narrative comedy relies on the limited self-awareness and outlook of its characters. None of us are fully aware of our flaws, and when we do point out a clear fault in others, they may see it differently. A racist may know that their views are broadly unacceptable but they draw a lonely superiority from the fact, telling themselves, 'I'm just saying what everyone knows is true, but doesn't have the guts to say'. This lack of insight can get us into a world of trouble and that's where comedy begins.

Characters who are aware of their faults are halfway to fixing them. Those who continuously stand back, see the big picture and make sensible choices have little place in comedy, unless they're about to be hit by a bus or savaged by lions. Only when normally capable characters lose their way do they instigate comic hijinks.

Key to any comic character's limitations is an inability to see the humour in themselves or their situation. Some of the funniest comic characters have no sense of humour at all (just ask Lucille Bluth, the wicked mother in *Arrested Development*). Tragic characters may fully appreciate the tragic dimensions of their situation, weeping and railing against the gods. Comic characters also weep and rail because they also think they're in a tragedy. And that's the way we like it. If Woody Allen's characters ever recognised the humour in their situation they'd be a lot less funny.

Consider it a rule of thumb that if a character laughs at their situation, the audience doesn't. And if they think they know something, they don't know the half of it.

Narrative Gags

Narrative gags are comic events that reveal character, confirm a situation, offer a new perspective or move the story forward. They're the bricks from which a comic narrative is built. Infinite in their variety, they are nonetheless governed by a limited number of time-honoured principles. These principles are not formulae but provide a framework within which anything is possible.

All narratives gags fall into seven categories:

- Negations
- Cover-Ups
- Limited World Views
- Taking Things Literally
- Distortions
- Running Gags
- Catchphrases

A sound knowledge of these principles enables a writer to enhance a script's comic moments, create a healthy mix of gags and select gags appropriate to the characters. Most of these gag principles will be familiar—but now you'll be able to give them a name.

Although the principles are limited, the gags they generate are infinite in their variety. For example, the first principle in this chapter, Negation, can govern a character's transition from safety to danger, dominance to subservience, rags to riches, love to fear, pride to humility, boldness to meekness. Negations reveal ignorance where knowledge was assumed and vice versa. It lays the mighty low and raises paupers to the throne. The possible transitions are endless and each transition can cover any number of gags.

The trick is to make the principles work for you, in your style. The only true limitation is imagination.

Once you know the principles, you'll see them everywhere, from classics like *Are You Being Served* to newcomers like *The Office*. This doesn't mean that observing the principles makes your script derivative—*The Office*, with its single-camera mockumentary style and character-based stand-alone sketches, is rightly regarded as a ground-breaking sitcom. The principles remain the same, but the characters, events and the ideas in any given script are as fresh as the writer's approach.

Neither do the principles overlap. For instance, at first glance it might seem that cover-ups and distortions cover similar ground, but they are distinct. When a guilty character distorts an accusation, their *intention* may be to cover up, but the gag itself remains a distortion.

Though some narrative gags may seem more suited to buffoons, they are just as easily applied to sophisticated characters. Both Shakespeare's clownish Bottom from *A Midsummer Night's Dream* and the complex and contradictory David Brent from *The Office* have high if ill-founded self-regard, unrealistic ambitions and a tendency to self-aggrandise by belittling others. These qualities make both characters suitable for comic exploitation using the same techniques, though to very different effect.

NEGATIONS

Negation is essentially an instantaneous comic reversal. It's a principle that had 'em rolling in the amphitheatre aisles way back when sandals were expensive and desirable.

The most common form is character negation. This occurs when a character changes their mind under pressure, when they undermine themselves inadvertently through their own behaviour or have their views inadvertently negated by the behaviour of another.

Character negation can also derive from the reversal of a character's accepted traits, for example a tough guy bursting into tears at the sight of a puppy.

The other form of negation is narrative negation. Here, the *writer* plays the joke on the character rather than the character negating themselves or being negated by another. For example one camper says to another, 'Relax, I checked the weather forecast: it's going to be fine for the next week'. Cut to the two campers huddled in their tent as the rain pours down.

Comic negations almost always pay-off instantly. If there's too much time between the set-up and its negation, the connection between the two can be weakened or lost and the negation becomes part of the natural flow of the story and not a gag at all. To get a laugh, the pay-off must immediately follow the set-up. Punch says, 'I am the master of my house' and Judy whacks him on the head. That's funny. Putting a song between Punch's remark and

Judy's whack dissipates the impact of the negation. The whack may get a wry smile (Punch always deserves a whack) but the surprise is lost and therefore so is the laugh.

Almost any motivation can force a negation. People play dirty when it comes to their pride, status or heart's desire. A desire to please or impress can have a character flipping cartwheels or turning their world upside down. A lazy employee can instantly transform into a 'workaholic' when the boss arrives. A normally honest man can become an outrageous liar in an effort to appear more intelligent, powerful or morally superior to a challenger. A muscleman can turn to jelly or a rocket scientist can become a mumbling idiot on meeting a supermodel. Similarly she might go to pieces when she meets them. The offer of free beer on Grand Final day can instantly turn a sworn enemy into a 'friend'. Money, guns, love and sex each have the power to corrupt or convert even the most stalwart characters, reminding us that the only constant in life is change.

Of course, sometimes people just act stupidly. But stupidity alone isn't enough to cause a credible and funny negation. 'Because he's an idiot' is no justification for any character's actions. Their stupidity must be coupled to an active quality such as pride or ambition. Even in the Farrelly brothers' *Dumb and Dumber*, the heroes are driven to embark on an adventure together because of their honest natures and loyalty to each other. Their choices are ill-considered because of their stupidity, but they are not driven by it.

Character Negations can be inadvertent or deliberate.

Sergeant Jones in *Dad's Army* manages to negate his own words *inadvertently* by the panic-stricken way he runs about shouting, 'Don't panic! Don't panic!'

In *Blackadder II*, while discussing the colour of elephants, Lord Melchett spins on a dime to save his neck:

> MELCHETT: Grey, I suspect, your Majesty.
> QUEEN ELIZABETH: I think you'll find they were orange, Lord Melchett.
> MELCHETT: Grey is more usual, Ma'am.
> QUEEN ELIZABETH: Who's Queen?
> MELCHETT: As you say, Majesty. There were these magnificent *orange* elephants ...
> —*Blackadder II* ('Head' by Richard Curtis and Ben Elton)

The Sydney Olympics official, John makes a quick choice between two problematic paths:

> JOHN: Does anyone have any questions that don't have anything to do with lacrosse?

REPORTER: How much over budget are the Games at the moment?

JOHN: Are there any more lacrosse questions?

—*The Games* ('In the Public Interest', by John Clarke and Ross
Stevenson)

Karen in *Will & Grace* is a flinty woman capable of lightning-quick Negations. She welcomes Will and Grace to a party at her home: 'I'm so glad you're both here!' As soon as their backs are turned, she hisses darkly to herself, 'What the hell are they doing here?!' ('Bathroom Humor' by Greg Malins).

Characters under pressure (most commonly from fear) may abruptly and deliberately reverse firmly stated moral positions. Sergeant Jones' panic is genuine—the Germans posed a real and constant threat to the Dads' Armies of wartime Britain. But other factors can drive negations. Karen's negation above is based upon self-interest.

Pressure is a reliable goad for a comic negation. To give a pressured negation comic punch, the pressure should be placed on a recognised weakness in the character. This weakness can be malign (e.g. lust or vanity), neutral (e.g. forgetfulness or gullibility) or benign (e.g. sensitivity or compassion). Pressure on a recognised weakness makes a change of heart believable and any subsequent trouble the character's own fault.

And there's nothing like a physical threat to change a character's mind:

MR HUMPHRIES *and* MR LUCAS *are counting money.*

MR HUMPHRIES *and* MR LUCAS: One for them and one for us, one
for them and one for us, one for them and one for us.

Man holds up knife threateningly.

MR HUMPHRIES *and* MR LUCAS: All for them and none for us, all
for them and none for us.

—*Are You Being Served?* ('Fire Practice' by Jeremy Lloyd and
David Croft)

Often, pressure-based negations are underpinned by hope: the character faces a seemingly impossible situation, they change their position in a transparent attempt to avoid consequences, yet throughout they cling to a shred of hope that they'll succeed.

Characters can undergo swift *emotional* reversals due to a new factor in their plight.

FRASIER: My wife had left me, which was painful. Then she came
back to me, which was excruciating.

—*Frasier* ('The Good Son' by David Angell, Peter Casey and
David Lee)

No character should ever change their mind for no reason, no matter how well this may suit the writer's story structure. Appropriate pressure or a realisation will reliably render a character negation reasonable and believable, but negations also reveal character. They are turning points, albeit small ones, that reveal how characters behave under pressure. Of the three quotes above, Frasier's line is arguably the funniest, simply because its negation is also an intelligent observation that reveals a human truth—that all relationships are a mixture of love and resentment. We laugh both at what it says about Frasier, and in recognition of an uncomfortable truth.

Pressure can drive a character to contradict their most obvious qualities, revealing deep character. When the childlike Rose in *The Golden Girls* reaches the end of her tether with a ruthless little girl who's been holding Rose's teddy bear to ransom, Rose gives the girl what seems to be a speech of surrender: 'Oh, dear … I guess there's a lesson to be learnt here. Sometimes life just isn't fair'. And with that Rose snatches the teddy and throws the little girl out the door, revealing that even the sweet-hearted Rose has her limits ('Old Friends' by Terry Grossman and Kathy Speer).

Negations that don't involve pressure or realisation include narrative negations, when a character makes a statement that is immediately contradicted by fate (like the two campers above), and character negations in which one character's words or actions are negated by another, or by themselves inadvertently. In *The Last Crusade* (by George Lucas, Menno Meyjes and Jeffrey Boam), Indiana Jones boasts to his German captors that his friend, Marcus Brody, can blend into any culture like a native. This is negated when the scene changes to Marcus wandering helplessly through a Turkish marketplace loudly asking for directions in English.

A character's personal qualities can inadvertently lead them to negate their own position. In *The Nanny*, the acerbic and gossipy butler Niles is asked if he can keep a secret. 'Well,' he replies, 'I'm good until I meet the next person' ('The Engagement' by Rick Shaw). The nutty farmer Owen Newitt in *The Vicar of Dibley* is affronted when it's suggested he may be, well, nutty. 'I'm not a lunatic', he insists. 'I have the psychiatric report to prove it' ('Election' by Richard Curtis and Paul Mayhew-Archer).

Then there's the classic negation gag in which one character scolds another for doing something, then does exactly the same thing. Maxwell Smart in *Get Smart* (Mel Brooks), regularly overrode the suggested courses of action from his partner, '99'. 'Ninety-nine, if you don't mind, I'd like to be the one who plans this.' But then Max would announce a course of action identical to 99's suggestion.

Clarity and stark contrast are the keys to comic negation. The change doesn't necessarily have to be to a *literal* opposite (a successful negation might be a transition from, say, fury to confusion), but the clearer and greater the contrast between the two states, the greater the chance of getting a laugh. For example, making a character's declaration or principle as lofty as possible gives them further to fall when they are undermined (when their overweening pride turns to embarrassment). Don't be squeamish. Boldness is called for. And, so long as there's a credible catalyst supporting the negation, the gag will work.

EXERCISE

Here are some lines suggesting a lofty moral position. Devise a pressure-based scenario that makes Bob *deliberately* change his mind. For example:

> BOB: (*to a* BAD GUY) I hate people who think violence is the solution to their problems.
>
> > *The* BAD GUY *points a gun at* BOB's *head*.
>
> BOB: But for you I could make an exception.
>
> BOB: I call a spade a spade.
>
> BOB: I stand by my friends.
>
> BOB: I always tell the truth.

EXERCISE

Here are more lofty positions. Devise a scenario in which Bob *inadvertently* reveals that he doesn't practice what he preaches. For example:

> BOB: Barbara, darling, I will be my own man, independent and strong … if that's what you want me to do?
>
> BOB: Beauty is skin deep. I prefer women with brains.
>
> BOB: Our society must take care of its poor people.
>
> BOB: Physical fitness is my obsession.

EXERCISE

Take a crack at your own *emotional* negations, making Bob go from one emotional state to another. For example:

> BOB *hears that he has to spend six weeks in quarantine*.
>
> BOB: (*aghast*) But I'll be cut off from my relatives and my wife … (*Suddenly joyous*) I'll be cut off from my relatives and my wife!

Bob is overjoyed to hear his wife, Barbara, is leaving him for his mate, Dick.

Barbara is told Bob has a week to live.

Barbara tells Bob her mother is coming to stay.

CONFIRMATIONS

The flipside to negation gags are confirmation gags, in which a character confirms a (generally negative) aspect of their personality, outlook or situation. For example, in *Will & Grace* the lascivious, pill-popping lush Karen confirms her character when she gives Jack a guided tour of her house, showing him the doors to 'the gift-wrapping room, meat locker, discotheque and car wash', all intriguing elaborations of her extravagant and quirky lifestyle. Then she points down the hallway:

> KAREN: Down here we have liquor storage, liquor collectibles, liquor dry goods, emergency liquors and … candles … dipped in liquor.
> —('Forbidden Fruit' by Janis Hirsch)

This particular character-confirmation gag plays upon the audience's natural appreciation of a set of three. There's a laugh when they hear 'liquor' for a fourth time—it suggests Karen's list of liquors is interminable. The mention of 'candles' makes for a humorous afterthought to the 'emergency' items (for most of us candles are a more obvious emergency item than liquor). But then Karen hits us with one last reference to 'liquor'. It probably doesn't matter to the writer that liquor-dipped candles are nonsense; the gag relies on the rhythm of the confirmations, and Karen's personality is strange enough to justify the oddness of dunking candles into booze. This gag turns on its unpredictable but accurate confirmation of the character's extreme behaviour.

It's a typical pattern and a useful model for confirmation gags: state something four times to over-confirm it, give a moment's relief, then seal the deal by mentioning it a fifth time.

The other character-confirmation gag pattern is the *ad nauseum* repetition of one word or line (see Chapter Two: 'Wordplay'). Bart and Lisa in *The Simpsons* confirm their tenacity when they beg their dad, Homer, to take them to Mount Splashmore Waterslide Park. 'Will you take us to Mount Splashmore? Will you take us to Mount Splashmore? Will you take us to Mount Splashmore …' It goes on day and night until Homer relents ('Brush with Greatness' by Brian K. Roberts).

COVER-UPS

Cover-ups are opportunities to tie your characters in knots as they try to stay one step ahead of exposure.

At their heart, cover-ups are lies, making them the sitcom writer's best friend. Lies must grow and change to survive. They're swiftly escalated and complicated, and can provide a satisfying catharsis when they're resolved.

Cover-ups occur when a character uses denial, concealment, diversion, a dishonest clarification or a change of context to protect themselves from exposure. The inadequacy of a cover-up may be apparent even to the character delivering it (as Kelso's stumbling delivery below suggests—he expects Red to spot the lie).

> KELSO *is looking through Red's garage.* RED *enters.*
> KELSO: (*nervously*) Red ... Hey ... Y-You're wondering why I'm going through your stuff.
>
>> RED *nods threateningly.*
>
> KELSO: Okay ... let's see ... I needed to ... borrow your saw because ... there's a rabbit stuck in a tree and I want to return that rabbit to the wild ... so it can lay its eggs.
>> —*That '70s Show* ('Hyde's Birthday' by Mark Hudis)

A comic cover-up may be barely convincing; nevertheless it tends to work for a time, usually because the other characters don't have the knowledge or opportunity to force its exposure. They have other things on their minds or are distracted by the further antics of the person employing the cover-up.

When cornered, the character covering up often explains themself with another cover-up. In the *Monty Python* 'Parrot Sketch', a pet-shop owner refuses to admit that a parrot he has sold to a customer is dead. First he insists the parrot is 'just resting'. When the customer refuses to accept this, the shop owner tries, 'It's stunned'. When this also fails, he suggests the parrot is 'pining for the fjords'. Each of these cover-ups is flimsy (the parrot is clearly an 'ex-parrot') but they buy time for the shopkeeper.

Cover-ups tend to follow the 'hope principle'. Despite the feebleness of their deceptions and distortions, the protagonist clings to a thin strand of hope that they'll get away with it.

A terrific episode of *Fawlty Towers*, 'The Anniversary' (by Connie Booth and John Cleese), is built largely on cover-up gags. Basil, having upset his wife, Sybil, on their wedding anniversary, is shocked when she storms out just as the guests arrive for her surprise party. Basil, embarrassed, tells the guests Sybil is sick in bed. In the face of their suspicion and determination to see their ailing friend, Basil uses cover-ups that become more elaborate and implausible as the episode progresses: Sybil is 'contagious', she's lost her voice, she's swelled up and doesn't look like herself, she's been seen by a doctor, actually it was a dentist ... Poor Basil buys time with every tactic, from pretending he's

TIM FERGUSON

choking to forcing the maid, Polly, to dress up as Sybil. When one of the guests claims to have just seen Sybil in town, Basil invents a woman 'from the north' who looks like Sybil, dresses like Sybil and drives a car exactly like hers. Brilliantly, when Sybil returns, all is not lost. Basil grabs her and swiftly leads her away from the party friends, gaily talking about 'the north', and locks her in a cupboard. Of course, this is a short-term fix. The episode ends with Basil forced to face Sybil's no-doubt cacophonous music. But by that time the audience has been treated to some of the funniest contortions of the truth and piling-on of pressures in sitcom history.

A single cover-up does not generally lead to the immediate exposure of a character's dishonesty. Instead, an initial cover-up tends to provoke a series that only crash to the ground (or sometimes culminate in unexpected success) when the character's credibility is at its lowest ebb.

a) Simple Cover-Up

A simple cover-up can occur when a character makes a Freudian slip or is caught talking to themselves, inadvertently revealing their true intentions and forcing them into an immediate correction. This chestnut works on a couple of levels: it tells us what is on a character's mind and adds desperation to their true purpose.

> SIDESHOW BOB *rubs* SELMA's *feet.*
> SIDESHOW BOB: (*quietly*) Soon I will kill you.
> SELMA: What?
> SIDESHOW BOB: Uh, '*Son pied sent il beau*'. That's French for 'Her foot smells lovely'.
> SELMA: Oh.
> SIDESHOW BOB: (*quietly*) Prepare to be murdered.
> SELMA: Huh?
> SIDESHOW BOB: '*Eipah deemeh moodu*'. That's Sanskrit for, 'Your toes are like perfume'.
> SELMA: Oh.
> —*The Simpsons* ('Black Widower' by John Vitti)

Selma is blinded by her love for Sideshow Bob, so her suspicions are not aroused by his murderous mutterings. But if the same Freudian slips were made by Basil Fawlty in *Fawlty Towers*, he'd be in deep trouble. Basil's wife, Sybil, is neither deaf nor stupid and is constantly suspicious of her husband's activities. It's likely Sybil would take issue with Basil's Freudian slip immediately. If this happened, Basil would have little choice but to take one of the available cover-up options: distract Sybil with a fresh topic, invent a benign context for

160

the word 'kill' ('I could *kill* you I love you so much') or invent an excuse for fumbling his words ('I'm experiencing lock-jaw'). Sybil's eye is as sharp as her tongue so Basil would be at significant risk of retribution. His objective would be to stay a step ahead of Sybil's reckoning for as long as he can. The writers would need to devise more cover-ups, divert Sybil's attention, or introduce a mitigating factor (such as a blow to Basil's head that would allow Sybil to put his Freudian slip down to disorientation).

b) Changing Context

Changing the context of an action can provide a cover-up:

> Tweety-Bird sits on a chair. He doesn't notice Sylvester the Cat preparing to hit him with a hammer. Granny walks in. Sylvester pretends to be fixing the chair with the hammer.

Sylvester's non-verbal cover-up is lame, but it saves him for the moment.

EXERCISE

Help Bob cover up his crime *non-verbally*. Don't be concerned if the cover-up is lame—use it to make the play more desperate. For example:

> Bob is caught staring closely at the cleavage of a woman on the bus. *He pretends he is blind and slowly feels his way off the bus.*

> Bob is caught by Barbara with his fingers in the cookie jar.

> Bob is caught giving the stiff middle finger to Barbara behind her back.

Basil Fawlty is a Jedi master of the cover-up. Here are two examples of verbal cover-ups from *Fawlty Towers*:

> BASIL *is lurking in a broom closet, hoping to catch a girl that a guest, JOHNSON, has smuggled into his room. He hears JOHNSON speaking (to another guest, the psychiatrist DR ABBOTT, not the girl). BASIL jumps out of the closet.*

BASIL: Right! The game is up!
> BASIL *sees who he's confronted, quails and looks at a point high up the wall.*

BASIL: Up there. A bit of game pie got stuck up there.
> BASIL *pokes a broom at a non-existent stain on the wall.*

BASIL: There we are. Right. Enjoy your walk.

DR ABBOTT *and* JOHNSON *continue walking.*

DR ABBOTT: (*to* JOHNSON) There's enough material there for an entire conference.

—*Fawlty Towers* ('The Psychiatrist', by Connie Booth and John Cleese)

Basil's re-interpretation of the key words in the euphemism 'the game is up' to their literal meaning is hardly credible, but he gets away with it because of a mitigating factor: the woman in Johnson's room is in fact his mother. Innocent of any wrong-doing, Johnson has no idea what 'The game is up' refers to, and in fact he and Dr Abbott have already concluded that Basil is insane.

Cover-ups generally backfire eventually, and when they do the price they exact for dishonesty outweighs that of the original crime.

EXERCISE

Help Bob cover-up his crime verbally. For example:

BOB *and* ESTHER *are on the couch kissing passionately.* BARBARA, *enters.* BOB *jumps up.*

BOB: (*calmly*) And so, Esther, those are the basics of resuscitation. You'll make an excellent Pool Guard.

BOB *is strangling* BARBARA'*s cat. She enters.*

BOB *is wearing* BARBARA'*s underwear. She enters.*

Distractions

A character can cover-up by distracting others from the truth. They can do this *non-verbally*. Or, they may distract others by talking their way out of trouble. The exercises below give examples of each type.

EXERCISE

Help Bob wriggle out of these awkward situations *non-verbally*.

BOB *is strangling* DICK *with a tea towel when he hears* BARBARA *approaching.* BOB *stuffs the tea towel into* DICK'*s mouth and shoves him in the cupboard.* DICK *can be heard banging the cupboard door. When* BARBARA *enters,* BOB *pretends to be tap-dancing to cover the noise.*

If Bob gets away with this pretence it should backfire later when, for example, his alleged tap-dancing skills are called upon.

BOB *winks at a pretty woman.* BARBARA *notices.*

Against BARBARA's *orders,* BOB *spits on the footpath. He turns to see* BARBARA *glowering.*

EXERCISE

Now help Bob to distract Barbara from his crimes *verbally*. For example:

BARBARA *has caught* BOB *with his fingers in the cookie jar.*

BOB: I can explain the whole thing.

He stops and looks at her.

BOB: You look pale. Have you been near someone with Bird Flu?

BARBARA: Don't be silly. I'm fine.

BOB *covers his mouth with a hankie, putting on a show of concern.*

BOB: Nonsense. Lie down. I insist! We can't take any risks.

BOB *pushes* BARBARA *onto the couch and covers her head with a towel.*

(Even though Barbara is fine and the issue of the cookie jar remains to be dealt with, Bob has escaped for now.)

BOB *is going through* BARBARA's *emails. She enters.*

BOB *is putting arsenic from a clearly marked bottle into* BARBARA's *dinner. She enters.*

Fixing the Faux Pas

Ever said the wrong thing to the wrong person at the wrong time? Trying to get the toothpaste back into the tube is an excruciatingly awkward exercise, which is why it's also comic.

While one character may attempt to save another by re-interpreting their *faux pas*, the ideal form of this gag has the character screwing things up all by themselves. This way, their discomfort is all their own work.

The most straightforward version of 'fixing the *faux pas*' occurs when only one word or phrase is re-interpreted:

BOB: When I think of the boss, I think, 'arsehole'.

BOB *turns to see the* BOSS *behind him.*

BOB: Uh ... By that, of course, umm, I mean you have a 'soul'. You're such a spiritual person and I admire that. No, really.

As with many dishonest or disingenuous acts in comedy, the more a character tries to fix a *faux pas*, the worse it gets. Ricky Gervais and Stephen Merchant, creators of *The Office* and *Extras*, are geniuses at this type of comic cover-up. Their comedy often explores the agony of everyday life and repeatedly shows that fixing a *faux pas* can be as agonising as it gets. Having inadvertently said the wrong thing, their characters have a devil of a time trying to re-interpret it:

> ANDY *kisses a* PRIEST's *hand.*
>
> PRIEST: Oh, you don't have to do that, I'm not the Pope!
>
> ANDY: No, old habits die hard. My old priest used to make me kiss him … on the ring… on his finger, not like that, there was none of that going on, and that makes me sick as well, people saying priests are paedophiles and kiddy-fiddlers, and it's probably … I mean, they probably are, you probably know some, but there's no percentage of perverts in … but, you know … there are all walks of life, aren't there? There are nonces everywhere, but let's not exaggerate the issue is what I'm saying. I've never been touched by a priest. I've been touched by God—not in that way—in the heart … but, you know, or … ah …oh … Condoms. Do we need them? Don't think so. Let the free seed of love gush forth.
>
> —*Extras* (Episode 3 by Ricky Gervais and Stephen Merchant)

Andy gets himself tied up in so many knots that even his desperate change of topic only makes things more excruciating.

EXERCISE

Devise re-interpretations for Bob's ill-timed comments:

> BOB: I am going to kill her with my bare hands. I mean it—I am going to throttle her in her sleep.
>
> BOB *sees* BARBARA *is standing behind him.*
>
> BOB: (*to* DICK) Barbara is a harpy from hell.
>
> BARBARA *overhears.*

Ideally, the cover-up itself forces the character into elaborately perpetuating their own fiction. For example, having convinced Barbara he is a resuscitation specialist, Bob might be forced to teach his wife the basics so that she can seduce him—the last thing he wants.

LIMITED WORLD VIEW

Douglas Adams (author of *Hitchhiker's Guide to the Galaxy*) said, 'The fact that we live at the bottom of a deep gravity well, on the surface of a gas-covered planet going around a nuclear fireball 90 million miles away and think this is normal is obviously some indication of how skewed our perspectives can be'.

We are all sometimes so caught up in our own little worlds that we can't see the full picture. Whether our lens is warped by our own desires, insecurities, selfishness, prejudices or personal limitations (such as innocence or a thin skin), we see the world how we *wish* to see it. A starving man will see a chocolate bar as a Godsend while a man on a diet will see it as the devil's taunt. A man blinded by love is capable of throwing his closest friends and worldly possessions overboard to win the object of his desires. A dim-witted man will misinterpret even the simplest commands. And, for a suspicious man, nothing is as it seems, no matter how implacably it may be proven.

A mafia don, a corrupt cop, a prostitute and a greenie will each have different views of what constitutes a moral breach. None of them can be completely right, but try telling them that (particularly the greenie). Each person's view will be limited by their experience; none will have a monopoly on the truth or a full and measured view of the world and their place in it. Consequently, any given stimulus may (and should) elicit a different response from each character.

Because no-one has a completely objective perception of themselves or the world, we can all see each others' shortcomings. Comedy's task is to clearly and accessibly present the diverse views of its subjects, and explore the trouble they can cause. The overall lesson we draw from watching limited world views in action is that our opinion can be our worst enemy. The more limited the outlook, the clearer, funnier and more pointed this lesson can be.

In *The Jerk* (by Michael Elias, Carl Gottlieb and Steve Martin), Navin Johnson is so innocent of the ways of the world that when he finds his own name in the phonebook he's elated to see his name 'in print' at last! A service station owner offers him an unpaid job with accommodation in a broom closet with the off-the-cuff provision that Navin will send him a postcard every once in a while. Navin mulls over the offer as if it was a high-level business deal.

When Kramer in *Seinfeld* meets a beautiful librarian, Marion, he falls madly in love. Upon reading her poetry, Kramer's convinced Marion is a literary genius. He convinces his friend Elaine to present Marion's poetry to a publisher, but the publisher rejects the poems as total garbage. Kramer's love limits his ability to assess her poetry objectively ('The Library' by Larry Charles).

Often a character will see the quality limiting their world view as a strength where the audience perceives a weakness, and vice versa. Ted Baxter in *The Mary Tyler Moore Show* is so convinced of his own wisdom that he refuses to accept the advice of others. This egotism leads Ted to make stupid mistakes he could have easily avoided had he simply accepted that nobody knows everything, especially newsreaders.

Limited-world-view gags immediately fulfil one of the imperatives of a narrative joke because they say something about character. A world view limited by innocence can drive a character to misinterpret phrases and euphemisms or take things literally:

> BETTY: You'll never guess what happened down at the shops!
> DAD: (*sarcastically*) Elvis dropped by for a cheeseburger and fries at the fish shop.
> BETTY: Did he? I didn't know that.
> —*Hey, Dad..!* ('Fair Cop' by Gary Reilly and John Flanagan)

Knowing Betty is what makes the 'Did he?' line funny—we must be aware of her innocence and gullibility for the line to work. Betty's lack of guile is so great it regularly surprises the audience.

Sometimes character limitations are so severe they depart from reality.

> MALCOLM: I gave him some food dye and told him they were chemicals.
> REESE: (*entering, elated*) Guys! I just made a discovery! When you mix blue and yellow, you get an entirely new colour.
> *He holds up a test tube filled with green liquid.*
> REESE: I'm gunna name it ... 'blellow'!
> —*Malcolm in the Middle* ('Experiment' by Alex Reid)

It's not credible that an apparently fairly functional teenager could be as dumb as Reese. So why does the audience accepts this lack of credibility? Because of their expectations from comedy.

One of the reasons we watch drama is to learn lessons we can apply to real life. To guarantee the lessons are valid, the characters have to come across as plausible. By definition, the actions of unrealistic characters have nothing to teach us about the real world. Even when the world of the dramatic story is not real (as in science fiction and fantasy), the characters must behave as though it is.

We don't, however, watch comedy to learn life lessons (although it's more satisfying if it has them). What is there to learn from Monty Python's 'The Parrot Sketch' or *Fast Forward's* Chenille and Janelle (Marg Downey and Magda Szubanski)? The sketches have themes and a narrative shape, but in terms of lived human behaviour, they're bereft.

We watch comedy to laugh, to experience the thrill of seeing the world turn antagonistic in some way without it representing real danger, or to witness aspects of life from a distance. Because we're watching for different reasons, we don't need to identify with every character. We can laugh at them without laughing with them, so their actions can be unrealistic (so long as they remain consistent). Reese is so dumb, in a drama his story would be very sad. He'd be in permanent care, incapable of looking after himself, a burden on his family, a young man with a limited future (certainly not in house-painting). In comedy, however, that doesn't happen. Reese is okay despite his shortcomings, because for us he is a puppet, not a person. We don't require him to be realistic so long as he's funny.

The other key to audience acceptance of unrealistic comic characters is consistency. Implausibly dumb characters like Reese, Betty, Woody in *Cheers*, Joey in *Friends*, Mike Moore in *Frontline*, Alice in *The Vicar of Dibley*, Rich in *Daas Kapital* and Earl's little brother Randy in *My Name Is Earl* are all consistently unrealistically dim-witted. They can all be relied on to see things the wrong way all the time.

So long as these idiots always act in accordance with their natures—and they're in a comedy—the extremity of their stupidity is accepted by the audience.

Writing limited-world-view gags requires boldness. Don't squib it in the name of credibility or political correctness. A character who's half-stupid only half the time is too close to reality and thus better suited to drama. Similarly, a character whose limitations (e.g. cynicism) waver from scene to scene will be too wishy-washy, undermining any gags that distil their limitation. For example, Red in *That '70s Show* remains cruelly cynical in any situation. If he lapsed into caring and sharing on a regular basis, as most fathers do, it would rob him of his identity in the show and fatally undermine the running gag of his cynicism. Unless the emotional or perspective change *is* the story, the character must remain true to their nature. In *That '70s Show*, the only time Red softens and says 'I love you' to his son Eric is when he's high on painkillers. The event becomes the catalyst for a story about Eric trying to deal with this declaration ('Kelso's Career' by Gregg Mettler). On any other day, however, Red's role is to constitute a threat to the other characters and to put the most cynical spin on any situation. While nobody is like Red all the time, we can all be cynical *some* of the time. So, even an extreme archetype such as Red can cause viewers to cry out, 'My dad is like that!' even though nobody's father could maintain Red's level of hard-heartedness.

Boldness, clarity and consistency will encourage viewers to invest in a character, no matter how unreal that character may be.

To illustrate how various limited world views can drive a character's responses, here are some examples in which each character responds to the same lead-in. Their outlook is conditioned by a personal quality.

The set-up is: character A visits the graveyard where their entire family is buried. On hearing this, character B says, 'That must have been a dreadful ordeal'.

INNOCENCE: Those were graves? I thought they were bike-stands.

SELFISHNESS: I'll say! There was no kiosk so I couldn't get a drink for the whole day.

PREJUDICE: I went to the graveyard but I didn't visit *them*. They're in the Protestant Section.

CYNICISM: They're dead? Tch. Typical of them not to tell me.

CALLOUSNESS: It was actually nice to see them all quiet for a change.

PETTINESS: It wasn't my *whole* family. My second cousin Arthur is buried in Sweden.

EXERCISE

Devise responses to the following for a character limited by a certain quality:

B: What did you think of the movie, *Titanic*?

B: Why don't you ever say you love me?

B: You owe me $22.38 for the concert ticket.

B: I think it may be your baby, probably.

B: Quick! The boathouse is on fire!

There's a common subset of limited world views in which a character offers a confirmation or solution that's technically correct but nonetheless inadequate due to their narrow view. These constitute a narrative version of Flawed Logic gags (see Chapter One, 'Flawed Logic'):

DOCTOR: Does it hurt when I tap you with a hammer?
PATIENT: Yes.
DOCTOR: Then avoid hammers.
 —*The Sunshine Boys* ('The Doctor Sketch' by Neil Simon)

JERRY: Four-thirty? Who eats dinner at four-thirty?
MORT SEINFELD: By the time we sit down, it'll be a quarter to five.
 —*Seinfeld* ('The Cadillac' by Larry David and Jerry Seinfeld)

HOMER: I'm sorry, Marge, but sometimes I think we're the worst family in town.

MARGE: Well, maybe we should move to a larger community.
—*The Simpsons* ('There's No Disgrace Like Home' by Al Jean
and Mike Reiss)

TAKING THINGS LITERALLY

Comedians and comic characters can inadvertently or deliberately take things
literally. A character with a world view limited by a quality such as naivety,
callousness and so forth is capable of *inadvertently* taking the wrong meaning
from an innocent, sarcastic, ironic or euphemistic statement (particularly if
they're not too bright). For example, a woman receiving an expensive birthday
present from her boyfriend might lovingly say, 'You're so naughty—I could kill
you for that'. Depending on the circumstances, if the boyfriend is sufficiently
naïve, paranoid or lacking in self-esteem, he'll hear the unintended, literal
meaning and wonder how his gift could prompt a threat of murder.

> Upon removing the [Barbeque Shapes] biscuits from their container, I
> was struck by the fact that, while uniform in shape, they resembled in
> no way any barbeque that I have ever seen.
>
> —Greg Fleet

STANLEY SMITH: My butt is on the line.
ROGER THE ALIEN: Well, that must be one massive line, 'cause your
butt is huge.
—*American Dad!* ('Roger Codger' by Dan Vebber)

JACK: When I said get a grip on yourself, I didn't mean get a grip on
yourself; I meant get a grip on yourself.
—*Shock Jock* ('What Goes Up' by Chris Thompson)

Characters can *deliberately* take a statement literally to suit their own purposes:

CAROLINE: Please can I have a quick word?
MAC: Zoom. Whoosh. There's two for you.
—*Green Wing* ('Rumours' by Robert Harley, James Henry,
Gary Howe, Stuart Kenworthy, Oriane Messina, Victoria Pile,
Richard Preddy and Fay Rusling)

RAY: (*to the* MAYOR) Everything was fine with our system until the
power grid was shut off by 'Dickless' here.
WALTER PECK: They caused an explosion!
MAYOR: (*to Peter*) Is this true?

PETER: Yes, it's true. This man has no dick.
—*Ghost Busters* (by Dan Ayroyd and Harold Ramis)

Here, Peter takes 'Dickless' literally, but also deliberately mistakes *which* fact the Mayor is querying.

This principle can also work well in reverse: one character setting up another to take the wrong meaning from a statement, then introducing new information that puts it in a totally different light:

NILES: (*about Maris*) She's been afraid to fly ever since her harrowing incident.

DAPHNE: Oh dear. Did a plane almost crash?

NILES: No, she was bumped from first class. She still wakes up screaming.
—*Frasier* ('Can't Buy Me Love' by Anne Flett-Giordano and Chuck Ranberg)

BRIGHTON SHEFFIELD: Yes, it just so happens that your voice carries.

FRAN: To your bedroom?

BRIGHTON: To Michigan.
—*The Nanny* ('Fran Gets Shushed' by Caryn Lucas)

PAUL: What did you say? I haven't been listening.

RICHARD: Well, I was just saying—

PAUL: No, I mean I haven't been listening for a couple of years.
—*DAAS Kapital* ('Chastity' by Richard Fidler, Paul McDermott and the author)

Finally, a character may *try* to correct, avoid or re-frame another character's intention, but there's no wriggling out of its true meaning:

A WOMAN *from the Make-A-Wish Foundation meets* KENNY.

WOMAN: So, Kenny, if you could have one wish, what would it be?

KENNY's *reply is muffled.*

KYLE: … He said his wish is not to die.

Long pause.

WOMAN: Okay … and what if you're gunna have *two* wishes? What would the second one be?
—*South Park* ('Kenny Dies' by Matt Stone and Trey Parker)

HENRY: Radar, do you know what kind of wood this is?
RADAR: Oak, sir?
HENRY: Nope—it's oak.
—*M*A*S*H* ('To Market, To Market' by Burt Styler)

Tommy and Dick are looking at babies at the nursery.
TOMMY: Which one is it?
DICK: It must be him—he's hideous.
MAN: Hey, that's my daughter!
DICK: I'm so sorry. *She's* hideous.
—*3rd Rock From The Sun* ('The Baby Menace' by Jim O'Doherty
and David M. Israel)

EXERCISE

Invent scenarios in which these common expressions are taken literally:

To walk softly and carry a big stick

To put yourself in someone's shoes

To look on the sunny side

Getting out what you put in

I need (this) like I need a hole in the head

DISTORTIONS

The discomfort experienced by a character who is distorting the truth, or having their own truth distorted, can be deliciously painful to witness.

LINDSAY: I guess (Mum) wanted me to have something new. Sweet old thing.
MICHAEL: Only two of those words describe Mum, so I know you're lying to me. And where did you get the outfit?
LINDSAY: Old thing got it for me.
—*Arrested Development* ('Not Without My Daughter', Mitchell
Hurwitz and Richard Rosenstock)

Following the comic principle of negation, *distortions* turn black to white, innocent to guilty, truth to fiction. They tend to follow the model of the non-hero striving against insurmountable odds with limited tools, yet clinging to hope (see Chapter Five, 'The Hope Principle') as the protagonist strives against all logic to maintain their view.

We've all been busted doing something we shouldn't. The temptation to re-frame our crime into something innocent is hard to resist. Like cover-ups, an inadequate distortion of the truth can be funny, so long as the audience knows that nothing very terrible is hanging on the outcome. (If the stakes are truly high, a *plausible* distortion could be a scary or thrilling moment, like the increasingly elaborate lies in Anthony Schaffer's *Sleuth*).

In the following, Bob invents a series of lame distortions to avoid Barbara's fury.

> BOB *is caught by* BARBARA *peeking through a curtain at girls.*
> BARBARA: You were perving on those girls.
> BOB: What girls?
> BARBARA: You were looking through the curtains—
> BOB: I was *checking* the curtains for moth holes.
> BARBARA: Then you pressed your nose against the glass—
> BOB:—As a way of checking the temperature outside—
> BARBARA:—And you whispered, 'Check her out'.
> BOB: 'Check *it* out', 'Check *it* out'.

Sometimes, even though we admit to our wrongdoing, others refuse to accept it. Mothers of criminals seem to be champions at this.

In the following, Bob's lawyer is driven by his desire for a not-guilty verdict. No matter how damning Bob's evidence, the lawyer finds a benign 'spin':

> BOB: I stabbed the bastard.
> LAWYER: You mean he threw himself on the knife.
> BOB: Twenty-six times.
> LAWYER: Twenty-six? So he was determined to kill himself.
> BOB: I stuffed the cat down his throat.
> LAWYER: He ate your cat? No wonder you feared for your life.

A character intent on damning themselves may distort another's efforts to comfort them.

> BOB: Everybody picks on me.
> BARBARA: Don't be silly.
> BOB: See? You're doing it now.

Conversely, what if we're accused of something and we are innocent? The facts are no help with someone who's made up their mind we're guilty.

Here, the detective has already decided Karl is guilty. No matter how solid his story may be, the detective twists Karl's words to suit his prejudice.

KARL: Listen, I just gave him a glass of milk.

DETECTIVE: Without asking if he was lactose intolerant? You scum.

KARL: We were just having breakfast as usual.

DETECTIVE: Nice of you to give him a last meal. What do you do when you're not killing your friends?

KARL: I teach biology at uni. Sort of an animal lecturer.

DETECTIVE: Did you say you're like Hannibal Lecter?

KARL: Look, I loved him. I gave him a kiss and the next thing I knew, he was dead.

DETECTIVE: That's what Judas said.

EXERCISE

In the following, Dick distorts Bob's admission in order to defend him:

BOB: I got sacked for having sex at the office Christmas party.

DICK: They should be sacked for *not* having sex at the Christmas party.

Provide Dick's distorting responses as he tries to defend BOB:

BOB: I smashed the photocopier.

BOB: Then I got caught piddling in the pot plants.

BOB: I got drunk and called our biggest client a 'total knob'.

In the following, Barbara negatively distorts Bob's compliments:

BOB: I love you like crazy.

BARBARA: So you have to be crazy to love me?

Provide Barbara's responses as she negatively distorts Bob's compliments:

BOB: You're as sexy as anything!

BOB: Anyway, I like something to grab a hold of.

BOB: Darling, I love every inch of you.

A good way to ensure a character's distortion survives scrutiny is to constantly shift the angle of defence or attack so that the other characters have no time to dwell on a distortion that would otherwise quickly unravel. Furthermore, shifting the focus to other aspects of the story invites new distortions, elaborating the joke.

RUNNING GAGS

A running gag is essentially a repeated narrative gag. In sitcom, these gags often comprise a minor story or a tag for a succession of situations in an episode.

They often occur when a character encounters the same reaction from a number of other people. Normally, the reaction doesn't please or help the character, even though it may be entirely innocent.

INT. BOB'S OFFICE. DAY.
BOB *has a new bushy haircut of which he is proud.*
TINA: Gee, Bob, you look like Krusty the Clown.

INT. THE HALLWAY. DAY.
BOB *is at the water cooler.*
JUDY: Please come to my party, Bob. Karl's coming dressed as Sideshow Bob so you'll make a perfect pair.

INT. JUDY'S HOUSE. NIGHT.
The party. KARL, *dressed as Sideshow Bob, sees* BOB, *dressed normally.* KARL *gives* BOB *a thumbs up and a wink.* BOB *is distraught.*

EXT. JUDY'S HOUSE—THE POOL. NIGHT.
A bunch of kids run up to BOB *and stare at him expectantly.* BOB *sighs, rolls his eyes and does a Krusty The Clown laugh.*
BOB: Hi kids!
> *The kids applaud, thrilled.* BOB *is miserable.*

Ideally, the running gag inadvertently comes to the rescue of, or finally condemns, the victim of the gag. Here, Bob's bad haircut comes to his rescue:

BOB, *his hair restored to normal, sits nervously in the courtroom.*
NEIGHBOUR: Your Honour, I saw the whole thing. The shooting took place right in front of me.
> BOB *quakes as he waits for the* NEIGHBOUR *to identify him.*
JUDGE: And who was the criminal?
NEIGHBOUR: Krusty The Clown.

Here, the running gag resolves to Bob's detriment:

BOB: Do you think I look like Krusty?

BARBARA: No. You look like someone who *wants* to look like Krusty.

BOB: You'll get used to it. Gimme a kiss.

BARBARA: Gimme a divorce.

Long-Running Gags

A gag can appear once each week, each time with a different spin. The ever-changing trumpet blast by Gonzo in the *Muppet Show* intro is a good example. A longer-form version of a repeating gag can be found at the end of each episode of *The Vicar of Dibley* when the Vicar tells a rude joke to her young friend Alice who never gets it.

Get Smart features several gags that appeared on an almost weekly basis. While the particulars of each joke changed, the framework remained the same. Maxwell Smart often back-pedals from a lie that isn't working and introduces a lesser lie with, 'Would you believe … ?' When *that* doesn't work, Max resorts to a lie that is so feeble it could never have the effect intended in his original lie.

MAX: At the moment, seven Coast Guard cutters are converging on
  us …

MR BIG: I find that hard to believe.

MAX: Would you believe six?

MR BIG: I don't think so.

MAX: How about two cops in a row boat?

  —('Mr Big' by Mel Brooks and Buck Henry)

Another regular *Get Smart* gag features Max insisting upon the literal meaning of his own words:

MAX: Don't tell me (… some undesirable news)

  An ally confirms the undesirable news.

MAX: I asked you not to tell me that!

CATCHPHRASES

A catchphrase is a line that appears regularly throughout a series. Most catchphrases are delivered by a particular character or characters and say something about their personality or outlook.

The common factor in successful catchphrases is versatility. They can be readily used in everyday life in a variety of situations. How many times have you adopted Arnold Schwarzenegger's Austrian accent to tell someone, 'I'll be back'? On the other hand, it would be hard to find myriad appropriate contexts for the more specific 'Whoops, me nuts are totally squished!', no matter how funny it might appear. Without regular opportunities to use it, the phrase has little chance of catching on.

To introduce a catchphrase, apply the magical number three. Pop it into an episode three times in different contexts and, hey presto, you've launched your catchphrase.

'Noice.' ('Nice')

—Kath and Kim

'Yeah, baby!'

—Austin Powers

'Yo, chicky-babe!'

—Wayne Lovett in *All Together Now*

'D'oh!'

—Homer Simpson

'Bewdiful!'

—Con The Fruiterer in *The Comedy Company*

Though catchphrases are often disparaged as cheap laughs, they work like a wheel. When catchphrases were parodied in *Extras* by repeating them ad nauseum, even the parodied catchphrases (e.g. 'Are you 'avin' a laff?') caught on. This worked beautifully for writers Ricky Gervais and Stephen Merchant— they gave the impression they were above such tricks while still reaping the reward.

Imperatives of Narrative Jokes

Just because it's funny doesn't justify its inclusion in the script.

In drama, every scene, beat of action or line of dialogue must perform at least one of four story functions: it must drive the story, reveal character, confirm the situation or offer a new perspective. In narrative comedy, the same is demanded of *every joke* in the show.

There are no exceptions to this rule.

A joke or gag is any event or dialogue that's specifically designed to inspire laughter—as opposed to a character whose personality remains a constant amusement. But unless it also meets at least one of the four story functions, even a genuinely funny joke will come across at best as irrelevant. At worst, it will break the flow of the action and undercut carefully established characterisation. While a joke that meets all four story functions is ideal, only one of the following functions needs to be fulfilled for the joke to justify its place in a script.

DRIVING THE STORY

In a comedy script, every joke is part of the story, so it's important that like other parts of the story, the jokes pull their weight narratively. An example of a gag that moves the story might be a negation in which after a character insists the situation is stable, the stakes are immediately raised. The transition from 'We're safe!' to 'We're in trouble!' is a story-moving gag.

Whether it starts trouble, deepens it, complicates or resolves it, a gag moves the action when it causes a degree of change in the fortunes of the characters. The *confirmation* of the stakes (i.e. 'You're right, we are definitely in trouble!') can also advance the story if at least one character becomes aware of their plight.

The following excerpt from *Men Behaving Badly* features a gag that raises the stakes when Deb's mum appears at the wrong moment. The poor lads then try a deliberate misinterpretation to rescue the situation:

> TONY *and* GARY *call out to* JONATHAN *as he leaves.*
> TONY: And just remember, eat plenty of celery!
> GARY: And help old ladies across the street!
> TONY: Yeah, except Deb's mum!
> GARY: Yeah, except Deb's mum!
> > DEB'S MUM *appears.*
> TONY: Because she's not old!
> GARY: Not old.
> TONY: Not in the slightest.
> GARY: In any way.
> TONY: At all.
> > —*Men Behaving Badly* ('Ten' by Simon Nye)

SAY SOMETHING ABOUT THE CHARACTERS

Gags can reveal the qualities of new characters. Eldin Bernecky in *Murphy Brown* reveals his self-confidence and disregard for social niceties on his first appearance in the series: Murphy is dancing in her living room, unaware there is a total stranger behind her. Eldin watches with bemusement when a bashful interruption of Murphy's embarrassing dance would be more appropriate. Murphy's embarrassment and this strange man's attitude both get a laugh ('Respect' by Diane English).

Most of the time, however, sitcom audiences know the regular characters' qualities, so the gags are not so much character-*revealing* as character-*displaying*. The characters are familiar and we enjoy simply seeing them at work. A line that would be just a sentence if spoken by another character is given dimension and context when spoken by a character that the line typifies.

While on her way to a funeral, the thrifty Maggie in *Mother and Son*, stops the procession so she can buy some cheap oranges from a roadside vendor. Clutching the bag of oranges she insists to her son, 'These were a bargain, Arthur, and I'm not letting them go' ('The Funeral' by Geoffrey Atherden).

When Frances O'Brien is told her daughter is to be expelled from school due to a 'three strikes and you're out' policy, she daintily responds, '...I thought that was a bit American. It should be "six and out", surely. Our country, our rules.' Knowing Frances and her Australia-first attitudes gives this line a comic boost (*The Librarians*, 'My Rock' by Robyn Butler and Wayne Hope).

Character-displaying jokes can be delivered by one character but designed to reveal an aspect of *another* character. In this next gag, the aged and irascible Sophia from *The Golden Girls* gives her view on the man-hungry Blanche:

> BLANCHE: My whole life is an open book.
> SOPHIA: Your whole life is an open blouse.
> —*The Golden Girls* ('The Truth Will Out [a.k.a 'The Will'] by
> Susan Beavers)

A narrative gag can feature a group of characters revealing themselves at once:

> MICHAEL: Okay, guys, um … they are going to keep Dad in prison until this gets sorted out. Also, the attorney said that they are going to have to put a halt on the company's expense account.
> *The others gasp.*
> MICHAEL: Interesting. I would've expected that after 'They're keeping Dad in jail'.
> —*Arrested Development* ('Pilot' by Mitchell Hurwitz)

SAY SOMETHING ABOUT THE SITUATION

A gag can directly sum up a situation. When a shamefaced Paul in *Daas Kapital* enters Rich's bedroom with a bucketful of tennis balls as a token of apology, Rich growls darkly, 'You've got a lot of balls coming back here'. Rich has summed up the situation literally and figuratively ('Faith' by Richard Fidler, Paul McDermott and the author).

A gag can illuminate the plight of a character. In *Blackadder Goes Forth* when Baldrick mentions that he burned his cat to stay warm, we get a strong impression of his desperate life in the trenches of World War I ('Captain Cook' by Richard Curtis and Ben Elton).

A change of context immediately casts a new light on a situation, pointing out an aspect we may not have noticed or illuminating a larger truth implied by the scene. When Murphy dances alone in her home, the sudden presence of Eldin Bernecky changes her dance from a joyful moment to a potentially embarrassing one. It also reveals a larger truth—Murphy is lonely.

REVEAL A NEW PERSPECTIVE

Characters can bring a fresh perspective to a situation. It might be sensible, flawed or total nonsense. Often this perspective is the product of a character's idiosyncrasies, allowing it to perform both character-displaying and new-perspective functions simultaneously. For a moment we inhabit the mind of the character and see the world in a different way. In *Mork and Mindy*, Mork is an alien who sees our world through innocent eyes. Because he takes things literally, common expressions can be turned on their heads, revealing contradictions and anomalies:

> MORK: Why do they call it 'rush hour' when nothing moves?
> —*Mork and Mindy* ('Mork in Love' by Gordon Mitchell and
> Lloyd Turner)

Naivety isn't the only way to reveal a new perspective. A new perspective can be cynical, bigoted, wise or even metaphoric:

> MIRANDA: So all I have to do to meet the ideal man is to give birth to him?
> —*Sex and the City* ('The Baby Shower' by Terri Minsky)

> TED BULLPIT: (*on his wife visiting a Catholic school fete*) Strike me green, woman—I'm not letting any wife of mine set foot inside that miniature Mick Vatican-ette.
> —*Kingswood Country* ('Aerial Warfare' by Doug Edwards)

> FRED DAGG: (*who has just silenced a pack of barking dogs to the wonderment of his mates*) What you do is, you wait till you reckon they're about to stop barking and you whistle just before it happens.
> —*Dagg Day Afternoon* (John Clarke and Geoff Murphy)

A change of context can also deliver a new perspective on an everyday event or ordinary character. In *M*A*S*H*, when Hawkeye and Trapper sip martinis amid the harsh environment of the Korean War, the drinks are symbolic of their rebellion against army discipline and of the world they've left behind.

ACTION, CHARACTER, SITUATION AND PERSPECTIVE

So, what about bringing all four of these imperatives together? *M*A*S*H*, arguably the best U.S. sitcom ever written, shows how it's done:

> FRANK: Are you going over my head?
> HAWKEYE: No, just through a hole in it.
>   —('Showtime' by Larry Gelbart and Robert Klane)

Here, Hawkeye (Alan Alda) a) pushes the story by revealing his intention to steamroll Frank; b) confirms his own sardonic personality and his dim view of Frank's; c) confirms the situation (a direct challenge to Frank's authority); and d) offers a new perspective on the euphemism 'going over my head'.

Though the four story functions are simple, their importance cannot be overstated. Without it a script is just a list of unrelated jokes: funny for a while but ultimately pointless and boring.

One more time for the peanut gallery: just because it's funny doesn't justify its inclusion in a script.

Metaphor

Comic metaphors equate or compare one thing with another, manifesting the qualities of a character, object, view or situation in something that would normally be seen as unrelated but is shown to have similarities. The purpose of a metaphor is to illuminate a larger truth about the subject.

FUNCTIONS OF THE COMIC METAPHOR

Comic metaphors turn up constantly as one-liners in dialogue:

> RED: You are about to read a book that my foot wrote. It's called 'On the Road to in your Ass'.
>   —*That '70s Show* ('On With The Show' by David Schiff)

Comic metaphors can however be more than simply gags in dialogue. They can be imposed upon an entire scene or character to reduce, typify or exaggerate the true nature of the character or scene. They can:

1. Reduce important things to the mundane or trivial:

In *Life of Brian* by Monty Python, a fire-and-brimstone prophet thunders graphically about the apocalypse and the Whore of Babylon. A second prophet rages in a thick brogue about a horned demon with a nine-bladed sword coming to destroy all sinners. The third speaks meekly in the tone and manner of a forgetful parent discussing a domestic issue involving naughty kids:

> PROPHET: ... At this time, a friend will lose his friend's hammer and the young shall not know where lieth the things possessed by their fathers that their fathers put there only just the night before, about eight o'clock ...
>
> —*Life of Brian* (Monty Python)

The predictions go from the hugely important horrors of the apocalypse to kids nicking hammers. The larger truth highlighted by the third prophet's mundane and trivial prediction is that one man's prediction is as good as another's. If you think about it, his prediction has the greatest chance of coming true, as any father who's lost a hammer will attest. We may laugh, but tarot card readers and their ilk will find no comfort in the jibe.

2. Equate something with something else of similar value:

Again, *Life of Brian* provides a fine example by equating ancient Rome's insurgents with university communist committees. The members of the People's Front of Judea (PFJ) gather to conspire in the overthrow of the Roman occupation. In a withering pisstake of all-talk-no-action communist university clubs, the cell members waste time squabbling.

One member, Judith, rushes in to tell them Brian is going to be crucified by the Romans. The other members agree the situation calls for immediate action—but not without first adhering to committee procedures. When they decide to kidnap Pontius Pilate's wife, they end up battling the People's Judean Front (PJF), whom they hate more than they hate the Romans. The PFJ and the PJF subsequently kill each other.

Both the PFJ and university communists feature similar characteristics. They talk too much, follow too many rules and are powerless to change things. Most apt of all, the Trotskyites hate the Spartacists more than they hate the Capitalists (surely their true enemy).

The PFJ–communist metaphor is saying directly that, rather than being romantic rebels, the Judean zealots were their own worst enemies: badly organised and completely ineffectual against the might of Rome.

It's important to recognise that this multi-faceted metaphor works better than a metaphor with only one similarity to its subject. Equating Jerusalem's rebels with a flock of squawking seagulls might be vaguely amusing, but likening them to a university communist society allows Monty Python to jab several sore points at once.

3. Exaggerate trivialities to high importance:

In *Father Ted*, Ted and eight other priests get lost in the lingerie section of Ireland's biggest department store. They're terrified they'll be seen looking at ladies' underwear. Their escape from the lingerie floor is played as a military escape from a jungle fortress. The priests react to every passing shopper as if to a patrolling enemy. The show's producers push the metaphor even further, adding exotic birdcalls to the soundtrack ('A Christmassy Ted' by Graham Linehan and Arthur Mathews).

The elevation of the situation to that of a life-or-death struggle works well. Priests and panties are already a funny combination but when they're given the importance of a military exercise, they become very silly indeed.

The larger truth being illuminated is that the Catholic Church takes sex far too seriously.

METAPHOR AND CHARACTER

The *Father Ted* 'jungle' scene shows how metaphor can be used to impose archetypal character traits upon established characters, even though those traits have little or no connection to the characters or the situation. For example, when one of the priests twists an ankle, he urges his comrades to go on without him and save themselves. Like brave Marines, they insist they won't leave a man behind and help him limp along with them.

Often, the dialogue used in such scenes is derived from the clichés associated with the subject. 'Leave me, I'll only slow you down' is exactly the type of dialogue you'd expect from a war film. A comic metaphor is there to be plundered for its broadly-recognised associations, seeing them in a new light.

The approach to crafting comic metaphors is similar to that of comic juxtapositions: they both involve connecting two things that don't normally go together.

IDENTIFYING A COMIC METAPHOR

Below is a six-step process for identifying a metaphor that can be imposed onto a scene. As an example, let's reverse the People's Front of Judea/communist-cell metaphor and impose the Roman metaphor upon a meeting of a contemporary communist cell.

1. Begin by interrogating the scene for its essential qualities:

- What are the components of the scene? The scene is a modern meeting of communists in which the leader is overthrown. The leader is overbearing, petty and convinced he's surrounded by idiots. He particularly loathes Bruno, the humble note-taker. The other cell members hide their common purpose.

- What is at the heart of this scene? The cell-meeting is a coup d'etat.
- What is the message of the scene? In politics, trust no-one.

2. Identify a situation that metaphorically typifies, reduces or exaggerates the scene and illuminates its message.

- Typify: A chessboard metaphor, with the characters acting as chess pieces, would typify the scene's fixed hierarchy and events, ending with the leader, in the role of a king piece, suffering checkmate. The message is highlighted when the cell leader is betrayed by the other pieces refusing to sacrifice themselves or break the rules.
- Reduce: A kindergarten election for the role of being at the front of the line in a game of follow-the-leader. After being praised for his tidiness and good behaviour, the cell leader is undone (and the scene's message is highlighted) by the childish squabbling and shameless cheating of his easily distracted colleagues.
- Exaggerate: Ancient Rome exaggerates the mundane communist society election to a struggle for the rule of an empire. The message is highlighted by the Romans' lofty ideals being undermined by their political infighting and intrigue.

In this example, ancient Rome is selected as the metaphor to exaggerate the proceedings, satirising the society members' grand perception of themselves.

3. As for any comic juxtaposition, list the broadly-known people, values, events, terms, sayings and songs associated with the metaphorical subject.

ROME:

PEOPLE
Julius Caesar
Brutus
Claudius Maximus (Russell Crowe in *Gladiator*)
Spartacus
Asterix (the comic-strip character)

VALUES
Greed
Gluttony
Political machinations

Bacchanalia
Military power

EVENTS
Assassination of Caesar
Nero fiddling while Rome burned
The sacking of Rome
Pontius Pilate washing his hands
Eating peeled grapes

TERMS
Centurion
Legion
Thumbs up or down
Visigoths
Emperor

QUOTES
'All roads lead to Rome.'
'I came. I saw. I conquered.'
'*Et tu, Brute?*'
'When in Rome, do as the Romans do.'

SONGS
'On an Evening in Roma' (Dean Martin)
'Three Coins in a Fountain' (Frank Sinatra)

4. Make a similar list of qualities for the communists.

5. Compare the characters and events in your cell-meeting scene with the associations you've made and identify connections.

The leader can be compared with Caesar, Nero fiddling, coming, seeing and conquering. The other characters can be associated with political machinations, thumbs up and down ...

You may see a way to base the scene upon an event associated with the metaphor. As the meeting involves an overthrow of the leader, the assassination of Julius Caesar seems a good place to start. The metaphor elevates an ordinary cell-meeting squabble to epic drama.

The meeting becomes an 'assassination' of the leader. Instead of literally stabbing him in the back, as the senators did to Caesar, the other cell members use the leader's back as a surface upon which to secretly sign a petition removing him from office.

The last is the poor note-taker, Bruno. Honest and faithful to the Party, he tearfully shows the leader the petition, then signs it himself.

The Leader, aghast, cries 'Et tu, Bruno?'

Okay, it's not Shakespeare, but the layering of one scenario over another is best kept simple. The obvious associations with a metaphor are the best tools for joke-building. Using too many obscure references can be deemed undergraduate or pretentious.

6. When you've settled on the structure of the scene, look for opportunities to exploit the metaphor within dialogue.

Possible lines might include:

'Et tu, Bruno?'

'Thumbs down, I'm afraid.'

'Peeled grape, anyone?'

LEADER: Where is my champion?

BRUNO: He came. He saw. He left.

Like any comic juxtaposition, imposing a metaphor that's diametrically opposed to a character or scene can work well. The fact that a group of priests is highly unlikely to engage in combat manoeuvres makes the *Father Ted* 'jungle' scene above even more comic.

Be clear about which scenario (explicit or metaphorical) you are mocking. The writers of *Father Ted* were not denying the gravity of a true wartime situation—that would needlessly offend the show's broad audience. Their rather affectionate deprecation is aimed at the Catholic Church.

The best place to start when building comic metaphors is to choose scenarios that are accessible, well-known events or situations. Otherwise you're comparing your scene or characters to something with which the audience has no ready association.

Sitcom Poignancy

Hollywood producer Thom Mount has a sign in his office that defines his criteria for a good script to all who enter:

Make Me Laugh

Make Me Cry

Make Me Cum

Make Me Think

Mount demands these criteria of any script that lands on his desk, be it comedy or drama. With all four fulfilled, he says, a film has every chance of satisfying its audience. This is because the criteria imply a big emotional journey.

Although TV comedy is not generally explicit, sexuality is a prime motivator of the drama. Even the older ladies of *The Golden Girls* provide a sexual zing. Blanche is an attractive and sex-obsessed man-eater, and Sophia has a deliciously dirty mind. In fact, the average well-written dom-com regularly delivers on all fronts.

Sitcom's more emotionally-detached sub-genres, however, farce and satire, while they deliver laughs, sexual tingles and food for thought, don't typically make us cry. In fact, the writers of *Seinfeld* had a 'No hugging, no learning' rule that served them well. The last thing they wanted was for the audience to shed a tear for George Castanza.

An exception to this rule is found in the final scene of the last episode of the satire *Blackadder Goes Forth*. In one of the most heartrending moments in sitcom, Blackadder and his chums go 'over the top' of a trench in World War I to certain death. The ghastly pointlessness of that war, until then a driving force behind the series' comedy, is laid bare. But this is the exception that proves the rule: poignancy is kept in check until the series' final scene. Having exposed the show's tragic undercurrent, there could be no return to hilarity.

However, an emotional journey *must* take place, so in lieu of tears writers of farce and satire generally aim for bleaker emotions. Disgust, dislike, pity, shame, frustration or anger are all emotional extremes equivalent to making Thom Mount cry.

Domestic-comedy, however, is up close and personal, so matters of the heart are its arena. It promises the full spectrum of family life, so moments of sadness, sympathy and reflection are vital. In dom-com, 'Make Me Cry' means exactly that.

This is where the most accessible (and underestimated) comedy sub-genre hits its biggest hurdle. As any writer of romantic comedy will tell you, the comedy's the easy bit—the romance can do your head in. A typical commercial dom-com has thirty minutes, periodically shattered by ad breaks, to generate an empathetic emotional response in its audience—as well as the laughs that the viewers have tuned in for! To achieve this, poignancy can be a most effective weapon in the comedy writer's arsenal. It must however be handled with care.

Sitcom poignancy relates directly to the episode's 'lesson' and is most often found in the final act, when the episode's theme and issues are established and the viewers have had a good laugh. The characters reach a point where only honesty will help them out of their fix. Having seen the lighter side of the issue at hand, the characters must resolve the issue by making a choice, usually between self-interest and the greater good. Poignancy is generated when characters choose the good over self-interest, and in this way poignancy usually brings about the resolution of the issue. To be effective, the issue should be one to which the audience can relate easily.

Many comedy writers fear poignancy like the plague, and for good reason. There's a real danger the episode will veer into the saccharine, the cheesy or the downright depressing.

The most reliable way to avoid these perils is to rely on your characters to take their own unique view of the issue at hand. This way, instead of a worthy lecture that could just as easily be delivered in a pamphlet, the episode's issue can be dealt with through the prism of the character's view. So, a lecture from Mum about being brave in the face of a loved one's death can instead become a more nuanced and fresh approach to the tragedy. Fear of mortality, anger at God or even relief at the fact that a death can cure many problems are credible perspectives that are far from cheesy. A character with their own prejudices and preoccupations is more likely to take an original perspective on the loss of a loved one. Even if a character does deliver a direct lesson (e.g. 'Death is a natural part of life'), there is always room for another to contradict them (e.g. 'Maybe, but it still sucks'). In this way, platitudes give way to more a more rounded appraisal.

In *The Golden Girls*, Sophia discovers her new beau, Alvin, has Alzheimer's disease. After making light of memory-loss and old age, Sophia must face the harsh reality of a future dealing with a partner suffering from a debilitating condition. She decides that, as much as she is fond of Alvin, she is too old and set in her ways to take on such a burden and allows his family to relocate him to a special home in faraway New York. This outcome is far from saccharine, and Sophia's actions are morally questionable—a romantic heroine would surely go with him. The issue is discussed by Sophia and Dorothy in a rational and informative way, but the resolution of the story is Sophia's own rather than a Hallmark moment. The final scene, in which Sophia visits the place where she first met Alvin and shows her stoic acceptance of his departure, is guaranteed to bring a tear to the eye ('Old Friends' by Terry Grossman).

As comedy must, 'Old Friends' faces the darkness and presents some painful truths: sometimes we must accept our own limitations, and all good things must come to an end.

Poignant scenes in sitcom are best kept short, and there should be no more than one per episode. This is comedy, after all.

Painting Pictures

The ancient Greeks would portray a battle onstage by having characters describe it. The pictures painted a thousand soldiers.

Comedy can work in the same way. In this scene from *Blackadder Goes Forth*, the trench soldier Baldrick paints a less-than-pretty picture.

BLACKADDER: (We have) new ladders?

GEORGE: Yeah, came yesterday. I issued them to the men, and they were absolutely thrilled. Isn't that right, men?

BALDRICK: Yes, sir, first solid fuel we've had since we burned the cat.

—('Captain Cook' by Richard Curtis and Ben Elton)

Whether it is a character who is often spoken of but never seen—such as Maris in *Frasier*, Old Mister Grace in *Are You Being Served* or Stan in *Will & Grace*—a line of dialogue or an entire story, a description can be a very effective tool for moving a story forward and defining a character or setting. '… since we burned the cat' shows Baldrick's desperate plight and his unsentimental stupidity in one shot.

In *The Golden Girls*, the elderly Sophia Petrillo tells the story of her experience running in a local marathon:

SOPHIA: So, finally, the race was under way. I start off slow, like a panther, but when the time is right, I pounce! The crowd is on its feet, 'Sophia! Sophia!'. My heart is pounding in my ears—but then again, it's always pounding in my ears. I could see the finish line … and then it happened, what every runner dreads. I hit the wall.

DOROTHY: You ran out of steam?

SOPHIA: No, I actually hit a wall.

—('And Then There Was One' by Russell Marcus)

The picture painted in the viewer's mind can be outlandish beyond any budget. Sophia's marathon, for example, would require a lot of extras, a stunt-double and a location shoot—all for a thirty-second scene. And, after all that trouble, the audience probably wouldn't enjoy the scene any more than her description of it.

Described images can also be more extreme than the audience would like to see portrayed. Importantly, sexual content far outside audience taste or broadcasting guidelines can be related by characters. George Castanza in *Seinfeld* tells the story of how his mother caught him masturbating and fell over in shock. It'd be difficult to depict this scene in a way that is either appealing or legal in a 7 p.m. timeslot. But the story of the event can be told, albeit in a way that goes over kids' heads.

Audiences can be more repelled by cruelty to animals than to humans. (When did you last see a serial-animal-killer movie?) Test audiences for the action film *Independence Day* (Dean Devlin and Roland Emmerich) witnessed aliens destroying Washington and New York but complained that, amidst the slaughter, a dog was killed. The film was re-cut to show the dog, a lovable Labrador named 'Boomer', surviving the alien firestorm without a scratch.

That said, animals have been treated cruelly in comedies. In the film

There's Something About Mary (by Ed Decter, John J. Strauss, Peter Farrelly and Bob Farrelly), Healy feeds a handful of Valium tablets to 'Puffy', a nasty little dog he needs to sedate. Puffy overdoses. In trying to revive the dog with power leads, Healy accidentally sets fire to him (not unlike Baldrick's tale of cat burning).

Sophia's accident, Baldrick's cat-burning and Healy's harsh treatment of Puffy are funny (and forgiven by the audience) for one reason: the audience is prevented from identifying with them. Sophia tells the story about herself, so she's clearly okay and we feel fine about laughing. The audience doesn't sentimentalise Puffy—he's a vicious brute who predictably survives his ordeal (whereupon he goes for Healy's jugular). And we never see Baldrick's cat, so we aren't given a chance to empathise. However, Boomer, a loyal family dog, is given sympathetic treatment and so cannot be harmed without his injuries becoming central to the drama.

In terms of painting pictures in viewers' minds, while some might not like to see Baldrick putting a match to a live cat to keep himself warm, they're happy having the tabby-torching left to their imaginations, where they can conjure images more graphic than anything the BBC Props Department could devise.

Kill the Baby Before It Kills You

Writers will always say they appreciate criticism. The good ones mean it. They know it's a process. The rest say it out of politeness and a desire not to look precious.

The curse of comedy is the act of cutting. It's called 'killing the baby' for a reason, though sometimes infanticide can look like the easier option. For some, the suggestion to cut a single line from a first draft can result in tears and recrimination, dark mutterings and fiery accusations of jealousy, stupidity or humourlessness. Editing can be a debilitating experience, particularly for new writers.

The truth is, even Shakespeare wrote some crap plays. *Coriolanus* for one has me reaching for the red pen. Writing comedy is as much about what you cut as what you write. In fact, cutting is the comedy writer's primary skill. No idea is beyond cutting. Besides, you're creative. There's always another idea around the corner.

So, don't get attached to your baby. It must live in the shadow of the axe. You must be prepared to hack off a line, a scene, a character or even an entire draft at any stage in the process.

Ernest Hemingway said, 'The first draft of anything is shit'. So, don't be too quick to say, 'It's ready'. Before you present a first draft to anyone, give yourself time to climb off the cloud of catharsis finishing the draft brings. Too often, a writer will present a first draft to a producer before the spell-check has fbinished. Put the draft in a drawer for a week, then read it again. Its lack of structure, style and clarity will horrify you. And it will seem as funny as Anna Karenina's teenage poetry.

The demands of comedy cannot be avoided, denied or ignored. A script is funny or it isn't. It appeals to its intended audience or it doesn't. There are no grey areas.

The risks in writing comedy are greater than that of drama. In drama, if the writing is bad, the audience goes to sleep. In comedy, if the script is bad, the audience gets angry.

Learn to look at your script the way a surgeon looks at a patient on the operating table. Don't make the mistake of imagining *you* are the patient, that your sense of humour is under the knife. It's not personal—it's business. Cut, cut, cut.

Chapter Seven:
Selling a Sitcom

PHONE: *You've reached Fox. If you're pitching a show where gold-digging skanks get what's coming to them, press 1. If you're pitching a rip-off of another network's reality show, press 2. Please stay on the line—your half-baked ideas are all we've got.*

—*The Simpsons* ('There's Something About Marrying' by J. Stewart Burns)

To get your show made, you'll have to approach a production company or television network. Networks tend to outsource the production of most of their comedy and drama shows, so for most writers a production company is generally the first option.

Whichever path you choose, the basic selling document for your concept is the 'series bible'. You may also wish to write a sample episode or segment from the show. If you have the skills and resources, you might also shoot a sample or 'pilot' episode or segment. And, finally, you pitch.

The Series Bible

A sitcom 'series bible' is, in essence, the best possible summary of the series in development. The bible should give a producer or network executive a clear understanding of the identity of the series, its intended audience, the characters and basic conflicts, and its creative potential.

A bible should be a stand-alone document. It may be passed to various departments (production, programming) and you won't be there to explain or clarify it. The potential for ongoing stories and character development should be clear.

Try to write the document in a style that captures the flavour of the series. This will make it more readable while also hinting at the show's sensibility.

Standard components of a bible:

1. THE COVER PAGE.

This should include the series name, logline, writer's details and copyright ownership. The logline is a one- or two-line pitch. The shorter the better. For example:

BOB and BARBARA
The Ropers meets *War of the Roses*.
© Beryl Barkly, 2007.
c/- BandB Management P/L
88 Barnaby Street
Bendigo VIC 3341
Australia
PH: (+61) 03–9999 8888
E-mail: bb@whatever.com.au

2. THE *ONE*-PAGE SUMMARY.

This should include:

- The ideal timeslot, series length, episode length and frequency (generally nightly or weekly).
- The series sub-genre (domestic comedy, farce, satire etc).
- The demographic most likely to watch the series. (The two major adult demographics networks aim for are ages 16–39 and 25–54.)
- The primary shooting location ('studio-based', an actual location, or a mix of the two).

This should be followed by a paragraph (100–150 words) describing the story premise. It should include:

- The series' main setting (the story locale as opposed to the real-world location above).
- The major characters or group of characters (e.g. 'the Benson family') around whom the action revolves.
- The ongoing conflicts that will drive the main action.
- The series' theme.

Below that, a paragraph (100–150 words) describing the essential qualities of the series. This should include:

- Points of difference with other series built around similar subject matter. (What is new about the style, setting and characters of your series? If the series takes place in a common setting, for example a family home, say how the perspective of the series is new and fresh. A 'Points of Difference' heading may be appropriate.
- The shooting style, if this is distinctive.
- The conflicts, themes and other qualities that will appeal to its target audience.

For example:

BOB and BARBARA

A 13-part half-hour weekly sitcom aimed at the 25–54 demographic in the 9 p.m. Friday timeslot. The series is shot on location.

Bob and Barbara both have two failed marriages behind them—with each other. Now it's third-time lucky for this pair of real estate agents. Bob's a buffoon, Barbara's a battle-axe. They've vowed to make the marriage work or kill each other trying.

Bob and Barbara takes a fresh look at how professional and personal competition causes conflict in a modern marriage. Shot in a junky hand-held style, it brings to life the fast-paced messiness of a modern marriage. The show's themes of love and rivalry, with a sprinkling of sex, will appeal to its adult audience.

3. MAJOR CHARACTER DESCRIPTIONS

These are short descriptions (no more than 100 words) of each major character. They should include:

- Their characterisation (their social role, e.g. 'mother', 'detective', 'failed astronaut', 'Olympic hopeful').
- Their motivating desire. (One desire is ideal in this section of the document. Two is acceptable for a central character, provided they are clearly incompatible. Three is too many, even for a character who's out of their mind.)
- Their unconscious need. What do they need to learn, gain or overcome?
- The chief character flaw that condemns them to regular conflict (e.g. 'a man whose determination blinds him to the feelings of others', 'a failure whose bitterness at the world has inspired a path of vengeance', 'a doe-eyed sweetheart whose naïve choices pave the road to Hell').

For example:

CHARACTERS

BOB: Bob Barrett is a well-meaning but clumsy real estate agent working for a shifty agency in Toorak. What he lacks in ability he makes up for in get-up-and-go. He loves his wife Barbara, knowing he'd be lost without her guiding hand. Bob wants success but after years of knockbacks and pussy whipping he's lost faith in himself. If Bob can overcome his meekness and self-doubt he'll take command of his life and become an equal to Barbara at last.

BARBARA: Barbara Barrett is Bob's wife and business partner. Ambitious and forceful, she hates losing anything—especially her husband. She loves Bob for his good heart but is maddened by his inability to focus and reach his full potential. A thin-skinned control-freak, Barbara often goes overboard in asserting herself. What she won't admit is that her dominant nature masks a fear that she is unworthy of her successes. She needs to take a good look at herself or risk alienating the only man who has ever truly loved her.

4. THE EPISODE SYNOPSES

For a series of more than ten parts it is not necessary to do a synopsis for every episode, however there should be at least six. Each should be:

- A single paragraph outlining the premise and developing conflict in the episode.
- Written in the present tense.
- 50–150 words and open-ended if the stories are self-contained (e.g. 'Bob and Barbara must race to get the toothpaste back in the tube …')
- Up to 500 words and complete if serial (ongoing) story elements predominate, or if the structure or story is unusual in some way.
- Free of dialogue. Fragments are okay if they are the most succinct way to encapsulate a scene, but even then a single line is preferable to an exchange between characters.
- Named or numbered. Episode names are not compulsory; you may simply number each episode.

For example:

Ep 1: The Eye of the Beholder

Bob and Barbara arrive home from their third honeymoon to find Bob's mother waiting for them. She holds a 'Bob + 1' invitation to a gala ball. Who will Bob take to the ball? To put it another way, who is he more eager to please?

5. A ONE-PAGE CURRICULUM VITAE FOR EACH MEMBER OF THE WRITING TEAM.

Dos and don'ts

Do:

- Keep it concise. Producers and executives are not known for their patience or literary appreciation.
- Mention successful precedents for the show. These precedents need not be sitcoms. (A crude but efficient convention is to put two contrasting precedents together to represent the overall thrust of the show, e.g. a series following the adventures of three amateur detective senior citizens might be described as 'The Golden Girls meets CSI' or

'*Murder She Wrote* meets *Seinfeld*'.) Choose these precedents carefully as producers frequently latch onto them when describing the show in a quick pitch to their associates or to executives. Choose one they don't like and it's all over.

- Where appropriate, use humour.
- Remember that some, if not all, of the producers and executives who will deal with your bible will specialise in fields other than sitcom. More likely they'll be experienced in light entertainment or drama. The ongoing conflict in the series will always be the element most readily grasped.

Don't:

- Go on about how wonderful and hilarious the show is. Producers prefer to make their own appraisals regarding a series' brilliance and potential for humour.
- Use irony or sarcasm! These are easily misconstrued.
- Tease. A bible is a working document, aimed at professionals who need a clear summary of the structure and intention of the show. Ambiguity or unanswered questions (e.g. 'Is Bob *truly* in love with his wife?' or 'Is it all really happening in Bob's head?') leave doubt in the reader's mind as to the show's identity and the writer's grasp of the material. (The exceptions, of course, are the episode synopses for which resolutions are not compulsory.)
- Include your dream cast in the bible. Actors will say 'Yes, darling' to many a speculative job until they actually have to do it, and if they do change their minds their names become an albatross around the neck of your project. Also, producers and executives usually have irrational yet unshakeable views on who is a ratings draw card. If you have profile actors interested in the project, save their names for the verbal pitch. Only include an actor's name in a bible if your series or a character is specifically based around them, and they've given their consent.

Spec Scripts

Short of an actual pilot episode, a 'spec script' (a sample episode or excerpt) is the strongest indicator of your show's identity. If the network is unfamiliar with your work, a spec script can also demonstrate your ability to write narrative comedy.

If they know your work then a spec script is less important than a soundly developed bible.

Shooting a Pilot

Producing a pilot episode or excerpt is the most tangible proof of the show's qualities. An excerpt can be a closed sketch, with beginning, middle and end, or it might be open-ended, raising the stakes and finishing at a point that leaves the viewer wondering 'What happens next?'.

The risk is that a poorly executed pilot will not do justice to your show. Pilots are always made on a shoestring and an example that is poorly shot or acted can leave too much to the imagination of the buyers. There's not much sales technique in saying, 'Imagine it's like this, except good!'.

To give a good impression on a low budget, always prioritise the sound quality. Poor vision is forgivable but bad sound (echoing rooms or unclear dialogue) always feels amateur. Use a professional-quality boom or lapel microphones and a trained recordist. Peter Moon and Brendan Luno's brilliant Australian sitcom *Whatever Happened To That Guy?* was successfully pitched with a pilot episode shot on a home digi-cam—with professional-quality sound.

If you don't know anyone with the resources you need, contact a local film society and ask them for the contact details of people who've made short films in your region. Short-filmmaking is often a no-budget exercise and such producers often have contacts that are open to donating their time for a worthy cause. The TV and film industry is more open than one might realise—and a good idea will always attract people.

Pitching

'Pitching' is the art of selling the right to produce your show to a network or production company.

You may already have a strong relationship with your customers so an informal 'elevator pitch', a pitch comprised of a logline and a brief summary of the setting, characters and conflicts that lasts as long as an elevator ride, may be enough. Newcomers will most likely be invited to give a more formal, longer office-based pitch.

Before the pitch, learn as much as you can about the network or production company you're pitching to. All networks have timeslots they must fill and demographics they must attract. Your pitch should deliver on both fronts. When pitching to a producer, you should select one that has made shows that appeal to you or that aim for the same audience you are targeting. This ensures they are appropriate for your show and vice versa, and you'll be able to pitch with reference to things they've done.

The first step in a pitch is the 'logline': one or two sentences that sum up the show in a nutshell (see 'Cover Page', 'The Series Bible'). This will give the listener a handle on the project and shows your understanding of the show's important elements.

Next, present clear and concise descriptions of the setting, the main characters and central conflicts.

A brief description of one or two episodes will give a sense of the show in action. You may also wish to mention the show's series arcs (developments in character, cast or the setting that occur throughout the series). For example, in Season Four of *Murphy Brown*, Murphy has a baby out of wedlock, a life-changing event that alters the focus of the series. On the other hand, your concept may feature no major series arcs at all. Some sitcoms, such as *Mother and Son*, start afresh each episode with few, if any, significant changes to the characters or setting.

Rather than referring to a document in the meeting, you should have all this material in your head so you can remain focused on the pitch recipient throughout. You don't need to be word perfect, but you should be fluent when outlining the elements that best describe the show.

Some famous pitches have been driven by simple stunts or props. There's a famous, perhaps, apocryphal account of the pitch for the movie, *Twins*. Legend has it that producer and director Ivan Reitman brought photographs of Danny DeVito and Arnold Schwarzenegger into Universal Studios, pointed at them, said 'Twins', and then left. True or not, it shows how a stunt can tantalise its target. If you do go for an audacious or gimmicky pitch, however, make sure you have a more detailed version ready to go so you can provide detail when it's asked for. Or a couple of A-list movie stars.

Above all, you'll fare best when you pitch a project that is well developed. Pitching half-baked concepts or scripts can end in a no-sale.

Brace yourself for the fact that your idea is likely to have many siblings. The producer or executive has probably had similar shows pitched to them before. Or shows they feel are similar, even if you don't. For instance, a domestic comedy set in a suburban home, or a political satire set in a politician's office, will both have famous precedents. There are, after all, only three comedy sub-genres: dom-com, farce and satire. It's possible your concept is a hybrid of some kind that hasn't been seen before, but the genres themselves are fixed.

That said, it's possible to come up with a thoroughly original hybrid by drawing upon the dynamics of a dramatic genre. For example, *Wilfred* is a comedy named after its central antagonist who is a dog, played by a man in a dog costume. But the dog/man is only one trademark feature of the show. It also boasts a genre-hybrid of domestic-comedy and psychological-thriller. All these aspects of *Wilfred* are original and intriguing, but they're not compulsory selling points for the show.

The true selling points of any narrative comedy are:

- The conflicts within and between characters
- The pressures the characters face
- The stakes the characters face
- Your firm grasp of these points and your plan to exploit them.

In *Wilfred*'s case, the dog is threatened by his female owner's new boyfriend and employs ruthless tactics to remain the favourite male in his owner's life. He constantly threatens her boyfriend with the destruction of the relationship through villainous means. Coupled with the talents of screenwriter/actors Jason Gann and Adam Zwar, it proved to be a fascinating combination of elements the network (SBS) couldn't resist.

PITCHING RULES OF THUMB

- Whether you personally know the producers or executives or are meeting them for the first time, feel free to chat with them for a while before you get into the pitch itself. This keeps the exercise relaxed and informal.
- If you've never pitched before, feel free to say so. This will make your nerves understandable and forgivable. If you don't know the answer to something, say so, but make your response positive, e.g. 'I haven't considered that question but it's a good one—I'll get you an answer asap'. This is not only polite and reasonable, it may buy you another meeting, or at least a discussion. You will have time to consider their question or suggestion and devise an appropriate, clear response.
- Don't expect love. You are after their money.
- Don't ask 'Do you like it?' The answer will be a polite 'Yes'.
- Don't ask 'Do we have a deal?' The decision will not be made in the room.
- Don't be put off by silence as you pitch. A pitch is not a conversation.
- Know when you are done. Once you've covered the essential aspects of the show, don't waffle or repeat yourself. Move directly to, 'Any questions?'
- When the questions do come, expect the unexpected. They may seem irrelevant (e.g. 'Is there are a bathroom on the set?') or left-field ('Have you considered the series as an animation?', 'What if all the characters are rabbits?'). They may seem at odds with the fundamental concept itself ('Can it include footballers?', 'Would it work as a kids' show?').
- Be firm about your ideas, but show that you can listen. If the producer suggests an idea you like, say so. If they suggest an idea that is totally at odds with your concept for the show, there's no need to argue the point

on the spot. Promise to consider their ideas and get back to them.

- The pitch is over when you say so. When you've gotten everything across, and any questions are dealt with, there's no need for too much small talk. Thank everyone, suggest you'll call them in, say, a fortnight to discuss the concept further, then leave.
- Above all, relax. Nobody in the room wants your pitch to go badly. A successful show is the dearest wish of every producer and executive, and they're hoping like mad that you're a creative genius who's come to save them from going broke or being fired. No matter how confident or intimidating they may appear, never forget they're terrified for their own careers and desperate for your show to be The Big One. If your concept is good they'll forgive any hiccups.

When the Boat Comes in

If a production company decides to take your show on, they may ask your permission to gallop straight to a network with only a handshake as their bond. This is generally okay if their handshake has credibility. Remember, you still own the copyright.

Alternately, a production company or network may offer to purchase an 'option' on your concept. This short legal document gives them the right to develop and produce your show within a finite timeframe, usually one year with an option for another year. Fees for options range from $100 to infinity (guess which is the most common). These agreements sometimes specify how much you'll receive as the series creator if the show goes into production. It may also give a no-obligation outline of any other role you may have in the production. Once the option agreement is signed, your concept is effectively owned exclusively by the producers for the life of the deal.

Be aware that an option agreement does not usually cover the terms of your future involvement in the project, if any. This is covered by another document, typically a 'writer's agreement', specifying your role or roles. At this point it's worth approaching an agent to negotiate a deal that remunerates you adequately and takes your experience into account.

A producer may also invest money in shooting a pilot episode or segment for presentation to a network.

Once the show's commissioned there's a good chance the producers and the network will want to make changes to your concept. They may attach other writers, editors or producers, each of whom will bring their own vision to the show. Your level of experience and the deal you've struck will determine how much influence you have over this process, but no TV show is entirely the child of a single imagination. Collaboration is inevitable.

This is not necessarily a bad thing. It's possible for a six-part half-hour series to be fully developed by a single writer, but the show's dialogue can become repetitive, the stories similar and the characters start to deal with familiar problems in the same old ways. The problem is exacerbated by the pressure under which most TV writing is produced. Once a show is commissioned, everyone wants everything yesterday, so there's not much time for reflection and renewal. To avoid these problems the producer, with the network's approval, will probably choose to bring in other writers and script editors. Rather than resist this, use your influence to bring in people whose work you respect and with the personal qualities that will make them lively and interesting collaborators. Most experienced television writers know how to work within a creative brief. Watching others expand your vision in ways you could not have imagined can be a joy and a wonder.

Of course, if you've collaborated on the concept from the beginning then you'll already have a writing 'team'. But don't automatically reject the suggestions of those outside the team, and be sure to work with a script producer or editor—their detachment is vital for clear communication with the audience.

Ideally, you've chosen your producers well and they have enough runs on the board to provide useful advice and creative guidance. The best producers listen to the writer/s who've developed a concept and try to convey that vision to the audience.

Above the production company are the network execs, the people who pay the big bucks for the show. Best-case scenario: they're former producers with experience in the field of narrative comedy and/or drama. Worst-case scenario: they're homophobic cricket enthusiasts who've come up through the ranks of the network's sales department. Either way, they represent The Money and can insist on the last word in any creative decision. No matter where they're from, there remains the *slight* chance they wouldn't know a joke if it headbutted them. That's television. Argue your case, but then move on.

Once you've completed the first scripts and production gets underway, brace yourself for the inevitable horror of the actors and directors demanding their own changes to your precious baby. Terrifyingly, some may want the freedom to improvise using your script as a springboard only. By and large the degree to which the director and cast can change a script is under the producer's control. Most of the time the producer will back the writer, particularly as the network has signed off on their version, not the actors'. Nevertheless, in the end it's the producer's call. Generally you won't be able to speak to the director or cast directly; rather the producer will insist you speak through them so there are no crossed wires. (This is why so many writers become producers of their own work. In the US and the UK the senior producers of most TV comedies and dramas are also writers. To its detriment, Australia has no such tradition. Australian writers should actively acquire production skills and fight for their right to produce!)

A Few Hard-Won Pearls

RESEARCH

- The more you know about sitcoms, the better. Watch as many as you can, particularly the successful ones. ('Successful' means they rate. The grim reality is that TV ratings indicate whether a sitcom reliably makes people laugh. For the networks, they are the only meaningful criterion.) Don't disregard a show because it's not to your taste: if it's a worldwide success, you need to work out why. In particular, don't be a snob when it comes to domestic comedies: they constitute television's most popular art form. Also, watch unsuccessful sitcoms to see where they went wrong.

- Use a stopwatch to time the length of scenes in popular sitcoms. Time how long it takes to establish a story, and how many seconds are spent on a given story throughout an episode. Time every little thing. You'll be surprised (and daunted) by the pace at which sitcoms move.

- Read as many sitcom scripts as you can. (The internet is a good resource for scripts and transcripts.) The best way to become a good writer is first to read. So it is with sitcom. Better to stand on the shoulders of giants than wander, blindfolded, about their feet.

- Talk to comedy writers and producers. Join screenwriters' guilds or internet forums—you'll have greater access to people who know their stuff. Most people in the industry are generous with their time, if only because everyone likes to sound knowledgeable. Even if you're a rookie, most professionals won't discount the possibility that you're the Next Big Thing. Be humble, but aim for the stars.

READING SCRIPTS

- The best way to read a script is out loud. If you're a producer, reading a sitcom script out loud gives it the best chance of communicating effectively. The pace will be regular and your natural timing will ensure that jokes won't be skimmed over. Reading aloud gives the characters greater definition and makes the rhythms of the script more apparent. Overall, the script will make more sense if you take the time to hear it. Reading your *own* scripts out loud is essential for the reasons above and because any mistakes, repetitions or dull patches will stick out like an ice-skater's nipples.

- Having someone else join you in reading your script is very useful. Ambiguous lines will bob to the surface when a reader who is unfamiliar with the script sees it for the first time. (Actors, in particular, seem to find things in a script that aren't apparent at first glance.) Having a reading partner is also a good way of seeing if the jokes make others laugh.

- Crucially, reading aloud, particularly in front of an audience, is the most accurate way to gauge the length of a script. Pause for three to five seconds after the best jokes to allow for laughter and applause. With as little as twenty-one minutes to tell your story, every line counts.

- As you read the draft, keep a red pen handy. Strike through dialogue you don't need and draw lines under dialogue you think you can tighten later. Keep an eye out for any line, word or even *syllable* that does not advance story or character. That includes 'Um', 'Aaah', 'Y'know', 'Kind of' and the amplification 'really'. Unless such padding is central to a joke or the character's speaking style, cut them. When in doubt about any line, cut it: if it turns out to be crucial, it will inevitably make its way back to the page. The more red lines you see at the end of reading an early draft, the better the writer you are. If you can't find anything wrong with an early draft, hire an editor and change medications.

- Be aware that reading the same script several times can blind you to potential changes. Challenge yourself. Always ask, 'Is there a sharper, shorter or punchier way to get through this page?' Always use a reading to identify problems, not to revel in sections that you like.

- You are the person who created the script, not the producer who will buy it or the audience who will watch it. Beware of optimism and vanity. Read as though you don't like the person who wrote it and are hoping it will not make sense or be funny.

- Identify the script's jokes by circling the last word in each punchline, then measure the distance between them. As a rule, a page without a gag should be cut or revised to include gags. (An exception might be a point in the story that calls for true poignancy—in which case one page of poignancy is plenty.) Ideally, there should be at least three punchlines or comic moments per page.

- Ensure there is a healthy mixture of gag types throughout the script. (A variety of cover-ups, obvious gags, negations etcetera.)

- Check the script against the principles outlined in this book, e.g. the Hope or Victim's-Fault principles.

- As you read, put yourself in the mind of one of your old school teachers—not someone you know well or personally. Ask 'What would Mrs Whatever think of this script?' The script may be funny to you, but you are a screenwriter, not an average audience member. Imagining how Mrs Whatever would think helps ensure you're not just writing a show *you* want to see—you're writing a show the world will want to see.

- Never, *ever* be daunted by the idea of chucking an entire draft into the bin and starting again.

WRITING FOR COMIC ACTORS

- Writing for a particular actor requires big ears. Listen to them at work, identify their verbal rhythms and ticks.
- Identify the gag principles (taking things literally, distortion, slapstick etcetera) that work best for the character portrayed by the actor, and employ them.
- Nevertheless, maintain a meaningful variety of narrative gag principles. For example, if there are too many put-downs in an episode, they lose their zest.
- Timing is crucial in comic performance. Comedy-writers can help actors by writing dialogue that follows recognisable and workable rhythms associated with the character and the show.
- Keep dialogue as clear and economical as possible. Let the actors do their work.
- In particular, keep longer speeches as short as possible. Thirty seconds is a long time in TV.
- If you are a new writer coming onto an established show, research the show to identify the traits of the characters, the show's moral themes, story structures, dialogue patterns, the works.

GETTING ADVICE

- When our pilots for a live comedy show were being pulled in all directions by various capable specialists, executive producer Peter Wynne insisted we follow our own instincts, saying, 'Opinions are like arseholes—everybody's got one'. It's a good idea to ask experienced people what they think of your project or scripts, but don't ask too many. Even great producers will suggest ideas that conflict with those of their peers—where one sees a puppet show, another sees an animation. Find a couple of experienced people you trust, hear their thoughts and don't be too proud to take their advice. Don't ask for feedback from your lover, mother or best friend unless they know what they're talking about. The affirmations of the ignorant can lead to disaster.

REJECTION

- Don't take rejection personally (unless instructed otherwise). Even if a reader says that your script is way off the mark, it's the script they're talking about. Take their ideas on board and see if they work. A writer's skill base must include an ability to take no for an answer without having a breakdown. Every rejection can be merely another chapter in your struggle-to-glory memoir.

- Of course, some of those who reject your project may be genuinely unqualified to do so. Or they may simply be competent drama producers who lack comedy experience and are wary of the challenges a sitcom faces. Even the hugely successful *Kath and Kim* was originally rejected by the ABC for being 'too broad'. Most of the time, however, producers and execs *do* know what they're talking about. If a script has made them laugh and want to keep turning the pages, they know it's good.

- Rejection may come with advice and an invitation to reapply. If so, be aware that every producer brings their own taste to your show. Even when their advice is valid, it may not be right for the project.

- Being good may not be enough to get a show to air. A sitcom can be rejected for reasons that have nothing to do with the concept. It may be that there are already shows that resemble it, the network schedule is full or they can buy a ready-made foreign sitcom for a fraction of the price of making one.

- Persistence pays. If your show is rejected, take it to someone else— there's no law to say how long you can try and sell something. On the other hand, there's an old Jewish saying: 'If six people tell you you're sick, lie down'. After multiple rejections there comes a point where you may have to face the fact that, no matter how good your show, it's not what the networks are looking for. Put it aside and have another idea. You can always come back to it later.

Copyright

Networks and producers are all too aware of the dangers involved in reading a spec script. Before touching your script or bible they will usually ask you to sign an agreement that you understand they may have other shows just like yours under development. This is normal and nothing to get paranoid about. When *Friends* hit the screen, comedy writers the world over cried out, 'Hey, that's *my* idea!' But it's not a huge stretch to imagine that more than one writer came up with the idea for a show about the trials of a bunch of twentysomethings living in an apartment block. It was a particular mix of characters that created the DNA that sets *Friends* apart—and only one writing team thought that up (David Crane and Marta Kauffman).

The only reason to withhold a script from a suitable producer is if it's not ready. The chances of having your sitcom ripped off by a network or production company are close to zero. A script is copyright as soon as you affix a copyright symbol (©) and show it to someone. Attaching it to an email and saving that email in your records works to prove the date of the copyright. Registering the concept with a writers guild is also useful for protecting your concept.

The truth is, a premise is only as good as its characters, and characters are only as good as the writer who creates them. Taking an idea away from its originator usually means killing the idea. Even if producers see potential but feel you aren't the person to execute it, generally they'll say no thanks. In the rare case where your premise is a work of genius but they're still convinced you lack the skills to bring out its full potential, they may offer to buy it from you. In this case, your own preciousness about your concept will decide whether they get their hands on it.

In the unlikely event that you do feel you've been ripped off by a network or company to whom you have pitched your concept and script … let it go. It would never have made it to the screen unless the network was very sure of its ground and you'll need a top-shelf barrister in any case. Ask yourself, 'Do I want to die young and poor?' and have another idea. Or find a cheap undertaker.

Conclusion

Comedy offers no specific path to success but once you've started on the journey, there is nowhere you can't go.

If there is a constant in a comedian's life, it is travel. I've played in, and been thrown out of, venues ranging from stadiums and pubs to laneways and public urinals in every continent but Antarctica (where punters are scarce). Funny business has paved my own path through TV, radio, film, music, performance, commentary, comic books and novels. This promiscuous journey is not uncommon—comedy works in any medium.

Moving from stand-up and musical comedy to writing narrative comedy proved exhilarating. Actors relish the challenge of comic performance and their ability to bring new dimensions to a character that has sprung from your own imagination never fails to surprise.

If you're a writer who wants to rummage around in the human soul, expose human weaknesses and social injustices, to create stories that hit hard and hold fast, to transmit themes dear to your heart in a way that is far from saccharine, look no further than comedy. Comedy is often labelled 'light entertainment' but a more accurate label might be 'light *and dark* entertainment'. Actor Zero Mostel claimed comedy is a rebellion 'against hypocrisy, against pretence, against falsehood and humbug and bunk and fraud, against false promises and base deceivers … against all evils masquerading as true and worthy of respect'. Mostel's view reveals a truth: the prime objective of many comedians and comedy writers is not to make audiences happy but to make them think.

Be warned: comedy makes friends and enemies faster than any other art form. Prepare for fans, sure, but thicken your skin for the slings and arrows of people you offend or for those who don't find you funny. I've lost track of the complaints my work and that of my comrades has provoked over the years. The most satisfying response to criticism that comedy writers have is to create more work—harder, darker and sharper. I've found that, eventually, those who are unamused by my work surrender to persistence and offer at least grudging respect. And those who are offended learn to use their remote controls. So listen to your fans and let critics fuel your creative fire.

Don't worry that working in the field of comedy will turn you into a depressed person. Trust me, comedians are depressed *before* we become comedians. Depression can stem from unresolved anger and as Zero Mostel shows, we all have a lot to be angry about. Writing comedy is a great way to get it out of your system. Nothing hits harder than a joke.

There are good financial reasons for becoming a narrative comedy writer. Sitcom writers tend to be paid more per page than soap writers. Devising dramatically satisfying stories is one thing; making those stories and their dialogue funny is another. Such skill is rare, and rarity has a price tag. Best of all, comedies appeal to large audiences. Sitcoms occupy primetime on most TV networks and on film no fewer than twelve of the twenty biggest box office hits in Australian cinema history have been comedies. Even stand-up involves being well paid for repeating written gags to an audience, or inventing them on your feet. There are worse ways to pay your mortgage.

I began the process of writing this book with the thought that everyone has their own sense of humour in the same way everyone likes their own blend of musical styles. The principles outlined in this book work for comedy in the way that harmonic structures, melodic patterns and rhythms work for music: they provide a framework within which infinite creativity is possible. With these principles in mind and your own 'cheeky monkey' as your guide, you'll create gags, characters, dialogue and narratives the world has never seen. You'll surprise yourself, and that's funny.

Appendix: Exercise Examples

A LIST OF NON-DEFINITIVE RESPONSES TO THE BOOK'S EXERCISES

COMIC IRONY

1. Brunhilde is a sweet and shy woman who wants to find a husband.
She arranges a date on the Internet but is too shy to turn up for it.

2. Vladimir is a chronic gambler who wants one last win.
He wins. Then he wants one last win again…

3. Rex is a superhero who wants to win a local weight-lifting competition.
Rex lifts 5000 kilograms, an impossible feat. He gets disqualified for suspected steroid abuse.

SITUATIONAL IRONY

1. Claudio is tired of being ignored. He wants to meet someone who will listen to his problems and arranges some dates over the Internet.
Claudio speaks endlessly about his problems and his dates all dump him.

2. Jemima is a realist. She wants her best friend, Sybilla, to abandon her belief in God. She takes Sybilla to a church and calls upon God to appear.
God appears to Jemima—but not to Sybilla. Jemima is 'saved' while Sybilla is now convinced there is no God.

3. The Archangel Gabriel is given a new assignment: impregnate a virgin in Sydney's western suburbs.
Gabriel goes from door to door but there are no virgins to be found.

DRAMATIC IRONY

1. Davo excitedly shows Suzie his plans for a bank robbery.
Suzie is an undercover cop.

2. Detective Smith leads the Chief of Police through a murder scene.
The Chief of Police is the murderer.

3. John weds Marsha.
Marsha is a man in disguise – and John is a woman in disguise.

OBSERVATION HUMOUR

Proposing marriage

Deconstruction: *The man puts the ring in a glass of champagne. Does he want to marry her or choke her? It's like they're married already.*

Perspective: *A woman believes everything is real when a man proposes. He dresses up, he doesn't talk about sport, he expresses his feelings… After proposing is the perfect time to sell her a bridge.*

Changing context: *Women should insist on their husbands going down on one knee whenever they want anything. (Going on one knee) Darling, can you pass the salt?*

Wooing a potential lover

Deconstruction: *We bat our eyelids, stare, wink, raise our eyebrows. If you're lucky, this sends the message, 'I like you' and not 'I can't see you.'*

Perspective: *Black Widow spiders have to be particularly attractive to woo a male. I mean, male Black Widows would have heard the rumours… Maybe that's why the females have so many eyes to wink.*

Changing context: *Imagine if dogs followed our example. They wouldn't get straight down to butt-sniffing—there'd be some chat. 'Do you pee on this pole often?' 'Can I get you a bowl of water?' 'I am so over the pussy-chasing scene.'*

Dumping a lover

Deconstruction: *We say 'It's not you, it's me', but we never specify what 'it' is. Then we say, 'You're a great person,' but that's how the whole thing started in the first place.*

Perspective: *While he's trying to think the way she's thinking, all she's thinking is 'What is he thinking?' or worse, 'What the hell was I thinking?'*

Changing context: *Dumping an employee is a much gentler process. Employers say 'The company is going in another direction' instead of 'We don't love you anymore.'*

SELF-REFERENTIAL

Archetype:

Pessimist: *Pessimism never does anyone any good.*

Sex addict: *I used to be a sex addict, but I thought 'Fuck that.'*

Crisis counsellor: *Why are crisis counsellors so calm? Don't they know they're in the middle of a crisis!*

Animal psychologists: *I gave up being an animal psychologist; they'd never answer my questions.*

Jockeys: *Jockeys are so high and mighty.*

Archetypal characteristic

Bad memory: *Is my memory bad? I forget.*

Political correctness: *Political correctness is a chick thing.*

Fear of public speaking: *(Into a megaphone) Now hear this! My fear of public speaking has reached extreme levels!*

Easily bored: *I think husband was accusing me of being easily bored, but I tuned out halfway through.*

Everything is predictable: *Everything is predictable. I bet you didn't expect me to say that.*

'I forget things all the time': *but I forget to remind myself of it.*

'I get lonely at parties': *so I hide in the bathroom till they're over.*

'I'm easily shocked': *and it's freaking me out.*

'I don't believe in ghosts': *My clairvoyant told me they're bogus.*

I wore a t-shirt saying 'Don't look at me!' ... *but nobody noticed.*

People told me blind optimism was naive ... *but I thought it had some positive qualities.*

Sure, I'm self-centred ... *but you have to see it my way.*

Am I secretive? ... *I'm not going to tell you.*

I could try to explain what it was like to be completely alone ... *but I guess you had to be there.*

FLAWED LOGIC

Hideousness: *Baby, you're not ugly, just a teensy bit hideous.*

Deafness: *I tried telling her she's deaf but some people don't listen.*

Secret: *If you tell me a secret, it's not really a secret anymore is it?*

Suicide: *If you commit suicide I'll kill you!*

Virginity: *The next time I lose my virginity, I'm gunna be sober.*

INCONGRUOUS JUXTAPOSITIONS

What do cats and porn have in common? *They're both fun to shoot.*

What's the difference between cats and porn? *The shape of their fur-balls.*

What do lawyers and cannibals have in common? *They both cost you an arm and a leg.*

What's the difference between lawyers and cannibals? *Cannibals eat* other people's *young.*

What do dwarves and blondes have in common? *They both look up to Barbie.*

What's the difference between dwarves and blondes? *Blondes are* all *Dopey.*

TWO MEANINGS

To be beside yourself: *I was beside myself until I realised I was standing next to a mirror.*

To drop off the perch: *Grandad dropped off the perch? I guess the fall killed him.*

To drive someone up the wall: *I drove my husband up the wall. Coming down the other side was the tricky bit.*

To go down for the third time: BOB *and* BARBARA *see a man and woman drowning.*
BOB: *Oh no! They're going down for the third time.*
BARB: *How can they think of sex at a time like this?*

To fall off the back of a truck: *I didn't ask for a clock that fell off the back of a truck. I ordered a stolen one.*

MALAPROPISMS

'One percent inspiration, ninety-nine percent perspiration.'
Writing a book is one percent inspiration, ninety-nine percent procrastination.

'Going at it hammer and tongs.'
They were going at it hammer and tongues.

'Pecuniary fund.'

My eccentric grandad left me a peculiar fund.

'Struck by cupid's arrow.'
He's been struck by Stupid's arrow.

'To move with alacrity'
He moves with a laxative.

MISINTERPRETATIONS

He's so dumb he thinks an 'IQ' is … *the latest billiard stick from Apple.*

She's so lascivious she thinks a 'square root' is … *sex with a rocket scientist.*

He's so out of touch he thinks 'J-Lo' is … *a brand of fruit juice.*

She's so selfish she thinks the 'Poor Box' is … *something the homeless can live in.*

He's so square he thinks the 'Lambada' is … *a kind of kebab.*

When lawyers say:	They mean:
'Hostile witness'	Someone who can't be bribed
'Memorandum'	A reminder to forget everything
'Criminal lawyer'	Any lawyer
'The Bar exam'	Testing your ability to get as drunk as a judge
'BMW'	Blood Money Wagon

OBVIOUS

The secret to a happy life is … *die young.*

Married people have the best sex … *before marriage.*

The best way to get off a deserted island is … *a speedboat.*

Cats use their tongues to clean themselves … *which proves they're not that picky about their food.*

John Lennon said, 'All you need is love' … *Bullet-proof jackets are handy too.*

Terrorist martyrs spend eternity with seventy-six virgins … *No sex is mentioned in the deal – just eternity with seventy-six virgins.*

The best marriages are arranged marriages … *That way you can blame someone else.*

I bought a sawn-off shotgun … *But the sawn-off bullets don't work.*

Let me offer a word to the wise … *Smartarse.*

Bad people go to Hell … *They probably cause trouble there, too.*

0.02% of grandmothers are convicted of murder … *The rest get away with it.*

Life is like a box of chocolates. You never know what you're going to get … *Unless you look at the back of the box.*

TRANSPOSITIONS

Fundamental: *Headline: Fundamentalist Neither Fun Nor Mental*

Postmodern: *Anyone who calls the post modern hasn't waited a year for their paycheck to arrive. 'Postmodern' is like saying 'public transport reliable'.*

Respond: *Why should I re-spond? I didn't spond in the first place.*

Decapitate: *I lost my head but I'm capitated now.*

Henchmen: *C'mon, fellas, the boss wants us to hench. Let's go a-henchin'!*

NEGATIONS

BOB is playing poker with some GANGSTERS.

BOB: I call a spade a spade.

He reveals a royal flush of spades. The GANGSTERS glare at him.

BOB: All I have is… a pair of clubs.

BOB: I stand by my friends.

Their angry Boss approaches. BOB races to the door.

DICK: Where are you going?

BOB: To stand next to a different friend.

BOB: I always tell the truth.
DICK: *But if you do, our wives will find out we went fishing instead of to work.*
BOB: *Fishing is a kind of work.*

BOB: Beauty is skin deep. I prefer women with brains.
A pretty woman walks by.
BOB: *She seems very brainy.*

BOB: Our society must take care of its poor people.
BOB *says this while stepping over a homeless person.*

BOB: Physical fitness is my obsession.
Bob says this while watching an aerobics show and chewing on a hamburger.

Bob is overjoyed to hear his wife, Barbara, is leaving him for his mate, Dick.
BOB: *(Overjoyed)* I'll never see her again. *(Distressed)* But I'll never see Dick again.

Barbara is told Bob has a week to live.
BARBARA: *(Happily) Free at last. (Disappointed) A whole week?*

Barbara tells Bob her mother is coming to stay.
BOB: *(Anguished) But now you'll both pick on me. (Whispering craftily to himself) But then they'll tire of that and pick on each other.*

COVER-UPS

Non-verbal

Bob is caught by Barbara with his fingers in the cookie jar.
BOB *pretends he is pulling a tiny bug out of the jar. He flicks away the non-existent bug.*

Bob is caught giving the stiff middle finger to Barbara behind her back.
BOB *closely examines his middle finger as if it has a paper cut.*

Verbal

BOB is strangling Barbara's cat. She enters.
BOB *(to the cat):* Breathe, little darling, breathe! *(To Barbara)* Furball.

BOB is wearing BARBARA's underwear. She enters.
BOB *blinks as if waking.*
BOB: *I must have been sleepwalking again.*

DISTRACTIONS

Non-verbal

Bob winks at a pretty woman. Barbara notices.
BOB *pretends he has something in his eye.*

Against Barbara's orders, Bob spits on the footpath. He turns to see Barbara glowering.
BOB *dabs the toe of his shoe in the spit and polishes it.*

Verbal

BOB is going through BARBARA's emails. She enters.
BOB: *Darn it, a computer virus keeps opening the wrong files. I insist we go to the computer shop and complain—right now.*

BOB is putting arsenic from a clearly marked bottle into BARBARA's dinner. She enters.
BOB: *Homeopaths think one drop of arsenic per million is good for you. I want this dinner to be very good for you. It's clear your blood pressure's rising right now.*

FIXING THE FAUX PAS

BOB: I am going to kill her with my bare hands. I mean it – I am going to throttle her in her sleep.

BOB sees BARBARA is standing behind him.
BOB: *I mean kill her with a cuddle and, er, throttle her with affection.*

BOB: (to DICK) Barbara is a harpy from hell.

Barbara overhears.
BOB: *By that I mean she's had a hell of a time and now she's harpy to be here.*

LIMITED WORLD VIEW

Innocence

B: What did you think of the movie, Titanic?
A: *The ending took me by surprise.*

Selfishness

B: Why don't you ever say you love me?
A: *You haven't earnt it.*

Prejudice

B: You owe me $22.38 for the concert ticket.
A: *It's typical of a poor person to put a price on such a wonderful experience.*

Cynicism

B: I think it may be your baby, probably.
A: *I think it may be your problem, probably.*

Pettiness

B: Quick! The boathouse is on fire!
A: *Don't you mean it's on water?*

TAKING THINGS LITERALLY

To walk softly and carry a big stick
DELORES: *I walk softly and carry a big stick.*
DICK: *(Looking about nervously) Is it an invisible stick?*

To put yourself in someone's shoes.
BOB: *Darling, put yourself in my shoes.*
BARBARA: *No way—I don't want tinea.*

To look on the sunny side
BOB: *You have to look on the sunny side of life.*
BARBARA: *It's night time.*

Getting out what you put in
DELORES: *You only get out what you put in.*
DICK: *But if I've put it in, why would I want to get it out?'*

'I need this like I need a hole in the head'
BOB *and* BARBARA *are in a sports shop.*
BOB: *I need a fishing pole like I need a hole in the head.*
BARBARA: *(To storekeeper) One fishing pole, please—two to be sure.*

DISTORTIONS

BOB: I smashed the photocopier.
DICK: *That's a lifelong dream fulfilled.*

BOB: Then I got caught piddling in the pot plants.
DICK: *You probably mistook them for lemon trees.*

BOB: I got drunk and called our biggest client a 'total knob'.
DICK: *Better than calling him a 'half-knob'.*

BOB: You're as sexy as anything!
BARBARA: *Anything? Like a hamburger? A car tyre? A dairy cow?*

BOB: Anyway, I like something to grab a hold of.
BARBARA: *I'll leave you to it.*

BOB: Darling, I love every inch of you.
BARBARA: *But not me as a whole?*

Want to Learn More?

Tim also offers stand up and narrative comedy writing masterclasses.

Visit www.cheekymonkeycomedy.com for more information

Tim Ferguson is represented exclusively by HLA Management Pty Ltd

www.hlamgt.com.au +61 2 9549 3000